丛书编辑委员会

总　编　张喜华

编　委　刘苏力　刘贵珍　马振涛　王元歌
　　　　　吴　英　李炳慧　陈发家　张喜华
　　　　　罗　晨　周建萍　赵　菁　徐　庆
　　　　　盖梦丽　董莉芳　翟润梅

一带一路·中东欧文化读本

罗马尼亚概况
Survey of Romania

赵 菁 / 主编

世界知识出版社

丛书总编序

　　东欧国家是我国"一带一路"国际合作倡议实施的重要参与国，也是"一带一路"经济带的重要组成部分。为了有效推进倡议的落地，必须高度重视文化先行的必要性和可行性，因而了解并探究中东欧国家文化就显得尤为必要。"一带一路"的内涵概括为"五通三同"。"五通"（政策沟通、设施联通、贸易畅通、资金融通、民心相通）中的"民心相通"是"一带一路"建设的社会根基，是其他四通的前提，也是我国和中东欧国家战略合作关系可持续发展的保障。文化互识、互鉴和交流是实现"民心相通"的重要抓手。"一带一路"沿线国家，尤其是中东欧的民众如果和我们"民心相通"，不仅会使整个合作机制获得广泛的支持基础，而且还会推动相关合作实践顺利开展。反之，则寸步难行。中东欧国家是我国"一带一路"国际合作倡议实施的重要合作伙伴和推动力量，我们有必要全面、客观了解中东欧国家文化，以便开展适当的、精准的高水平文化交流和合作活动，为倡议的实施打下文化互识的基础，创造良好的合作氛围。

　　随着中国－中东欧国家合作机制的建立，中国与中东欧国家的合作迅猛发展，对中东欧文化的关注日渐增强，中国与中东欧国家的全方位合作交流日益频繁。然而，国内对中东欧国家的研究还比较零散，系统介绍这些国家概况的文献尚属空白。我国在"中国文化走出去"方面开展了大量的工作，取得了显著的成绩，但是，要获得更好的"走出去"效果，还需要"知己知彼"。本丛书的编写初衷正在于此：知己知彼，民心相通，共建命运共同本。编委们希冀通过对这些国家文化的梳理，让我们对它们的文化概况有一个基本把握，为对它们的深入研究和理解打开一扇大门，助力我国和中东欧国家的"民心相通"，借以增进彼此合作和理解，以共同推进"一带一路"建设。

丛书以中东欧国家文化为观照，旨在促进国内知己知彼，开展后续比较研究。丛书为这个领域的研究做出了文献资源上不可或缺的贡献，为拓展国内的国别和区域研究提供了新的系列文献。丛书深化了我们对中东欧国家文化状况的了解，对服务于"一带一路"倡议的实施具有跨文化交流的现实意义，有利于中国与中东欧国家在政治、经济、文化等领域的深入了解和合作。丛书也有利于提高中国文化走出去的针对性和传播效果，从而提升我国在中东欧地区的文化软实力。

虽然丛书的编撰研究具有一定难度（例如，所涉区域广、国别多、对象国语言障碍多，国内研究文献不足等），但是北京第二外国语学院跨文化研究团队在国家大力发展小语种人才培养的政策引领下，在学校领导的大力支持下，结合复语人才培养工作的需求，开始了本丛书的编写工作。在为期三年的研究中，团队核心成员与中东欧国家驻华使馆人员和对象国大学同行们进行了多次交流，并自费走访匈牙利、捷克、波兰、立陶宛、拉脱维亚、爱沙尼亚等国家，广泛查阅对象国有关权威部门（如外交部、驻外使馆）官网公布的资讯以及原文文献，以确保信息可靠，语言地道。

中东欧国家（按汉语拼音顺序）包括阿尔巴尼亚、爱沙尼亚、保加利亚、波黑、波兰、黑山、捷克、斯洛伐克、克罗地亚、拉脱维亚、立陶宛、罗马尼亚、马其顿、塞尔维亚、斯洛文尼亚、希腊、匈牙利。丛书以这些国家为研究对象，各国单独成卷。丛书内容涵盖对象国地理、历史、语言、政治、经济、教育、文学、音乐、舞蹈、绘画、体育、习俗、节庆活动、与中国的合作，等等。

丛书总编序

丛书以英语撰写乃基于以下几点考虑：第一，有利于文化交流实践。大部分读者并不一定知晓对象国的语言，但如果通过中文撰写，读者或研究者到达对象国或者与对象国人士进行交流时依然存在语言障碍，需要翻译转化过程，从而大大影响交流效果。英语作为国际通用语言，能够让读者借助丛书内容和知识，直接和对象国人士沟通交流，达到互识互信的文化交流效果，提高跨文化交际效果，促进我们和对象国之间的"民心相通"，服务中国－中东欧国家的国际合作需要。第二，有利于复语人才的培养。目前国内外多语种人才培养中英语是必要的复语，毕竟小语种的使用对象和使用范围都具有一定局限。本丛书为对象国语言专业学习者提供了与本专业内容相关的英语复语文化读本，符合多语种复合、跨专业复合的外语人才培养特点。第三，有利于信息的真实和完整。丛书文献都来源于对象国国家部门或者对象国研究公开出版的权威刊物，语言表述精准，信息传达到位，符合对象国实际情况。

丛书的出版旨在打开一扇窗户，帮助读者了解中东欧文化概况，提升文化素养，拓展国际视野，促进文化交流，做到知己知彼，达到民心相通的跨文化理想。每个国家的民族文化都有着自己的发展脉络、历史渊源、丰富形式和独特内涵；每个国家的文化又都是动态发展的，文化意义因政治、社会、历史语境的变化而变化，因此，丛书难以做到面面俱到，相关专题的细致和深入发掘还有待后续研究。

本丛书的出版得到了北京第二外国语学院"一带一路"专项（200078）经费的资助，属于学校国别与区域研究成果，特此致谢！

张喜华

2019 年 11 月 30 日于北京

CONTENTS

Chapter 1	Introduction	003
Chapter 2	History	022
Chapter 3	Climate and Environment	032
Chapter 4	Culture and Customs	046
Chapter 5	Social Life	074
Chapter 6	Government and Politics	097
Chapter 7	Economy and Trade	125
Chapter 8	Transportation and Communications	164
Chapter 9	Education	191
Chapter 10	Religion	211
Chapter 11	Sports and Outdoor Activities	235
Chapter 12	Entertainment	249
Chapter 13	Current Issues and Challenges	262

Romania
Basic Information

- Area: 238,397 km^2
- Borders with other countries: Bulgaria, Moldova, Ukraine, Hungary, Serbia.
- Major regions: Bucharest, Wallachia, Transylvania, Moldavia, Maramures, the Banat and Crisana, the Delta and the coast.
- Population in 2018: 21,457,116
- Spoken languages: Romanian (official language, which belongs to the Indo-European family). The various minority ethnic groups speak their own language like Hungarian, Ukrainian, Turkish, Bulgarian, Croatian, etc. English, French, German and Italian are some of the foreign languages spoken in Romania.

Chapter 1
Introduction[1]

Romania is a European country located on the western shore of Black Sea between Bulgaria and Ukraine. Romania boasts of plenty of natural beauty which also has a rich cultural heritage. As is a part of NATO and EU politically, Romania is also a great tourist destination with economy doing well in the last decade.

Bucharest is the capital and the largest city of Roman. It's also the financial, industrial and cultural center of Romania. Located on the Dambovita River in the southeastern part of Romania, Bucharest is a historical city which has seen a great economic development in recent years.

Here are some basic elements about the country.

---

1 https://www.dookinternational.com/about/romania

County Profile

The Coat of Arms[1]

The coat of arms of Romania was adopted in the Romanian Parliament on 10 September 1992 as a representative coat of arms for Romania. It is based on the Lesser Coat of Arms of the Kingdom of Romania (used between 1922 and 1947), redesigned by Victor Dima. As a central element, it shows a golden aquila holding a cross in its beak, and a mace and a sword in its claws. It also consists of the three colors (red, yellow and blue) which represent the colors of the national flag. The coat of arms was augmented on 11 July 2016 to add a representation of the Steel Crown of Romania.

Picture: The Coat of Arms
SOURCE: https://en.wikipedia.org/wiki/Romania#/media/File:Coat_of_arms_of_Romania.svg

---

1 https://en.wikipedia.org/wiki/Coat_of_arms_of_Romania

Chapter 1 Introduction

Picture: The National Flag of Romania
SOURCE: https://kids.kiddle.co/Image:Flag_of_Romania.svg

The Flag

The Romanian flag consists of tricolor of vertical stripes — dark blue one, yellow one and red one. The red, yellow and blue stripes represent Moldova and Walachia, the two principalities that united to form Romania in 1859. The colors are found in the coat of arms of these former states.

The National Day

Great Union Day is a national holiday in Romania, celebrated on 1 December, marking the unification of Transylvania, Bessarabia and Bukovina with the Romanian Kingdom in 1918.

The National Anthem

The name of Romania's national anthem is "Deșteaptă-te, române!" This has various translations, include "Wake up, Romanian!" and "Awaken thee,

Romanian!" The lyrics for the song were written in 1848 by Andrei Muresanu. The music was created by Anton Pann in the same year.

Geography[1]

Situated in the northeastern equidistant from the most westernly part of Europe—the Atlantic Coast—and the most easterly part of Europe—the Ural Mountains, Romania is the 12th largest country in Europe with an area of 238,391 square kilometres. Of its 3,195 kilometres of border, Romania shares 1,332 kilometres with the Soviet Union to the east and north. In the southeast, 245 kilometres of Black Sea coastline serves as an important outlet to the Mediterranean Sea and the Atlantic Ocean. The Carpathian Mountains[2] encompass about and the Atlantic Ocean. The Carpathian

PICTURE: Rasnov Fortress
SOURCE: http://romaniatourism.com/images/rasnov-fortress.jpg

---

1 R. D., Bachman, & E. K. Keefe, *Romania: A Country Study,* Washington D.C., United States Govt Printing Office, 1991.

2 The Carpathian Mountains or Carpathians (/kɑːrˈpeɪθiənz/) are a mountain range system forming an arc roughly 1,500 km long across Central and Eastern Europe, making them the second-longest mountain range in Europe (after the Scandinavian Mountains, 1,700 km) [Source: Wikipedia].

Mountains[1] encompass about one-third of the country, surrounding the Transylvanian Plateau and disunite it from the other two main regions: Moldavia in the northeast and Walachia in the south. In the central region are the Transylvanian Alps[2] which contain the highest peak, Mount Moldoveanu. Regions in the eastern and southern Romania are characterized by rolling plains. As the second-longest river within the EU, the Danube River[3] stretches through the country for 600 miles, constituting its southern border with Serbia and Bulgaria and emptying into the Black Sea in the east. It is a source for irrigation and hydroelectric power for people living along with it. Traditionally, Romania falls into six historic regions which do not fulfil any administrative function any more. On the easternmost is the region of Dobruja that expands from the northward course of the Danube to the shores of the Black Sea. Moldavia stretches from the Eastern Carpathians to the Prut River on the Soviet border. Walachia reaches south from the Transylvanian Alps to the Bulgarian border and is divided by the Olt River into Oltenia on the west and Muntenia on the east. The Danube river serves as a natural boundary between Dobruja and Muntenia. The west-central region, known as Transylvania is delimited by the arc of the Carpathians, which separates it from the Maramures region in the northwest; by the Crisana area, which borders Hungary in the west; and by the Banat region of

---

1 The Carpathian Mountains or Carpathians (/kɑːrˈpeɪθiənz/) are a mountain range system forming an arc roughly 1,500 km (932 mi) long across Central and Eastern Europe, making them the second-longest mountain range in Europe (after the Scandinavian Mountains, 1,700 km) [Source: Wikipedia].

2 The Transylvanian Alps are a group of mountain ranges located in southern Romania. They cover the part of the Carpathian Mountains located between the Prahova River in the east and the Timiș and Cerna Rivers in the west. To the south they are bounded by the Balkan mountain range [Source: Wikipedia].

3 Europe's second-longest river, after the Volga River. It is located in Central and Eastern Europe. The Danube was once a long-standing frontier of the Roman Empire, and today flows through 10 countries, more than any other river in the world. Originating in Germany, the Danube flows southeast for 2,860 km, passing through or touching the border of Austria, Slovakia, Hungary, Croatia, Serbia, Romania, Bulgaria, Moldova and Ukraine before emptying into the Black Sea [Source: Wikipedia].

| 罗马尼亚概况 | Survey of Romania |

the southwest, which adjoins both Hungary and Yugoslavia. It is the west of the Carpathians that contain the highest concentrations of the nation's largest ethnic minorities—Hungarians, Germans, and Serbs.

  Mountains constitute one-third of Romania's territory. The principal mountain chain consists of the Eastern and Southern Carpathians, which form an arc that is more than 750 kilometres in length, open toward the northwest and with its point close to the country's centre, extending southeastward from near the Ukrainian border, then west to the Iron Gate[1] that frames the Danube's entry into Romania. The Eastern Carpathians extend into Romania from the Ukrainian Carpathians to the north, with a spur westward into Transylvania called the Rodna Mountains. Where the Eastern Carpathians extend southward between Transylvania and Moldavia, their western side features Alpine meadows and lakes of volcanic origin, notably Red and St. Ana Lakes. Two major passes pierce them. The first, the Borgo (Romanian: Bârgâu) Pass, connects Bistrita in northern Transylvania with the valley of the Moldavian river also named Bistrita and is immortalized in the opening scenes of Bram Stoker's Dracula. The second, the Predeal Pass, provides the rail route for most travellers from central Transylvania to Bucharest with dramatic views of the Bucegi Mountains. Smaller passes between these, through the Bicaz Gorge near Red Lake and the valleys of the Oituz and Buzau, connect the Szekely region of eastern Transylvania with central Moldavia. The Southern Carpathians (or Transylvanian Alps) are less accessible to travellers because they have fewer passes and are by-passed by major thoroughfares. West of Bucegi, the Fagaras massif (including Moldoveanu, the country's highest peak at 2,543 meters)

---

  1 A gorge on the Danube River. It forms part of the boundary between Serbia (to the south) and Romania (north). In the broad sense, it encompasses a route of 134 km; in the narrow sense, it only encompasses the last barrier on this route, just beyond the Romanian city of Orşova, that contains two hydroelectric dams, with two power stations, Iron Gate I Hydroelectric Power Station and Iron Gate II Hydroelectric Power Station. At this point in the Danube, the river separates the southern Carpathian Mountains from the northwestern foothills of the Balkan Mountains. The Romanian side of the gorge constitutes the Iron Gates natural park, whereas the Serbian part constitutes the Đerdap national park [Source: Wikipedia].

Chapter 1 Introduction

presents an almost impenetrable barrier, of which air travellers between Sibiu[1] and Bucharest may gain an uncomfortably close view. Equally hair-raising is the Trans-Fagaras Highway, built in the 1960s south of Sibiu, which rises up and through the range near its highest point. Further west, the Olt River Gorge provides the only passage of a major Transylvanian river through the Carpathians at Red Tower Pass. The Fagaras, Paring, and especially the Retez at massif and its national park, west of the Olt, attract hardy mountaineers to their glaciers, lakes, and wildlife: brown bears, chamois, and lynx. After the Carpathians, lower, older mountain ranges present less substantial obstacles within the historic provinces: the Moldavian and Getic Subcarpathians to the east and south, and the Western Mountains (sometimes called the Western Carpathians) in several ranges from north to south, to the east of the present Hungarian border. Only the highest of the Western Mountains, the Bihor range, reach heights above 2,000 meters. Unlike these other mountains, for most of recorded history, the Eastern and Southern Carpathians constituted a political and cultural frontier between Hungarian lands and the principalities of Walachia and Moldavia, where Romanian statehood first arose.

Walachia arose from the historical regions of Oltenia and Muntenia, to the west and east of the Olt, formerly seats of viceroys but for many centuries no longer distinct administrative units. The northern part of Walachia is mountainous country populated seasonally by shepherds and their flocks, by occasional hermitages or larger monastic establishments, and the first capital towns of the medieval and early modern era. The Alpine country gives way to hills and tableland, conducive to fruit (especially plums and apples) and viticulture, punctuated by a series of rivers that broaden as they flow south or east into the low, fertile (Romania's maize and wheat are grown here) plain of the Danube: the Motru, Jiu, Oltet, Olt, Vedea, Teleorman, Arges, Dimbovita and

---

1 A city in Transylvania, Romania, with a population of 147,245. Located some 275 km north-west of Bucharest, the city straddles the Cibin River, a tributary of the river Olt. Now the capital of Sibiu County, between 1692 and 1791 and 1849–1865 Sibiu was the capital of the Principality of Transylvania [Source: Wikipedia].

Ialomita Rivers. Ancient and medieval accounts reveal that the Danube plain was previously covered with forests, as are the foothills today. The draining and rerouting of river backwaters have also made the Danube plain less productive for fishing than it once was.

Oltenia's principal city, Craiova, rose to prominence as the seat of a viceroy when it moved down from the hills to the newer town on the middle Jiu that was better situated for east-west communications. Its major industries in recent decades have been automobiles, aircraft, and thermal power. Targu Jiu, in the northwestern mountains, is the country's main mining centre. After heavy development of many years, it is now environmentally blighted and has been the site of industrial unrest in recent decades. Drobeta-Turnu Severin, whose name refers to its ancient origins (remnants of its Roman bridge across the Danube are still visible), is a transport centre east of the Iron Gates and known for the rose gardens in its city centre. Muntenia constitutes two-thirds of Walachia's territory. Bucharest, the capital, is the cultural and industrial centre. Other urban and industrial centers are Ploiesti (long one of the major oil-extracting centers of Europe) and Piteşti (auto-manufacturing and textiles) to the north and west. Giurgiu is a smaller industrial centre (chemicals) and port on the Danube that was heavily polluted under the communists. Several of Romania's largest lakes are backwaters of the Danube in southern Walachia.

North of Walachia and facing the Carpathians from the east, Moldavia bears the same name in Romanian—Moldova—and the same historical origin as the independent state to its northeast on the other side of the Prut. As in Walachia, Moldavia's Carpathian borders slope irregularly to lower mountains, hills, and the plains. Relatively few rivers (the Bistrita, Oituz, Trotus, and Buzau) flow down from these mountains, and the principal rivers, the Siret and Prut, run parallel to them and form a maize-growing plain before emptying into the Danube. Romania's largest Danubian ports are in Moldavia, Galati, and Braila. Galati is also an iron and steelmaking centre, and its deep harbour enables it to service oceangoing vessels. The hill country of Moldavia boasts two of Romania's most important wine regions, Vrancea in the south and Cotnari northwest of Iasi. Iasi, the historical capital of the province, is the country's second-largest city and, like Bucharest, a centre of diverse branches of industry. The independent nation of Moldova, largely but not completely synonymous with Bessarabia, is a low land between the Prut and the Dniester. Modest hills in its centre are home to major winegrowing regions, but Moldavia (Romanian: Moldovia)'s principal crops are maize and sugar beets. The capital city is Chisinau (Slavic: Kishinev). The Transdniester (primarily Slavic) and Gagauzi regions of Moldavia, near its southeastern border with Ukraine, are virtually though not de jure independent. The area across the border, which was ceded to Ukraine in 1940, has a Romanian minority.

One-third major region is Dobrogea (Slavic: Dobrudja) in the southeast, bounded by the Danube, the Bulgarian border, and the Black Sea. The two major coastal towns were founded by the ancient Greeks and contain extensive archaeological remains: Mangalia (Greek: Kallatis) near the Bulgarian border and Constanta (originally Tomis) further north, Romania's largest Black Sea port and near the mouth of the Danube-Black Sea Canal, completed in 1984. The inland of Dobrogea is dry, with a few ranges of hills and a restored Roman monument at Adamclisi to the conquest of the area from the Dacians by Emperor Trajan[1]. Further north, Histria was a Greek port at the mouth of the Danube before it silted up in the 7th century. For most of the modern era, this region was ruled directly by the Ottoman Empire, as evidenced by the presence of mosques and Turkish place-names such as Techirghiol and Medgidia, the latter founded under Sultan Abdul Mejid in 1840. Still further north, the Danube Delta is not a part of Dobrogea either historically or geographically but is commonly included with it. East of the port town of Tulcea on the Ukrainian border, the Danube divides into three arms before it reaches the sea. The Chilia arm forms the border and is the longest, frequently branching arm; the Sulina arm, artificially straightened, is favoured by shippers but requires periodic dredging, while the

---

1 Roman emperor from 98 to 117 AD. Officially declared by the Senate optimus princeps ("the best ruler"), Trajan is remembered as a successful soldier-emperor who presided over the greatest military expansion in Roman history, leading the empire to attain its maximum territorial extent by the time of his death [Source: Wikipedia].

St. George arm is furthest south. This is a sparsely populated region of reedy marshes with more than 300 species of birds. South of St. George, Lakes Razim and Sinoie are salt-water lagoons. After excessive harvesting of the reeds, overfishing, and an ill-conceived project to gain cropland through draining the area, UNESCO inspired the establishment of the Danube Delta Biosphere Reserve Authority in the 1990s that controls development and tourist access.

Bucovina, historically part of Moldavia, was created in1775 through the cession of this territory northwest of Iasi to Austria. While it came to united Romania in 1918, its northern part, with a large Romanian population, was ceded to Soviet Ukraine in 1940. Southern Bucovina is in the northernmost part of current Romania, in the upper reaches of the Siret, Suceava, and Moldavia Rivers. Due to isolation near the frontier and the Carpathian barrier to the west, the region is relatively undeveloped. This, along with UNESCO designation as artistic treasures, has helped preserve Bucovina's painted monasteries, founded by Moldavian Prince Stephen the Great in the 15th and 16th centuries. The influence of 143 years of Austrian rule may be detected in a residual German element of the population and in the appearance of some of the towns.

The mountains extending into Ukraine from Romanian Bucovina separate it from the region of Maramures. Maramures and three other regions formed part of Hungary from the high Middle Ages until 1918: Crisana, Banat, and Transylvania. All four regions already contained a predominant Romanian element at that time. With the assimilating impact of the Romanian educational system and economic development, their adherence to Romania is secure today, but the influence of their earlier history is evident in the religion, work ethic, political preferences, and customs of all groups of society, as well as in the appearance of the towns. Superior rates of economic development benefited the Romanians and the non-Romanian populations, there were superior educational opportunities, and the legal and administrative framework favoured the development of civic awareness.

In Maramures, as in Bucovina, geographic isolation because of the mountains and the proximity of the frontier has limited the development of industry in recent decades and enabled rural communities to maintain their

Chapter 1　Introduction

character. The Gutai, Tibles and Rodna Mountains separate the province from Transylvania to the south, and administratively it formed part of Hungary proper rather than the relatively autonomous Transylvania. The earlier self-governing villages of free peasants and minor nobility have retained their separate consciousness, folk customs, and traditional garb to a surprising extent. These villages populate the valleys of the Iza and Viseu Rivers, while to their north the upper Tisa River forms part of the Ukrainian border before flowing into the Hungarian plain. The major town, Baia Mare, is a mining centre whose population suffered severely through the construction of metallurgical plants upwind of the city centre. The second city, Sighet, on the Ukrainian border, was the site of the country's main detention centre for political prisoners in the 1950s.

Crisana, further south, unlike Maramures and Transylvania, was not a historical region but a term of convenience for parts of several counties separated from Hungary in 1918 around the Somes and the three branches of the Cris Rivers. This region is geographically indistinguishable from the great Hungarian plain. It is a maize-growing, wheat-growing, and rye-growing area. Its major towns, Satu Mare on the Somes and Oradea on the Crisul Repede are seats of Roman Catholic bishoprics, hard on the Hungarian border, that bear the imprint of baroque and fin de siècle[1] architecture.

The Banat originated as a regional governorship that emerged in the Hungarian Mid-Middle Ages but gained its modern dimensions after the Austrians reconquered the area from the Turks in 1716. Having been depopulated by centuries of Turkish-Christian warfare, it was now colonized by the Habsburgs with German, French, Romanian, Serbian, and other settlers who received incentives to develop agriculture and crafts. The major towns, Arad on

---

1　A term commonly applied to French art and artists, as the traits of the culture first appeared there, but the movement affected many European countries. The term becomes applicable to the sentiments and traits associated with the culture, as opposed to focusing solely on the movement's initial recognition in France. The ideas and concerns developed by fin de siècle artists provided the impetus for movements such as symbolism and modernism [Source: Wikipedia].

the Mures and Timisoara, were largely rebuilt by the Habsburgs, with French-style fortifications and Central European squares. The Mures and Timis Rivers both flow into the Danube on Hungarian territory. The southern plain meets the Danube in the Banat by the old town of Oravita, while further east the mining town of Resita is a foretaste of Targul Jiu.

Transylvania was associated with the Hungarian Crown from its first documented mention in the 12th century until its union with Romania in 1918. The geographic unity of the province greatly contributed to the separate identity it enjoyed over the centuries, and to some extent still does today. The Eastern and Southern Carpathians formed a natural frontier toward Walachia and Moldavia, while the Western Mountains performed this function to a much lesser extent toward Hungary proper. North of the Bihor Mountains, the hills do not pose much of a barrier. The Somes flows through a wide valley to Satu Mare, while south of these mountains the Mureș, the longest river of Transylvania, flows through an even wider valley before entering today's Hungary near Arad. Central Transylvania is a well-watered plateau with several major river basins, north to south the Bistrita, two branches of the Somes, two branches of the Mures, two branches of the Tarnava, and the Olt, that helped, along with the defense needs of Hungarian kings, to define administrative and cultural units in this extremely diverse region. In the north, the headwaters of the Somes and Bistrita became the seat of a Saxon district, while further east the headwaters of the Mures and Olt formed the core of the Szekely or Szekler district, the middle expanse of the Olt formed the bulk of the Saxon zone, and border regiments of Szekely and Romanians guarded the Carpathians to the east and south. Central Transylvania too has its characteristic administrative and ethnographic regions. The major towns, Cluj-Napoca, Sibiu, Targu Mures, and Brasov are largely Romanian today but with significant remnants of the ethnic groups associated with much of their older Gothic, baroque, and art nouveau architecture. Gold, salt, iron, and copper mining are significant in various parts of Transylvania. Partly in consequence, some of the most polluted towns are in the metallurgical centres Zlatna and Hunedoar and the carbon works at Copsa

Mica. Transylvania's relatively high altitude means it has shorter growing seasons than the rest of the country does, but it is well watered and hence well suited for livestock as well as rye, maize, plums, and vineyards. Plum brandy is the Romanian national beverage, and it is produced in every region.

Peoples[1]

The differing history and date of integration into Romania of its regions has contributed in large part to its ethnographic variety. According to the 1930 census, minorities made up 28% of the population. Much of the minority population was permanently lost in 1940 with the secession of Bessarabia, but powerful assimilationist trends have also been at work. Ethnic self-identification, language, and religion must all be considered in describing the population of Romania. In March 2002 Romania held its twelfth census since the beginning of the 19th century. In terms of ethnicity, mother tongue, and religious identification, the census showed the following.

PICUTURE: Romanian girls in ethnic costumes
SOURCE: http://unirea.org.au/images/3566328314_8cf6e73321_z.jpg

---

1 T., Burford & N. Longley, *The Rough Guide to Romania*, London: Dorling Kindersley Ltd, 2011.

Romanians

Romanians are the predominant ethnic and linguistic group in every region of the country. While there is no consensus among scholars about the length of their residence in the country's territories, their presence is documented since the 13th century.

Most Romanians belong to the Romanian Orthodox Church, which is contiguous with the territory of the country, led by a patriarch in Bucharest, and divided into thirteen archbishoprics and bishoprics. Romanian Orthodoxy, with its Byzantine rite liturgy chanted in Romanian, rich tradition of icon painting and architecture, and association with dynastic and military history, is closely associated with national identity. It enjoyed an expansion of Orthodox seminaries and publishing, but it also meekly accepted the destruction of many historic churches in the 1980s. This attitude damaged the prestige of the church among many Romanians, and consequently, it has not been in a position to aid in the restoration of Romanian morale in the face of social and economic stagnation since the establishment of the new government.

Greek Catholics, whose church was organized in 1700 in Transylvania, live overwhelmingly in that province and are mostly Romanian. Their liturgy and artistic traditions resemble those of the Orthodox, but they recognize the authority of the pope. They numbered roughly 1.4 million, about half the Romanian population in the lands formerly part of Hungary, at the time of the suppression of the church in 1948. Although the church was restored to legality in 1990 and its previously clandestine bishops returned to public life, it has failed to regain possession of most church buildings expropriated in 1948. Doubts raised by the Orthodox about the loyalty of the church to the nation (ecclesiastical ties to the Roman Catholics made it relatively open to Hungarian cultural influence, although Uniate schools and writers were generally bulwarks of Romanian culture under Hungarian rule) and stubborn defence of Orthodox Church property have kept the Uniates on the defensive. To some degree, neo-Protestant churches have filled the void, attracting members from the traditional but embattled Romanian churches. The more than half-million strong Pentecostal, Baptist, 17th-Day Adventist, and Evangelical Churches have grown rapidly since 1990 and are primarily Romanian. Roman Catholic Church members are mostly Hungarian but include growing Romanian minorities in Moldavia and to a lesser extent in Walachia, where Latin rite parishes and bishoprics function in the Romanian language.

There are many Romanian ethnographic regions with distinctive folk arts that have inspired writers, painters, and composers. To mention only a few, Vrancea in southwestern Moldavia is known for its folk music, Gorj in Oltenia for its architecture, Tara motilor in the Western Carpathians for its carved wooden objects and annual mating fair, and Maramures for its carved wooden gates. The monasteries and villages of the Carpathians and especially their shepherds are powerful images in Romanian culture.

Hungarians

The large Hungarian minority is a legacy of the lands ceded from Hungary after World War I, where Hungarians had settled in medieval times. Though Romanians have predominated in these lands throughout the modern period and into the present, there is a Hungarian majority in two counties of the Szekely region of Transylvania and substantial minorities in most other counties that formerly belonged to Hungary. Miercurea Ciuc (Hungarian: Csíkszereda) and Sfintu Gheorghe are the largest towns with Hungarian majorities, but Targu Mure and Cluj-Napoca have large Hungarian minority populations. The decline of the Hungarian population below 1.5 million in the 2002 census is attributed by both Hungarians and Romanians to emigration, especially to Hungary, but economic stagnation and emigration have caused an absolute decline in the Romanian majority as well. The Hungarian political party, the Democratic Union of Hungarians of Romania, provides Hungarians with a large degree of political unity, and their cultural institutions enjoy the support of the Hungarian government, in which the Romanian government increasingly acquiesces.

Hungarian churches and bishops have served as protectors of minority culture. Most members of the Roman Catholic, Reformed (Calvinist), Unitarian, and Synodal Lutheran Churches are Hungarians. There are small Hungarian minorities in Moldavia and Walachia.

Two special ethnographic groups of the Hungarians are the Szekely (or Szekler) people and the Csangos. The Szekely owe their origins to a Turkic people[1] that was once distinct from the bulk of the Hungarians, but in modern times it has spoken a form of standard Hungarian and expressed Hungarian political consciousness. Szekely towns and rural communities are prized by Hungarians for the traditions of their schools and churches as well as (like the Maramureş Romanians) their carved wooden gates. The Csangos (Romanian: Ciangai) are a Roman Catholic people living in the valley of the Trotus River and around the towns of Bacau (Hungarian: Bákó) and Targu Ocna in south-central Moldavia. The Csangos are probably of Hungarian origin, though today most speak a local variant of Romanian and are distinguished primarily by their strong Roman Catholic faith. A subgroup of Csangos lives in southeastern Transylvania near the town of Brasov.

Roma (Gypsies)

The enumeration of Romania's Roma, or Gypsies, is difficult. The Budapest-based European Human Rights Foundation estimates the Roma population at 1.9 million, the largest in any country. Official census figures are much lower, but it is likely that anti-Roma sentiment in the general population discourages many Roma from declaring this identity to census takers. Market conditions after 1990 have enabled some Roma to do quite well in business

---

1 The Turkic peoples are a collection of ethno-linguistic groups of Central, Eastern, Northern and Western Asiaas well as parts of Europe and North Africa. They speak languages belonging to the Turkic language family.They share, to varying degrees, certain cultural traits, common ancestry and historical backgrounds. The most notable modern Turkic ethnic groups include Turkish people, Azerbaijanis, Uzbeks, Kazakhs, Turkmen and Kyrgyz people [Source: Wikipedia].

or music and to build gaudy "palaces" in the Roma quarters of some towns, but even larger numbers of Roma have failed to establish a firm footing in the Romanian economy. They suffer from poverty, homelessness, and inadequate education. Tens of thousands of Roma from Romania died in the camps in Auschwitz and Transnistria in World War II. Discrimination against Roma today, including mistreatment by the Romanian police, has been documented by Amnesty International.

The variety of ethnic groupings among the Roma also weakens Roma identity. The 2002 census reveals that only half the self-identified Roma indicated Romanes as their mother tongue. Most of the others are speakers of Romanian and, in Transylvania, Romanian or Hungarian. The Roma are politically disunited, with at least four Roma political parties in the country and a rival "king" and "emperor" in the Transylvanian town of Sibiu. Roma are distributed among the churches dominated by the Romanians and Hungarians in their respective regions. "King" Florin Cioaba is a Pentecostal minister. The majority of Roma live in settled urban or rural communities, and only a minority still follow a migratory lifestyle.

Ukrainians and Russians

The 100,000 eastern Slavs in the country are concentrated in two regions, the Ukrainiansin Maramures and adjoining parts of Bucovina, and the Russians (Lipovani[1]) in the Danube Delta. The political importance of these minorities is heightened, and their status either worsened or improved, according to the nature of Romania's relations with Ukraine and the Republic of Moldova, where

---

1 Descendants of the Old Believers who left Russia around 1772 to avoid religious persecution, the Lipovani (identifiable by their blond hair, blue eyes and, among the men, beards) were once dispersed all over the Delta but are now found only at Periprava, Mila 23, Mahmudia and Letea, as well as Jurilovca and Sarichioi on Lake Razim. Adapting to their environment, the Lipovani became skilled fishermen and gardeners, speaking a Russian dialect among themselves but equally fluent in Romanian [https://www.roughguides.com/destinations/europe/romania/delta-coast/lipovani/].

Ukrainians and Russians exercise strong influence over the fortunes of the Romanians living in those countries. The Ukrainians in Romania's northwest adhere primarily to the Ukrainian Orthodox Church, but a minority are Greek Catholics. The Lipovani are Russian Orthodox Old Believers, who came to the delta at the time of Peter the Great to escape religious persecution.

Germans

At its height, during the interwar period, Romania's German minority was ten times larger than its current size. The ancestors of some Germans were brought to Transylvania by Hungarian kings in the thirteenth century to settle and defend the southern borderland of the province, while others came in the eighteenth century to help revive the economy of southeastern Hungary after its liberation from the Turks. Today perhaps two-thirds of the Germans are Roman Catholic Swabians (Schwaben) residing in the Banat, while less than 20,000 Lutheran Saxons (Sachsen)[1] remain in southern Transylvania. Many Germans fled westward at the end of World War II, and a large portion of those who remained was deported to the Soviet Union. Most deportees returned to Romania in the 1950s but began to emigrate in the 1970s with the collusion of the Romanian and West German governments, which paid a ransom (nominally in remuneration for their education in Romania) for each person. Although the ransom system ended with the fall of communism, German emigration became a flood in 1990. Many abandoned Saxon villages have been occupied by Roma, while their historic churches are preserved by foundations based in Germany or have been purchased by Romanian congregations.

Turks and Tatars

Turks and Tatars are remnants of larger settlements in Dobrogea and the Lower Danube that arose during the period of Ottoman domination in Walachia

---

1 A group of Germanic tribes first mentioned as living near the North Sea coast of what is now Germany in the late Roman Empire [Source: Wikipedia].

and Moldavia. Their Muslim religion has proven more tenacious than their language and ethnic identity. Two mosques in Constanta were built in 1868 and 1910; there are older mosques in Mangalia and Babadag. Romania's growing economic relations with Turkey have helped ensure the preservation of these monuments and modest support for Turkish and Tatar cultural organizations.

Jews

Romania's Jewish population, like that of the Germans, was once much larger. Jews were a majority of the population of Iasi in the late 19th century, and they accounted for much of the commercial activity in Moldavia. Romanian anti-Semitism was correspondingly strongest there. It gained powerful influence in Romanian political life during the interwar period, although Jewish-Christian relations had been relatively peaceful in Bucharest. Jews east and south of the Carpathians were Sephardim, while those in the formerly Habsburg lands were Ashkenazim. The Holocaust took a heavy toll on both these groups, the former being deported by Romanian troops to Transnistria and the latter by the Hungarians to Auschwitz. Still, more Jews survived the Holocaust in Romania than in any other country in the region. As with the Germans, a ransom system (financed by Israel) facilitated the emigration of most survivors by the 1980s. Fewer than 10,000 Jews remain in Romania, but the country's ultranationalists still find anti-Semitism(often paired with anti-Hungarianism) a useful tool.

Chapter 2
History

Every country has a story. Some are longer than others, but there isn't a place with borders in the world that doesn't have tales of war, immigration, development, and independence in its past, and Romania is no different. The area today known as Romania was first settled by a people known as the Dacians. The Dacians formed a significant empire that reached its peak in the 1st century BC, and plenty of evidence of their structures and culture can be found to have littered all over Romania. Unlike some areas, the Romans conquered, however, Romania was located in an advantageous spot, rich in gold deposits and geographically located along trade routes and near (or in) the Balkan peninsula. As a result, something happened in Romania that didn't happen in many other areas: It became heavily Latinised as Romans moved in, establishing cities, building roads, and importing Roman culture. Rome's dominance over Romania only lasted about two hundred years, but in those centuries it had an incredible impact on the people and country.[1]

The history of Romania can then be divided into the following periods:

Ancient History / Roman Period (3600 BC – 500 AD)

Middle Ages / Byzantine Period (500 – 1500)

Early Modern / Ottoman Period (1500 – 1750)

Mid Modern Period (1750 – 1914)

Contemporary Period (1914 – present)

History[2]

Located in Southeast Europe, Romania is bordered by Ukraine on the north, Moldavia in the northeast, Hungary on the northwest, Serbia on the southwest, Bulgaria on the south, and the Black Sea on the southeast. The earliest evidence of human habitation in Romania dates back to Stone Age. Since then, Romania has been controlled by various empires. But a recorded form of information is not available until the time when the present-day Romania was known as Dacia[3] after its inhabitants, the Dacians or the Getae[4]. The Dacians suffered the first major invasion from the Greeks between the seventh and sixth centuries BC. Several centuries later, most of Romania became the Roman province of Dacia in about AD 100. After reigning over Dacia for decades, the Roman power came

---

1 https://www.onehourtranslation.com/translation/blog/short-history-romania

2 Frucht, R. C. (Ed.). (2005). *Eastern Europe: An Introduction to the People, Lands, and Culture* (Vol. 1). ABC-CLIO.

3 In ancient geography, especially in Roman sources, Dacia (/ˈdeɪʃiə, -ʃə/) was the land inhabited by the Dacians. The Greeks referred to them as the Getae (east of Dacia) and the Romans as Daci. Dacia was bounded in the south approximately by the Danubius river (Danube), At times Dacia included areas between the Tisa and the Middle Danube. The Carpathian Mountains are located in the middle of Dacia. It thus corresponds to the present day countries of Romania and Moldova, as well as smaller parts of Bulgaria, Serbia, Hungary, Poland, Slovakia and Ukraine [Source: Wikipedia].

4 The Getae /ˈdʒiːtiː/ or /ˈɡiːtiː/) were several Thracian tribes that once inhabited the regions to either side of the Lower Danube, in what is today northern Bulgaria and southern Romania [Source: Wikipedia].

crashing down as a result of barbaric invasions [1] and left the soil in AD 271. This incident started a new chapter of power struggle over Romania and waves of nomadic tribes began sweeping across the mainland, including the Goths[2], Vandals[3], Huns[4], Slavs[5] and Magyars[6]. Coming from different parts of Europe and Asia, these tribes occupied Romania at different times. Consequently, their arrivals, settlements, conflicts and integration of different cultures and races significantly influenced the demography of the country. Gradually, the mainland

---

1 The Romans referred to people groups outside the Roman Empire as barbarians who had different cultures from the Romans. They dressed differently, ate different foods, and had different religions. They did not have the same level of government, education, or engineering as the Romans. The Romans fought the barbarians at the borders of the Roman Empire for many years. In some cases, barbarians became part of the Roman Empire. In other cases, they fought wars and, eventually, sacked the city of Rome bringing about the end of the Western Roman Empire [in https://www.ducksters.com/history/ancient_rome/barbarians.php].

2 A member of a Germanic people that invaded the Roman Empire from the east between the 3rd and 5th centuries. The eastern division, the Ostrogoths, founded a kingdom in Italy, while the Visigoths went on to found one in Spain.

3 An East Germanic tribe or group of tribes, first appear in history as inhabiting present-day southern Poland, but later moved around Europe, successively establishing kingdoms in Spain and in North Africa in the 5th century [Source: Wikipedia].

4 A nomadic tribe whose origin is unknown but, most likely, they came from somewhere between the eastern edge of the Altai Mountains and the Caspian Sea, roughly modern Kazakhstan. Huns became one of the primary contributors to the fall of the Roman Empire, as their invasions of the regions around the empire, which were particularly brutal, encouraged what is known as the Great Migration (also known as the "Wandering of the Nations") between roughly 376–476. This migration of peoples, such as the Alans, Goths, and Vandals, disrupted the status quo of Roman society, and their various raids and insurrections weakened the empire [Source: Wikipedia].

5 An ethnic group of people who share a long-term cultural continuity and who speak a set of related languages known as the Slavic languages (all of which belong to the Indo-European language family). Today, a large number of Slavic languages are still spoken including Bulgarian, Czech, Croatian, Polish, Serbian, Slovak, Russian, and many others, stretching from central and eastern Europe down into Russia.

6 A nation and an ethnic group native to and primarily associated with the Hungarian people. Magyar tribes, the fundamental political units in which the Hungarians lived during the time they still occupied the Tarim Basin and later the Ural Mountains, prior to the establishment of the Principality of Hungary [Source: Wikipedia].

Romania disintegrated into three principalities. The northern region developed into a principality called Transylvania, the south into a principality called Walachia, and the east into Moldavia.

Till 11th century, the Magyars, the ancestors of today's Hungarians, dominated the Transylvanian region, while the Romanians who fled Transylvania established the independent principalities of Walachia and Moldavia in the 13th and 14th centuries. Hungarian historians proclaim that Transylvania was an uninhabited land when the Magyars first settled there; Romanians, however, allege that their ancestors dwelled in Transylvania after Rome's exodus and that Romanians should be acknowledged as the region's aboriginal inhabitants. This discrepancy was the source of a conflict that blemished relations between Romania and Hungary throughout the 20th century.

Throughout the 14th and 15th centuries, Walachia and Moldavia suffered repeated invasions by the Ottoman Empire[1]. They eventually succumbed around 1500 and remained under Turkish rule for more than 300 years. In 1526, a battle took place between Hungary and the Ottoman Empire, which is the Battle of the Mohacs[2]. Following this battle, Ottoman Empire occupied all three regions from the 16th to the late 17th century. In 1601, the principalities of Moldavia, Walachia,

---

1 An empire created by Turkish tribes in Anatolia (Asia Minor) that grew to be one of the most powerful states in the world during the 15th and 16th centuries. The Ottoman period spanned more than 600 years and came to an end only in 1922, when it was replaced by the Turkish Republic and various successor states in southeastern Europe and the Middle East. At its height, the empire encompassed most of southeastern Europe to the gates of Vienna, including present-day Hungary, the Balkan region, and parts of Ukraine; portions of the Middle East now occupied by Iraq, Syria, Israel, and Egypt; North Africa as far west as Algeria; and large parts of the Arabian Peninsula [in https://www.britannica.com/place/Ottoman-Empire].

2 The Battle of Mohács on 29 August 1526 marked the beginning of the Habsburgs' Turkish Wars, which lasted until well into the 18th century and reached their climax in the two Turkish sieges of Vienna, the first in 1529, the second in 1683. The battle, which led to some 10,000 people being killed or driven from their homes, resulted in an expansion of the Habsburg territories. Among the dead was King Louis II of Hungary and Bohemia; his territories passed to Ferdinand I, who later became Holy Roman Emperor [in http://www.habsburger.net/en/events/battle-mohacs-1526].

and Transylvania were united for the first time under Prince Michael the Brave[1]. During Michael's reign, Romania maintained a degree of sovereignty, but after his death, the Turks again dominated the region. They ruled through Greek officials who abused their power to exploit the peasants. In the late 1700s and early 1800s, the Ottoman Empire was weakened by a series of defeats to the Russians. Afterwards, Austria's Habsburgs[2] gained full control of Transylvania, while Walachia and Moldavia came under neighbouring Russian protection. After the Russo-Turkish War of 1828−1829[3], Walachia and Moldavia became Russian protectorates and remained under Russian influence until the Crimean War (1853−1856)[4] ended the protectorate. In 1859, Walachia and Moldavia merged to form Romania, and it became a unified kingdom in 1881 when Karl of Hohenzollern[5], a German prince, was chosen as the country's ruler and

---

1 The Prince of Wallachia, Prince of Moldavia and de facto ruler of Transylvania. He is considered as one of Romania's greatest national heroes, and he is seen by Romanian historiography as the first author of Romanian unity [Source: Wikipedia].

2 The House of Habsburg, also called House of Austria was one of the most influential and outstanding royal houses of Europe. The throne of the Holy Roman Empire was continuously occupied by the Habsburgs between 1438 and 1740 [Source: Wikipedia].

3 The Russo-Turkish War of 1828−1829 was sparked by the Greek War of Independence. The war broke out after the Sultan closed the Dardanelles to Russian ships and revoked the Akkerman Convention in retaliation for Russian participation in the Battle of Navarino [Source: Wikipedia].

4 War fought mainly on the Crimean Peninsulabetween the Russians and the British, French, and Ottoman Turkish, with support from January 1855 by the army of Sardinia-Piedmont. The war arose from the conflict of great powers in the Middle East and was more directly caused by Russian demands to exercise protection over the Orthodox subjects of the Ottoman sultan. Another major factor was the dispute between Russia and France over the privileges of the Russian Orthodox and Roman Catholic churches in the holy places in Palestine [https://www.britannica.com/event/Crimean-War].

5 Also as Carol I, the ruler of Romania from 1866 to 1914. He was elected Ruling Prince (Domnitor) of the Romanian United Principalities on 20 April 1866 after the overthrow of Alexandru Ioan Cuza by a palace coup d'état. In May 1877, he proclaimed Romania an independent and sovereign nation. The defeat of the Ottoman Empire (1878) in the Russo-Turkish War secured Romanian independence. He was proclaimed King of Romania on 26 March 1881. He was the first ruler of the Hohenzollern-Sigmaringen dynasty, which ruled the country until the proclamation of a republic in 1947 [Source: Wikipedia].

became King of Romania (Carol I) after the Congress of Berlin. Transylvania and Hungary were reunited by Austria in 1867.

In 1914, King Carol died and Ferdinand I was crowned. With the outbreak of the First World War, Romania changed its initial neutral stance and allied itself with Britain, France and the other Allies. The aim was to get hold of the territory of Transylvania and it succeeded in doing so with the Treaty of Trianon[1] in 1920. After the war, the Trianon Treaty doubled the size of the country, uniting Moldavia and Walachia with Transylvania, Banat, Bessarabia (present-day Moldova), and Bucovina (today in southern Ukraine). In the years after World War I, public dissatisfaction with the regency mounted when Romania was plunged into economic crisis by the Great Depression, the global economic crash that began in 1929. The Guard's fanatical members were known as legionnaires. Jackbooted and wearing green shirts with little bags of "sacred" Romanian soil hanging from their necks, they assaulted leftists and Jews, assassinating premiers in 1933 and 1939. When Ferdinand died in 1927, his son Carol II succeed his throne in 1930. To aid his consolidation of power, he forged informal and ambiguous links with the Iron Guard. But when the candidates of Iron Guard won major victories in the 1937 elections, Carol II eventually felt threatened by the Guard's power. In 1938, he cracked down on the legionnaires, arresting thousands of them and the head of the Iron Guard was executed on his order.

In August 1939, Hitler signed a non-aggression pact with Soviet leader Joseph Stalin, which freed Hitler to launch his invasion of Poland in September, starting World War II. The pact also included a secret clause giving Moscow a free hand to reclaim Bessarabia. On 26 June 1940, the Soviets gave Romania a

---

1 The peace agreement of 1920 to formally end World War I between most of the Allies of World War I and the Kingdom of Hungary, the latter one of the successor states to Austria-Hungary. The treaty regulated the status of an independent Hungarian state and defined its borders. The treaty limited Hungary's army to 35,000 officers and men, while the Austro-Hungarian Navy ceased to exist [https://www.nationstates.net/page=dispatch/id=447849].

24-hour ultimatum to turn over not only Bessarabia but also northern Bukovina, a region that had never been under Russian control. King Carol II was left with no choice but to give in to the Soviet demands. In August, under German, Soviet, and Italian pressure, Romania was forced to return southern Dobruja to Bulgaria and northern Transylvania to Hungary. Within three months, Romania was swiftly dismembered, losing one-third of its national territory and four million of its citizens. This national humiliation proved to be the end for Carol. In a last-ditch effort to retain power, he named pro-legionnaire Marshal Ion Antonescu[1] premier. But Antonescu, in league with the major political parties, army officers, and the Iron Guard, and with the full backing of Nazi Germany, forced Carol to abdicate on 6 September 1940. He fled into exile, leaving his now 19-year-old son, Michael V (1940–1947), to take the throne.

Although Michael took the throne in 1940, the real power fell to Ion Antonescu. In an effort to recoup Soviet-occupied territories, the country aligned itself with the German forces, participating in the invasion of the Soviet Union in 1941. Along Fascist orders, Romania was reorganized and about 270,000 Jews were massacred. In 1944, a coup supported by the King Michael was staged, Antonescu was overthrown and the Germans were expelled. Romania joined the Allied forces and in following years the Romanian army helped to liberate its neighbours, Hungary and Czechoslovakia.

After the Second World War ended in 1945, most of the occupied territories

---

1 Former prime minister of Romania for most of World War II, after leading the overthrow of Carol II in 1940. He nominally was co-head of state with King Michael, but most of the actual power rested with Antonescu. A firm anti-Semite, Antonescu independently implemented policies, based on the Nazi model, that were responsible for the deaths of some 40,000 Jews. Under Antonescu, Romania entered the War on the side of the Axis. He survived one coup attempt by the Iron Guardparty, a like-minded politicial rival whom Antonescu smashed with the aid of Germany. Antonescu allocated troops for the invasion of the Soviet Union in 1941. When the tide turned against the Axis, Antonescu attempted to reach a peace with the Allied Forces in 1944, but was instead successfully toppled by a coalition led by King Michael. He was tried in 1946 for war crimes, convicted, and executed [http://turtledove.wikia.com/wiki/Ion_Antonescu].

were returned, but the Russian communists retained control in Romania. They abolished the monarchy in 1947, replacing King Michael with a puppet government under the leadership of Petru Groza[1], turning Romania into a communist Peoples Republic. Business and industry were nationalized, and farmland was taken from the peasants and reorganized into government-run collectives. In 1955, Romania joined the Warsaw Treaty Organization and the United Nations. In 1965, Nicolae Ceausescu[2] became the General Secretary of the Romanian Communist Party. He actuated large-scale development projects, mainly with money borrowed from other countries. Many of those projects floundered, leaving Romania drowning in debt. Ceaucescu attempted to pay off by exporting virtually everything the country produced, leading to dire shortages of food and fuel. The secret police kept the people in line through terror while Ceausescu and his family, who controlled most of the government, continued to plunder the country for personal gain. In the 1980s, worsening food shortages, along with the toppling of other regimes in Eastern Europe, stirred unrest among people. Protests in 1987 were put down with a combination of military force and extra food distribution. In December 1989, protests in the city of Timisoara were met with gunfire, and hundreds of citizens died. Other protests broke out across the country, and the situation escalated until troops refused to follow orders and joined the protesters. Ceausescu and his wife attempted to flee the country but were halted by the army and brought to trial. Both were found guilty of murder and put to death by firing squad on Christmas Day 1989. A party called the National Salvation Front then assumed power, and in 1990 free elections

---

1 Romanian politician, best known as the Prime Minister of the first Communist Party-dominated government under Soviet occupation during the early stages of the Communist regime in Romania.

2 Romanian Communist politician. He was general secretary of the Romanian Communist Party from 1965 to 1989, and hence the second and last Communist leader of Romania. He was also the country's head of state from 1967, serving as President of the State Council, from 1974 concurrently as President of the Republic, until his overthrow in the Romanian Revolution in 1989 [Source: Wikipedia].

were held. Ion Iliescu[1], the leader of the National Salvation Front and a former Communist Party member, won the presidency, and a new constitution was adopted in 1991. Although there was widespread dissatisfaction with Iliescu's leadership, he won reelection in October 1992. Four years later, he was replaced by the reform-touting Emil Constantinescu[2] of the Democratic Convention of Romania. Despite positive changes during his term, the December 2000 elections became a contest between Iliescu and Corneliu Vadim Tudor[3] of the right-wing Greater Romania Party (PRM), who espoused a hard-line fascist ideology. In this election, an angry electorate returned to power Iliescu and his Social Democratic Party (PSD) with a huge vote for the ultra-nationalist Greater Romania Party to form a coalition government. In 2002, the EU[4] announced that Romania could join in 2007. By 2003, it was obvious that this was being pushed through, mainly due to Romania's strategic position close to the Middle East. By 2004, around 300 people closely tied to the PSD controlled approximately a quarter of Romania's economy; nevertheless, the EU decided the country had

---

1 Romanian politician, who served as President of Romania from 1989 until 1996, and from 2000 until 2004. From 1996 to 2000 and from 2004 until his retirement in 2008, Iliescu was a senator for the Social Democratic Party (PSD), whose honorary president he remains. Iliescu is widely recognized as a predominant figure in the first fifteen years of post-revolution politics. During his terms Romania joined NATO.

2 Romanian professor and politician, who served as the third President of Romania, from 1996 to 2000.

3 The leader of the Greater Romania Party, poet, writer, journalist and a Member of the European Parliament. He was a Romanian Senator from 1992 to 2008. He was born and died in Bucharest [Source: Wikipedia].

4 EU is an abbreviation for the European Union, which is a political and economic union of 28 member states that are located primarily in Europe. It has an area of 4,475,757 km^2 , and an estimated population of over 510 million. The EU has developed an internal single market through a standardised system of laws that apply in all member states. EU policies aim to ensure the free movement of people, goods, services, and capital within the internal market, enact legislation in justice and home affairs, and maintain common policies on trade, agriculture, fisheries, and regional development. Within the Schengen Area, passport controls have been abolished. A monetary union was established in 1999 and came into full force in 2002, and is composed of 19 EU member states which use the euro currency [Source: Wikipedia].

a functioning market economy. Romania joined the EU on New Year's Day of 2007, largely for geopolitical reasons, even though they could not assume fully the rights and obligations of membership. After reforming its military forces to implement NATO[1]'s standards and interoperability objectives which include restructuring the military bureaucracy, adjusting the size and design of the force, and implementing NATO assessment processes to measure efficiency, Romania joined NATO in 2004, promising to participate actively in NATO combined exercises and exploit the training opportunities of NATO's Partnership for Peace.

1　NATO is an abbreviation for the North Atlantic Treaty organization, also called the North Atlantic Alliance, which is an intergovernmental military alliance between several North American and European states based on the North Atlantic Treaty that was signed on 4 April 1949. NATO constitutes a system of collective defence whereby its member states agree to mutual defence in response to an attack by any external party. NATO is an alliance that consists of 29 independent member countries across North America and Europe. An additional 21 countries participate in NATO's Partnership for Peace program, with 15 other countries involved in institutionalized dialogue programs. The combined military spending of all NATO members constitutes over 70% of the global total. Members' defense spending is supposed to amount to at least 2% of GDP by 2024 [Source: Wikipedia].

Chapter 3
Climate and Environment

Owing to its distance from open sea and position on the southeastern portion of the European continent, Romania has a climate that is temperate and continental, with four distinct seasons. There are some regional differences: in western sections, such as Banat, the climate is milder and has some Mediterranean influences; the eastern part of the country has a more pronounced continental climate. In Dobruja, the Black Sea also exerts an influence over the region's climate.

Romania is bounded by Ukraine to the north, Moldova to the northeast, the Black Sea to the southeast, Bulgaria to the south, Serbia to the southwest, and Hungary to the west. There is a certain symmetry in the physical structure of Romania. The country forms a complex geographic unit centred on the Transylvanian Basin, around which the peaks of the Carpathian Mountains and their associated subranges and structural platforms form a series of crescents. Beyond this zone, the extensive plains of the south and east of the country, their potential increased by the Danube River and its tributaries, form a fertile outer crescent extending to the frontiers. There is great diversity in the topography, geology, climate, hydrology, flora, and fauna, and for millennia this natural environment has borne the imprint of a human population.[1]

Climate[2]

Romania's location in the southeastern portion of the European continent gives it a climate that is transitional between temperate regions and the harsher extremes of the continental interior. In the centre and west of the country, humid Atlantic climatic characteristics prevail; in the southeast the continental, influences of the Russian Plain (East European Plain) make themselves felt; and in the extreme southeast, there are even milder sub-Mediterranean influences. This overall pattern is substantially modified by the relief, however, and there are many examples of climatic zones induced by changes in elevation.

The average annual temperature is in the low 50s F (about 11 °C) in the south and in the 40s F (about 8 °C) in the north, although, as noted, there is much variation according to elevation and related factors. Extreme temperatures range from about 112 °F (45 °C) in the Baragan region to −37 °F (−38 °C) in the Brașov Depression.

Average annual rainfall amounts to about 25 inches (640 mm), but in the Carpathians it reaches about 55 inches (1,400 mm), and in the Dobruja, it is only about 16 inches (400 mm). Many regions are subject to periodic drought and flooding. Since the early 1990s, Romania's northern regions have been affected by severe rainfall and flooding. In 1998 and 1999, an unprecedented amount of rain fell in the Retezat Mountains, resulting in landslides, flooding, and widespread destruction and loss of lives. On the other hand, the southern areas of the country have suffered drought and high temperatures since the 1990s.

---

1 https://www.britannica.com/place/Romania
2 https://www.britannica.com/place/Romania

These conditions have been exacerbated by injudicious agricultural practices.

Humid winds from the northwest are most common, but often the drier winds from the northeast are strongest. A hot southwesterly wind blows over western Romania, particularly in summer. In winter, cold and dense air masses encircle the eastern portions of the country, with the cold northeasterly wind blowing in from the Russian Plain, and oceanic air masses from the Azores, in the west, bring rain and mitigate the severity of the cold. Romania enjoys four seasons, though there is a rapid transition from winter to summer. Autumn is frequently longer, with dry warm weather from September to late November.

Environment[1]

The soil of Romania varies greatly. The most fertile soil is the black earth of the plains, but much of the country is covered by brown forest soil of moderate fertility. The soils of the mountain and hill regions are the least fertile. Romania has many mineral resources. Petroleum extraction began in the 1850s, and reserves are now either exhausted or negligible. Natural gas reserves are much larger. There are limited coal supplies including hard coal and lignite.

Metallic minerals include copper, lead, zinc, bauxite, iron ore, chromium, manganese and uranium. Gold, silver and other rare metals are also found. Most of these deposits are sufficient for domestic requirements. The country does not have enough iron ore for its needs, however, and some must be imported. Romania has frequent earthquakes; the most severe are in the south and southwest. In March 1977, Romania experienced an earthquake that registered 7.2 magnitude Richter-scale. In 1991, a 5.7 magnitude earthquake hit western Romania. Additionally, the country's geologic structure and climate promote landslides following heavy periods of rain. Flooding is common and often severe, particularly during spring thaw and summer thunderstorms.

Romania has several serious environmental problems including air, water,

---

1 http://ejc.net/media_landscapes/romania

Chapter 3 Climate and Environment

and soil pollution, reflecting decades of industrial and economic growth with minimal effort to protect the environment. Moreover, the economic and political difficulties of the 1990s caused Romania to exploit natural resources. About one-fourth of the country is covered by forests, of which about 60% is in the mountains. Fir and spruce are the most common trees in the mountains while the lower slopes have forests of deciduous trees such as beech and oak. The plains and plateaus have grass vegetation with few trees. The Danube Delta has vast areas of reeds and other aquatic plants.

The rivers of Romania are virtually all tributary to the Danube which forms the southern frontier from Moldova Noua to Calarasi. Nearly two-fifths of the total Danubian discharge into the Black Sea is in fact provided by Romanian rivers. The final discharge takes place through three arms—the Chilia (two-thirds of the flow), Sfantu Gheorghe (one-fourth) and Sulina (the remainder)—that add to the scenic attraction of the delta region. The most significant of the Romanian tributary rivers are the Prut, Mures, Olt, Siret, Ialomita and Somes. The rivers have considerable hydroelectric potential although there are great seasonal fluctuations in the discharge and few natural lakes to regulate the flow. The total surface-water potential of the tributary rivers is dwarfed by the volume discharged at the Danube mouth which is more than five times as large. Subsoil waters have been estimated at an annual volume of some 250 billion cubic feet (700 million cubic metres).

The total theoretical hydroelectric potential of Romania—given optimum technological conditions—is tremendous, but for technical and economic reasons only a fraction of this potential can be developed. Geographically, the hydroelectric reserves of Romania are concentrated along the Danube and in the valleys of rivers emerging from the mountain core of the country. Other hydrographic resources include more than 2,500 lakes, ranging from the glacial lakes of the mountains to those of the plains and the marshes of the Danube delta region. The main effort since the 1940s, however, has been on the Arges, Bistrita, Lotru, Olt, Mare, Sebes and Somes rivers as well as on the Danube at the Iron Gate.

罗马尼亚概况 | *Survey of Romania* |

Wildlife[1]

Thanks to its antiquated agriculture and extensive areas of untouched native forest and wetland, Romania is uniquely important for wildlife in Europe. While the image of the country abroad is of industrial pollution, the reality is that it is far more pristine than much of Europe. Climbing into the hills, you enter a world where pesticides and fertilizers have never been used and where meadows are full of an amazing variety of birds and wild flowers—a landscape representative of Europe two or three centuries ago.

That said, the country has suffered, and there are numerous industrial plants that cause immense local damage. Some of the worst offenders such as Copsa Mica's carbon-black plant and the Valea Calugareasca fertilizer plant (east of Ploiesti) were built in the capitalist period while the Resita and Hunedoara steelworks and the Zlatna copper smelter date back to the 18th century.

With the establishment of the new government, new problems have appeared due mainly to the return of woodland to the families of the previous owners and the subsequent felling of more than half a million hectares of forest. Coupled with extreme weather, this has led to disastrous flooding and landslides. In 2005, floods caused more than a billion euros of damage with at least 70 deaths. In January 2006, temperatures fell to $-30°C$, causing 45 deaths while heatwaves killed 56 in 2005 and at least 35 in 2007 when temperatures were over $40°C$ nationwide and up to $45°C$ in Bucharest.

Habitat

One-third of Romania is mountain, largely forested and this is where most of the more interesting flora and fauna are to be found. One-third of the country is hill and plateau, and one-third is plain, mostly intensively farmed.

The Carpathian mountains form an arc sweeping south from Ukraine and

---

1 https://info.publicintelligence.net/MCIA-RomaniaHandbook.pdf

Chapter 3　Climate and Environment

around Transylvania to end on the Danube at the Iron Gates. At lower levels (up to around 800 m) the natural vegetation is the forest of oak, hornbeam, lime and ash, a kind of forest that has largely disappeared elsewhere in Europe. Even the hill farmland at this height—largely grazing and hay meadows—is comparatively rich in wildlife, with an abundance of butterflies. Above 800 m, beech becomes increasingly common, and at around 1400 m it forms an association with silver fir and sycamore known as Carpathian Beech Forest. Spruce is dominant above this, and above 1700 m comes the lower alpine zone, characterized by dwarf pine, juniper and low-growing goat willow, and then, from 1900 m upwards, the higher alpine zone of grass, creeping shrubs, lichen, moss and ultimately bare rock.

　　Elsewhere, particularly on the Transylvanian plateau, there is much more oak and beech forest although much has been cleared for farming. Until the 20th century, large areas of eastern Romania—particularly southern Moldavia and Dobrogea—were covered by grassy steppes, the majority of which went under the plough after World War II, though remnant areas can still be found, some (such as Cheia Dobrogea, 38km northwest of Constanta) protected as nature reserves.

　　In the southwest of the country, near the Iron Gates of the Danube, the spectacular Cerna Valley is notable for its more Mediterranean climate with Turkey and downy oaks, Banat pine and sun-loving plant species on limestone rocks.

　　The Danube Delta is a unique habitat. Formed from the massive quantity of sediments brought down the river, it is Europe's most extensive wetland and the world's largest continuous reedbed. It is a uniquely important breeding area for birds as well as a wintering area and a key stepping stone on one of the most important migration routes from northern Europe via the eastern Mediterranean to Africa.

　　Nature reserves have existed in Romania since the 1930s, and some 6.6% of the country is now protected. These reserves range from vast uninhabited areas to relatively modest but still valuable sites including caves, rocks and even

罗马尼亚概况 | *Survey of Romania* |

individual trees. The Retezat and Rodna mountains and the Danube Delta have been named as part of UNESCO's worldwide network of Biosphere Reserves, and at least ten other national parks are yet to be designated. These include the Bicaz and Nera gorges, the Cerna valley and the Apuseni, Piatra Craiului and Căliman mountains.

Flora

In springtime, the mountain meadows of Romania are a riot of wild flowers, 12% of which are endemic to the Carpathians. Between April and July, depending on altitude, you should be able to find spectacular scenes of clover, hawkweed, burdock, fritillary and ox-eye daisy covered in butterflies and, at higher levels, gentians, white false helleborine, globeflower and crocus. Alpine plants include campanulas, saxifrage, orchids, alpine buttercup, pinks and, in a few places, edelweiss. The hay meadows lying below the mountain forest are also extremely rich in flowers.

In the warmer southwest of the country, the Turda, Cerna and Nera gorges and the Retezat mountains are home to sun-loving rarities. One of the most accessible flower-rich sites is the wonderful Zanoaga Gorge in the Bucegi mountains.

The Danube Delta is home to more than 1,600 plant species of three main groups. The floating islets (plaur) that occupy much of the Delta's area are largely composed of reeds (80% Phragmites australis), with mace reed, sedge, Dutch rush, yellow water-flag, water fern, water dock, water forget-me-not, water hemlock and brook mint. In the still backwaters, wholly submerged waterweeds include water-milfoil, hornwort and water-thyme; while floating on the surface you'll find water plantain, arrowhead, duckweed, water soldier, white and yellow waterlily, frog bit, marsh thistle and curly pondweed. The river banks are home to white willow and poplar, with isolated strands of alder and ash, while the more mature forests of Letea and Caraorman also contain oaks, elm, aspen and shrubs such as blackthorn, hawthorn and dog rose. The Romanian peony can be found in woodlands such as Babadag Forest, just to the south.

Birds

Europe's most important wetland, the Danube Delta, serves as a breeding area for summer visitors, a stopping-off point for migrants and a wintering ground for wildfowl; permanent residents are relatively few. Dedicated birders come from the end of March to early June, and from late July to October—but the Delta and the more accessible lakes and reedbeds to the south are worth a visit with binoculars at any season. The Delta lies on the major migration route from Africa via the eastern Mediterranean and northwards along the rivers of Russia to the Arctic.

The spring period, especially May, is an excellent time to visit, with the rare breeding species-black-winged pratincole, pygmy cormorant, glossy ibis, white and Dalmatian pelicans, and warblers-all arriving. The reedbeds are alive with the returned songbirds, most obviously the very noisy great reed warbler. These are accompanied by large numbers of waders on passage to wetlands far to the north, such as little stints, five species of sandpipers and vast flocks of ruff. By this time, the great colonies—of herons (night, grey and squacco herons, great white and little egrets), and of both species of cormorant—are at a peak of activity; the lower Danube holds most of the world population of the endangered pygmy cormorant. The wader colonies are also very active, and you will be scolded loudly when near the nests of avocets and black-winged stilts.

High summer is a good time to see the first of the returning waders, and the population of summer visitors peaks immediately after breeding. This is an excellent time to see formation-flying white pelicans (and the rare Dalmatian pelican) as well as birds of prey such as the colonial red-footed falcon, lesser spotted eagle, marsh harrier and long-legged buzzard.

| 罗马尼亚概况 | *Survey of Romania* |

PICTURE: Dalmatian Pelican
SOURCE: http://whc.unesco.org/?cid=31&l=en&id_site=588&gallery=1&index= 25&maxrows=12

In winter, the number of visiting birds in the Delta area is reduced but still impressive. Main visitors include most of the European population of great white herons (or egrets), at times the entire world population of red-breasted geese (around 70,000 birds) and up to one-third of a million white-fronted geese; there are significant populations of other wildfowl including the exotic-looking red-crested pochard as well as pintail, goldeneye, wigeon, teal, smew and red-throated and black-throated divers; just offshore the sea can teem with wintering black-necked grebes, and rough-legged buzzards are a common sight on roadside wires in open country.

On the inland plains, some species indicative of steppe country still persist, such as short-toed and calandra larks (the largest European lark), while summer visitors include the exotic-looking hoopoe, lesser-spotted and booted eagles, red-footed falcons, European rollers, bee-eaters and lesser grey shrikes—the last three often seen on roadside wires in Dobrogea and the lowlands.

Away from the Delta, the most worthwhile nature reserves are inevitably in the mountains; golden eagles are now rare, but ravens are common. On the tree line, black and three-toed woodpeckers can be found together with ring ouzels in summer while on the highest crags there are alpine accentors and wallcreepers together with the common black redstart, water pipits and alpine swifts and, in some lower crags, crag martins and rock buntings. There are also birds usually associated with more northerly regions such as shore larks and dotterel (breeding only in the Cindrel mountains).

Mountain forests are home to the very shy capercaillie as well as the (slightly easier to see) hazel grouse and (in the north around dwarf pine areas) black grouse. Restricted to the vast forests is the nutcracker as well as the crested, willow and coal tits and the crossbill. The forests are also home to raptors (including buzzards, honey buzzards, sparrowhawks and goshawks) and a number of owls (including the Ural owl, eagle owl, pygmy owl and Tengmalm's owl). The relatively healthy state of Romania's conifer forests favours some birds now rare elsewhere (for example in Scandinavia), notably the white-backed woodpecker.

Romania's extensive lowland deciduous forests harbour huge numbers of common European woodland birds—chaffinches, hawfinches, nuthatches, song thrushes, treecreepers and great, marsh and blue tits. Oak woods are home to the middle-spotted woodpecker, joined in summer by nightingales, wood warblers, chiffchaffs and common redstarts.

Romania is also a refuge for the white stork whose large nests are characteristically built in the heart of human habitations on telephone poles and chimneys. The much shyer and rarer black stork breeds in extensive areas of forest near water, for example along the Olt in southern Transylvania.

Animals

Romania has the most important national populations of large carnivore species—bear, wolf and lynx—in Europe. Having been protected under Ceauşescu for his own personal hunting, there are now five or six thousand brown bears in Romania, particularly in the eastern Carpathians. Although they do raid garbage bins on the outskirts of Braşov and in Poiana Brasov—as well as any mountain hut near or below the tree line—they are generally afraid of humans and will keep well clear unless you come between a female and her cubs in April or May. Whilst they will take prey as large as red deer (not to mention sheep, cattle and horses), they are by diet omnivorous, famously raiding wild bees' and wasps' nests not only for honey but also for the larvae. They will also eat carrion, especially wolf-kill, large amounts of wild fruit (occasionally raiding apple orchards), and beech mast. Bears are hunted, but in a strictly controlled way, and the population is at a healthy level.

There are currently around 3,000 wolves in Romania, generally restricted to forests. Their prey consists almost entirely of deer, occasionally boar, chamois and the odd sheep, they pose no danger to humans. They are hunted, especially in winter, when their tracks can be followed in the snow. Lynx are fairly widespread (but very hard to spot) in hill forests and are the most specialized large predator of all; they take roe deer in forest areas and chamois above the tree line.

Red deer can be found in some lowland forests but are most common in spruce forest in hill areas. The stags' mating cries echo through the valleys in September and October, and it's sometimes possible to observe their ritual conflicts from a distance. Above the tree line in the Transylvanian Alps and the Rodna, the most visible mammal is the chamois, seen grazing in flocks with a lone male perched on the skyline to keep watch. Wild boar are also widespread from the Delta and lowland forests all the way up to and beyond the tree line in the mountains. They appear mostly at night and can leave a clearing looking as if it has been badly ploughed when they have finished digging for roots. Weighing up to 200 kg, they have a reputation for aggression when protecting their young in the springtime.

Other mammals include the European bison (kept in a semi-wild state in several areas), the golden jackal (now spreading from its stronghold in the south, especially in Dobrogea), the wild cat (which occurs commonly in lowland forests as well as up to the highest mountain forests), the red fox (which is even more widespread from the forests of the Delta to the highest mountain summits) and the badger (which is widespread but very uncommon). There are three species of polecat, all very shy, and pine martens in the mountain forests, are common as are beech martens in lower-altitude woods.

The Danube Delta is one of the last refuges of the European mink (still thriving there), and also home to enot (or raccoon dog), coypu and muskrat, all North American species that have escaped from fur farms in the former Soviet Union. European beaver was native to Transylvania and has recently been reintroduced there. Romania's predators depend to a large extent on rodents for their prey; in European souslik, Romania's very own gopher. Three kinds of hamster occur including the endemic Romanian hamster, and hikers in the Fagaras, Retezat, Rodna and a few other areas will encounter the alpine marmot living in colonies well above the tree line. In forest areas, there are no fewer than four kinds of dormouse. Stoats and weasels are also widespread as are bats.

The most frequently seen amphibians are the abundant little Bombina toads: yellow-bellied toads in the hills and fire-bellied toads in the lowlands. More unusual amphibians include two species of spadefoot toad, the moor frog and the agile frog. The amazingly loud frog chorus of the Danube Delta and other lakes and reedbeds is produced by male marsh frogs. Newt fanciers find heaven in Romania's myriad ponds and watercourses; as well as the familiar warty, smooth and alpine newts there is the endemic Montandon's newt, restricted to the Eastern Carpathians. Fire salamanders with their vivid black and orange colouring are easily seen in the woods during or just after rain while the exotic-looking green toad (with its trilling call) is frequently seen under village street lights as it hunts for bugs that are attracted by the light.

There is a healthy population of snakes—the commonest being the grass snake, found in the Danube Delta and up to some altitude in the mountains. In coastal areas is the more aquatic, fish-hunting dice snake; other non-venomous species include the smooth snake, four-lined snake and the impressively large whip snake. Europe's most venomous and fastest-moving snake, the horned

PICTURE: The Danube Delta
SOURCE: http://whc.unesco.org/?cid=31&l=en&id_site=588&gallery=1&index=25&maxrows=12

viper, occurs near Baile Herculane, and the common viper (or adder) is more widespread, particularly in hill areas. The steppe viper (or Orsini's viper) survives in the Delta, for example in the woods north of Sfântu Gheorghe.

The warmer climate of the southern Banat and Dobrogea is especially suitable for other reptiles—not just snakes but also some exotic-looking lizards such as the Balkan green lizard, the green lizard and the Balkan wall lizard. More everyday species (such as the sand lizard and viviparous lizard) are widespread. The aquatic European pond terrapin is common around the edge of lowland lakes and in the Danube Delta, and there are two species of tortoise: the rare Hermann's tortoise (found only in areas of the southwest such as the Cerna valley) and the more widespread spur-thighed tortoise (fairly common in woods in Dobrogea).

With little in the way of industry and an absence of fertilizers and pesticides in almost all hill areas, the river systems have impressive populations of fish, for instance, grayling in Carpathian hill streams. Six species of sturgeon occur in the Danube, and the picture for these is less rosy as the Iron Gates dam prevents migration upstream. Rainbow trout have been less widely introduced than in western Europe so that the native brown trout is much more common; the endemic Danube salmon or huchen is now very rare.

It is scarcely possible to avoid fish when in the Danube Delta; the common species caught are common carp, crucian carp, pike (especially in autumn), pikeperch or zander, and catfish or wels. In fact, the Delta is a remarkable place for fish, with catfish around 2 metres long often caught and confirmed accounts of even larger specimens showing some interest in taking village women fetching water from channel banks. Sturgeon migrate through the Delta as do Danube mackerel. Several fairly rare goby species also occur, especially in lakes and lagoons south of the Delta. Most of these species have declined to some extent due to pollution, overfishing and eutrophication of the water due to algal blooms. For this reason, several areas of the Delta have become strictly protected reserves with great efforts made to preserve the water quality.

Chapter 4
Culture and Customs

The culture of Romania is the product of its geography and its distinct historical evolution. It is theorized and speculated that Romanians and the Vlachs (Aromanians, Megleno-Romanians, and Istro-Romanians) are the combination of descendants of Roman colonists and people indigenous to the region who were Romanized. Modern Romanian culture visibly reflects a tremendous amount of both Balkan and Eastern European influences. In addition, Romanian culture shares several similarities with other ancient cultures such as that of the Armenians.

Each geographic region in Romania has its own culture, which reflects and is the product of regional history. Transylvania and the Banat were ruled for many centuries by Austria and Hungary, and their architecture reflects Romanesque, Gothic, and Baroque styles. Moldavia in eastern Romania has a culture that reflects its proximity to Ukraine and Russia though traces of Tatar and other

Central Asian influences have been identified in its folk art. The loggia, an open-air porch that evolved in the Mediterranean, was first incorporated into homes in Romania in Walachia. The region also traditionally absorbed influences from the Byzantine Empire and the Islamic Middle East. The Hungarian, German and Roma minorities, who are scattered throughout the country, maintain their own traditions, which are reflected in their folk arts, cuisine, and dress.[1]

Popular and High Culture[2]

The twin foundations of popular and high culture in Romania are the traditions associated on the one hand with the peasantry and rural life, and on the other with Romania's religious communities. The artistic expressions that grew from these foundations are evident in the work of the leading artists and writers of modern Romania. One-third foundation, national ideology, arose in the 18th century and has accentuated the distinctiveness of national cultures while undermining their commonalities. In addition to these three, external cultural influences have proven increasingly important with the onset of modern communications. Paradoxically, proponents of national integrity have enlisted French, German, and Russian political thought for their purposes.

The secular origins of Romanian folk culture should be sought in migratory shepherds (*ciobani*) in the Danubian Principalities before the rise of large-scale field agriculture beginning in the 18th century. The portrayals of ancient Dacians in Trajan's Column and the Roman monument at Adamclisi suggest they wore the same woollen breeches and fur caps as shepherds do today. It is much more difficult to establish other continuities with the Dacians. It is known that the unsettled military and political conditions in south and east of the Carpathians, and the domination of Hungarians and Germans on the other side left the development of autonomous Romanian folk culture in the hands of migratory

---

1 https://en.wikipedia.org/wiki/Culture_of_Romania & https://www.britannica.com/place/Romania/Political-process

2 M. Sanborne, *Nations in Transition: Romania*, New York: Facts On File, Inc, 2004.

shepherds astride the mountains. Centuries of transhumance probably account for the lack of dialectal variation in the Romanian language. The archetypical Romanian ballad, *Miorița* (*The Little Sheep*), has been documented in different versions in many regions. *Meșterul Manole*, on the other hand, is the Romanian variant of a construction myth (walling-in sacrifice) that is well documented in Southeastern Europe, also among the Hungarians. Landlords are absent from *Miorița*, as they were in the lives of free peasants in the foothill villages who helped preserve the *cioban* culture.

Settled village communities proliferated after the 18th century and multiplied the local styles of peasant dress, fabrics, woodcarving, and ceramics. The Hungarian, German, and Slavic communities were more sedentary and concentrated, but also developed variations in their designs as well as some interethnic influence in the use of colours or floral, vegetal and geometric motifs. Peasant homes and their interiors became more ornate if an agricultural

PICTURE: *Miorița*
SOURCE: https://costiceni.blogspot.com/2014/11/alecsandri-russo-si-balada-miorita.html

surplus permitted it. Well-off homes would feature little-used rooms heaped with embroidered pillows and bedspreads. Unless sumptuary laws forbade it, wealthier peasants might imitate the clothing and home decoration of the nobility or burghers. In ethnically mixed areas, social-climbing prefigured and often motivated linguistic assimilation.

Religious communities were an important marker of ethnic identity in villages of mixed population. First, their ecclesiastical calendars determine the times of major fasts and feasts that set one community apart from the others. Aside from saints and observances particular to one church, the difference of more than a week between the Gregorian and Julian calendars meant that even the major feasts that the Christian churches shared were usually celebrated at different times. Therefore the religious difference between the Orthodox Christians (Romanians, but also Serbs, Ukrainians, and Russians) and the other Christians was particularly strong. Religious differences were at least as important as linguistic ones as an obstacle to intermarriage among ethnic groups in traditional communities. Differences of calendar and diet separated the Christians even more strongly from the Jews.

The similarities of Romanian folk music to that of the Middle East owe much to the period of several centuries of the Danubian Principalities association with the Ottoman Empire. There are various forms of flute, bagpipe, and cembalom. The tekerőlant (hurdy-gurdy) is peculiar to the Hungarians while the best-known Romanian folk instrument is the pan flute or panpipe. Ancient depictions including a passage in Ovid's *Tristia* indicate the pan flute was played by shepherds on the territory of the country already in Dacian and Roman times, though the Romanian term commonly used today for pan flute, *nai*, it may have come from Persia via the Turks. The earliest professional pan flute association was registered in Bucharest in 1843. Fanica Luca was the first internationally known pan flautist from Romania. He performed at the world fairs in Paris and New York in 1937–1939 and taught the instrument at the Music Lyceum in Bucharest for 15 years before his death in 1968. His most famous student was Gheorghe Zamfir, whose recordings and performances are well known in North America. Damian Draghici-Luca, a grand-grand nephew of Fanica Luca, has performed and recorded since the age of 10.

The documentation of folk customs and songs began in the 19th century. Authorities founded the Romanian Folklore Institute in 1949, and ethnography gained a respected place in scholarship. The institute sponsored the excellent folk music orchestra Barbu Lautaru. The careful collection and study of folk music helped preserve it despite the rapid urbanization and industrialization, but the genre also became an instrument of political manipulation. Trade unions and houses of culture had organized a reported 44,000 music, dance, and dramatic ensembles by 1959. In 1975, the government established the cycle of organized music festivals called *Cîntarea României* (Song of Romania) that performed an

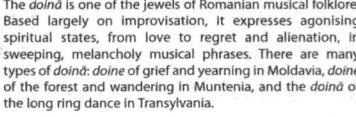

Doina

The *doină* is one of the jewels of Romanian musical folklore. Based largely on improvisation, it expresses agonising spiritual states, from love to regret and alienation, in sweeping, melancholy musical phrases. There are many types of *doină*: *doine* of grief and yearning in Moldavia, *doine* of the forest and wandering in Muntenia, and the *doină* of the long ring dance in Transylvania.

PICTURE: Romanian Folk Music Players
SOURCE: www.panacomp.net

amalgam of genuine folk music and paeans to the Ceausescu. The more traditional performances were carefully shorn of any religious or otherwise politically objectionable content and recorded in the most spectacular costumes and scenery with dubbed audio. Because of the fakery associated with Cintarea Romaniei and an excess of *Tezaurul folkloric* (The Folkloric Treasure) broadcasts on television during that era, many educated Romanians feel distaste for folk music despite the undeniable beauty and originality of the genre.

Formal or higher music owes a debt to ecclesiastical, folk, and Western formal influences. Valentin Bakfark (1507–1576) was a German/Hungarian lutenist from southern Transylvania whose compositions and performances were renowned during his time. Renaissance and baroque music was known in the courts of the Danubian Principalities as well as independent Transylvania. Baron Samuel Brukenthal invited the leading members of 18th-century Transylvania and Walachia to performances of the works of contemporary German composers in his palaces in and near Sibiu. Transylvania's towns became provincial centres of the musical culture of the Habsburg monarchy in the 19th century, and philharmonic societies were founded in the principalities as well. In the mid-19th century, Ciprian Porumbescu was the first distinguished modern Romanian composer. His few compositions were influenced by folk music. The foreign visitors Johannes Brahms and Franz Liszt toured the region and became aware of Romanian folk music, but its influence on the Hungarian composer Béla Bartók was even greater. He was born in the west of Arad and helped establish the folk music archives in the mixed Hungarian-Romanian region of Kecskemét in modern-day Hungary.

The master composer of the Romanians was George Enescu. A composer impressed by his precocity convinced his parents to enrol him in the Vienna conservatory at the age of seven; then upon his graduation, he studied in the conservatory in Paris under the tutelage of Jules Massenet and Gabriel Faure. Enescu composed his best-known works, *Romanian Poem* and the first two

Romanian rhapsodies, with their strong folkloric elements, between 1898 and 1901. In addition to composing, Enescu was a distinguished conductor (including at the New York Philharmonic in 1937–1938), violinist and tutor to Yehudi Menuhin. Other well-known musical performers of 20th-century Romania were the pianists Dinu Lipatt and Radu Lupu and the opera singers Ileana Cotrubas and Angela Gheorghiu. Several Romanian cities feature philharmonic orchestras and opera houses.

The key architectural monuments of the country are its churches and mona-steries. The monasteries set the tone for Orthodox spirituality, with a clergy that (unlike that of the parishes) is unmarried, renowned for its other worldliness, and attracts the faithful for festive liturgies in venerable, even grand surroundings. The oldest, 14th-century churches in Walachia at Tismana, Cozia and Curtea de Arges are of Serbian and Byzantine inspiration, formed around a square Greek cross. The bishop's church in Curtea de Arges dates from the early 15th century, whose fascinating decoration has Caucasian, Arabic, and Persian elements. The churches of Moldavia also follow the Byzantine model but are longer and higher with pitched shingle roofs and towers with cones at their top, showing a Gothic influence in their shape that is unusual in the Orthodox world. This Gothic influence is much more pronounced across the Carpathians. The wooden churches of formerly Greek Catholic Romanian villages in Maramures share not only the internal plan of other Orthodox churches but also high steeples found elsewhere only in Western Christian churches. Among the oldest surviving such churches is the one in Surdesti built in 1724 with a disproportionately high tower of 45 meters that long made it the highest wooden structure in Europe. Lacking government patronage and even suffering destruction during the religious strife of the 18th century, Romanian monasteries were fewer and less influential in Transylvania than in the Principalities.

Chapter 4   Culture and Customs

PICTURE: The Fortified Church in Dârjiu
SOURCE: www.romaniajournal.ro

Western Christian architecture in Transylvania followed the Romanesque, Gothic, Renaissance and baroque models of Catholic Europe. The Catholic cathedral of Alba Iulia has a Romanesque tower dating to 1247–1256, a Gothic choir and two Renaissance chapels. The second Gothic church in Transylvania is St. Michael's in Cluj, completed in 1432 with an impressive buttressed nave that dominates the main square of the city. These and the major Gothic churches of the south Transylvanian towns were actually built by the Saxons. Many Saxon churches, though abandoned by most of their congregants who have emigrated to Germany, still boast impressive winged altar paintings and Turkish carpets on the walls that recall the centuries when Saxon towns were outposts against Ottoman assaults. Saxons and to a lesser extent Szeklers fortified their rural churches with thick walls whose apartments could accommodate most villagers and their livestock in case of attack. The most impressive Saxon citadel churches

| 罗马尼亚概况 | Survey of Romania |

are in Prejmer and Biertan. The focal point of small Hungarian towns in western Romania is often a Reformed church decorated with an ornate wooden cassette ceiling and a carved stone pulpit created by the Renaissance artist Daniel Sipos.

The reign of Stephen the Great[1] in Moldavia (1457–1504) was one of the high points for Romanian ecclesiastical architecture. He built more than 30 churches and monasteries, many of which were in southern Bucovina and subsequently painted on their exterior as well as interior walls. The "painted monasteries" of Moldovita, Sucevita and Voronet are renowned for the brilliant colours and striking images of their exterior frescoes portraying Genesis, the Tree of Jesse, the Last Judgment and the siege of Constantinople. Moldavian church architecture experienced another great period in the 17th century with the construction of the monasteries of Dragomirna (1609) and Trei Ierarhi (1639), notable for their ornate lacework facades. During the 17th and 18th centuries, the closer relations between the two Danubian Principalities were reflected in greater similarity of their church architecture.

Due to the unsettled conditions in the Danubian Principalities, more important secular buildings survived from earlier times in Transylvania. In the Gothic style, these include the town hall in Sibiu and the castles in Hunedoara (of which a partial replica exists in the Budapest city park since the late 19th century) and Bran in the Carpathians south of Brasov. With its angular shape and prominence along the highway to Bucharest, Castle Bran is sometimes referred to as "Dracula's Castle" despite its tenuous connection with Vlad the Impaler. Renaissance monuments in Transylvania include private houses in Cluj and Sibiu and the royal fortress in the middle of the southern Transylvanian town of Fagaras. Sibiu, whose Saxon inhabitants have largely emigrated, is architecturally the largest German town in Southeastern Europe, with a partially intact city wall and characteristic window vents known as roof eyes (Dachaugen) on the pitched roofs of older buildings. In the Principalities, the major 16th-

---

1 Stephen III of Moldavia, known as Stephen the Great was voivode of Moldavia from 1457 to 1504. He was the son and co-ruler of Bogdan II of Moldavia who was murdered in 1451 [Source: Wikipedia].

Chapter 4　Culture and Customs

century fortress of Piatra Neamt in Moldavia has survived, but there are only ruins from the Walachian princely courts in Targoviste and Bucharest.

There were regional styles in the domestic architecture of the common people. The porches in Brancovenesc buildings may have arisen in imitation of Romanian homes. At the end of the 19th century, professional architects began to take more notice of popular styles and attempted a synthesis of folk and modern architecture in their work. The leading representative of this tendency in Romania was Ion Mincu, who built various restaurants and private homes in Bucharest and restored the Stavropoleos Church in 1906. The Transylvania Hungarian Karoly Kos studied in Budapest, where he became an advocate of a style that resembled Mincu's in its objectives but sought to revive Hungarian regional styles. His most notable building is the Szekely National Museum in Sfântu Gheorghe. The Palace of Culture in Targu Mures is another example of Hungarian folk revival architecture, whereas the National Theater in Cluj is an example of Habsburg art nouveau. Many Bucharest houses and even apartment buildings of the interwar period are examples of these styles. After 1920, Kos and the Bucharest sociologist Dimitrie Gusti worked independently for the preservation of folk architecture. Kos published a highly regarded collection of meticulous drawings of Transylvanian village architecture in 1929, while in1936 Gusti founded the remarkable Village Museum in Bucharest that is a collection of village houses and wooden churches from all over the country. It was the third open-air museum of its type in Europe. The Museum of the Romanian Peasant arose from earlier institutions founded in 1875 and 1906–1912. It was associated with the Village Museum after 1978 but became an independent institution once more in 1990.

The dominant trend in Romanian architecture since1918 has been an international style that is largely functional. The Ceauşescu era brought the great expansion of most cities with prefabricated apartment houses accommodating a great influx of population from the countryside. The provision of modern housing and conveniences was a significant benefit to large numbers of people. There was a wide range of quality in these new buildings both aesthetically and in their building materials and durability. The Scinteia House, the centre of Romanian publishing built in the wedding-cake style of the Lomonosov University in Moscow, became the most characteristic monument until the construction of the Palace of the People during the 1980s. The Palace of the People, having been built with the best materials and for the ages, now houses the Romanian Parliament.

Sculpture is a less prominent art form than in many countries because Orthodox Christianity provided no place for religious statuary alongside icons and frescoes. Consequently, for most centuries we find sculpted human figures in stone and wood only in association with the Western Christians of the former Habsburg and Hungarian lands. On the other hand, there was a strong tradition of stone carving for external decoration on church and secular architecture across the Carpathians. As previously noted, there was great regional variation in folk ceramics among the Romanians and other peoples. Objects for use were also carved from wood in the mountainous regions. The ornately carved wooden gates of traditional homes are a famous feature of Szekler communities in eastern Transylvania and Romanian ones in Maramures. Equestrian statues and busts of historical personages arose on the streets of Romanian as well as Hungarian cities in the 19th century.

Modern secular painting in Romania has closely followed Western models. Romantic and realistic painters of the first half of the 19th century favoured historical themes but increasingly devoted their attention to the life of the peasantry. Theodor Aman was the founder of modern Romanian painting and director of the art academy in Bucharest. His most famous successor, still known as the greatest Romanian painter of the 19th century, was Nicolae Grigorescu. After earning a living briefly as a self-taught painter of icons and then studying in Aman's academy, he spent several months in France where he learned to paint in the style of the Impressionists. Many of his works are pastoral landscapes, but he also painted realistic portraits of the Romanian peasantry and scenes from the War for Independence of 1877–1878, in which he participated as a war artist. Under the influence of the later, Impressionists were Stefan Luchian, Theodor

Chapter 4　Culture and Customs

Pallady and the more abstract Iosif Iser.

Constantin Brancusi was the most famous Romanian contributor to the international avant-garde, but others including the painter and architect Marcel Iancu and the poets Tristan Tzara and Ion Vinea also did it. Iancu, Tzara and Vinea helped found the Dada movement in Zürich in 1916. Iancu returned to Bucharest in 1922 and created a sensation with an exhibition of his post-Cubist paintings. He founded the modernist journal *Contimporanul* (*The Contemporary*) and organized a notable modernist exhibition in 1924 featuring Brâncuși, the surrealist Victor Brauner (who lived in Parisa after 1930) and the Transylvanian Saxon Hans Mattis-Teutsch, a graphic artist influenced by the German expressionists. Iancu moved to Palestine in 1941 and lived out his days in Israel.

The tank assault on the works of Brâncuși was inspired by the rejection of modernist art in general, many of whose exponents had already left for more congenial environments. The proletarian themes of socialist realism became the standard material of Romanian painters until complemented beginning in the 1970s. Since 1990, there has been a modest revival of the interwar Romanian avant-garde.

As elsewhere in Eastern Europe, literary life has played a stronger role than the fine arts in the definition of Romania's ethnic and national cultures. The standardization of literary languages and the presentation of national ideals for popular consumption were necessary components of the process of definition. As with other art forms in Romania, however, the national literature had their pre-Christian folk elements and Christian forms before they became national. They included sermons, saints' lives and other religious texts.

The Protestant Reformation in the Hungarian lands inspired an expansion of vernacular publishing among the Hungarians and Germans that also affected the Romanians. Scripture and the liturgy were translated into Hungarian and German, and writings addressing controversial religious issues appeared in these languages. The Saxon scholar and Lutheran preacher Johannes Honterus (1498–1549) became the leading figure in Transylvanian German publishing with the patronage of the Transylvanian princes, while the Reformed preacher Gaspar Karoli translated and published the first complete Hungarian *Bible* in 1590. Under the influence of these initiatives, Transylvanians also published the first books in Romanian. In the 17th century, the princes of Transylvania inspired the creation of a Romanian Reformed church, which failed to make lasting converts but further stimulated the use of the vernacular. Vasile Lupu, the prince of Moldavia, founded a printing press to counteract the influence of Protestant propaganda through the dissemination of Orthodox texts. Lupu was not yet printed in Romanian, however, the first publication in this language was a textbook printed in Transylvania in 1699.

The 17th century also brought the rise of the first important secular genre, historical chronicles and memoirs. The most important Romanian authors of these chronicles, not yet histories in the modern sense, were Moldavians: Miron Costin and Ion Neculce, while Dimitrie Cantemir, who also briefly ruled as the prince of Moldavia, deserves the title of historian because of his much more sophisticated use of sources. His *Description of Moldavia* broke new ground not only in describing the country but in examining its early history. His *History of the Rise and Fall of the Ottoman Empire* was translated into many languages. Notable historians of the Transylvanian Saxons and Hungarians included Johann Troester, Lorenz Toppelt, Istvan Szamoskozy, and Janos Bethlen, often still writing in Latin rather than the vernacular and recording imaginative genealogies and contemporary reports rather than formal history.

French literary models of memoir literature were dominant in the early 18th century, mediated in the Principalities by the Greek ruling elite. Later in Transylvania, the influence of the Austrian Catholic Enlightenment was more important, giving rise to a more critical awareness of religious and ethnic identity. Historians gave the name Transylvanian School to the group of Romanian linguists and historians active at this time. Its leading figures, Samuel Micu, Gheorghe Sincai and Petru Maior, presented important findings concerning the Latin origins of the Romanian language and the history of the Romanians in Transylvania. The Transylvanian School had a lasting impact

Chapter 4 Culture and Customs

on Romanian national consciousness. The debate between Romanian and Hungarian writers about the theory of Daco-Romanian continuity has raged since this time. The implicit threat in the Romanian arguments to Hungarian cultural predominance in Transylvania contributed in large degree to the vigour of the response.

The centre of Hungarian and Romanian literature moved from Transylvania, however, to Hungary proper and the Danubian Principalities. Romanian writers, many themselves graduating of Greek schools, rejected Greek and Russian influence and turned instead to France. Contemporary engravings of notables in the 1830s showed an interesting mixture in costume that was emblematic of the culture's reorientation. Some men wore Ottoman-style caftans and trousers while others wore frock coats in the French style. Gheorghe Asachi in Moldavia and Ion Eliade Radulescu in Walachia were leading proponents of national Romanian literature in the era of the Revolution of 1848. Later, but of more lasting influence, was Vasile Alecsandri, the author of popular patriotic verses at key points in the struggle for unification and a major playwright.

A debate about Romania's cultural roots and relationship with the West has enlivened Romanian cultural life since this era. The rejection of Ottoman costumes occurred within a generation, but the new debate lasted longer and was more ambiguous. Some polemics oversimplified the contest as one between Westernizers, who believed Romania must follow liberal, industrial Europe in order to prosper, and traditionalists who wanted to protect indigenous Romanian culture. The debate about language reform added an ambiguous note, with patriots in Transylvania favouring an unnatural spelling of the language to emphasize Latin origins, and the no less patriotic Junimea opposing it. The liberal Alecsandri was a notable collector of folklore, though Junimea placed more emphasis on village traditions. The greatest Romanian writers of the late 19th century were associated with Junimea: Mihai Eminescu, Ion Creanga, Ion Luca Caragiale and Ioan Slavici.

These four classics of Romania's greatest literary era made distinctive contributions. Eminescu[1] is known as the national poet. Influenced equally by his collecting of folk poetry in Moldavia and his study of German philosophy in Vienna, he is best characterized as a late romantic. Creanga recorded his childhood memories of his native village in northern Moldavia. Caragiale was a Bucharest writer of Greek origin who wrote popular plays satirizing the Romanian middle class, living his last years in Berlin when a wealthy inheritance permitted it. Slavici was born in the Banat and studied in Budapest and Vienna, then became a journalist, a leader of the Romanian National Party in Hungary, and author of stories of village life. All four lived tempestuous lives, and only Caragiale died in comfort. Slavici was persecuted by the Hungarian authorities for his political activity but sided with the Central Powers in World War I and documented his year of captivity in Greater Romania in the biting work *My Prisons*. As diverse as the traditionalist camp was among Romanian writers within Hungary, it found itself in ethnopolitical as well as philosophical opposition to the modernist and urban Hungarian writers. The Transylvanian poets of rural opposition to the Hungarian city were George Cosbuc and Octavian Goga. In contrast to Slavici, Goga took his opposition to the Hungarian government into exile in Bucharest in 1913 and lived 20 years in Greater Romania.

The development of Romanian theatre is closely linked to that of literature. Theater provides the opportunity for spontaneous expression in societies. Travelling troupes of the Romanian minority in Hungary before 1918 and of the Hungarians and Germans after this served this purpose. Vasile Alecsandri was the first director of the National Theatre in Bucharest and others were founded in Iași and Craiova. Theater was especially popular among the urban upper classes although the comedies of Caragiale pilloried them. Every ethnic minority had its theatre.

---

1 Mihai Eminescu was a Romantic poet, novelist and journalist, often regarded as the most famous and influential Romanian poet. Eminescu was an active member of the Junimea literary society and worked as an editor for the newspaper Timpul (*"The Time"*), the official newspaper of the Conservative Party (1880–1918) [Source: Wikipedia].

Chapter 4 Culture and Customs

Language[1]

Romanian is basically a Romance language with grammar similar to Latin. This familial resemblance makes it easy for anyone who speaks French, Italian or (to a lesser extent) Spanish to recognize words and phrases in Romanian, even though its vocabulary also contains words of Dacian, Slav, Greek and Turkish origin with more recent additions from French, German and English.

German may be understood — if not spoken — in the areas of Transylvania and the Banat traditionally inhabited by Saxons and Swabians[2]; and many educated Romanians have learned the language for professional reasons, although the tendency among students nowadays is increasingly towards English. Foreigners who can speak any scrap of Hungarian will find it appreciated in the Magyar enclaves of Transylvania, but not, which is, even more, the case with Russian — a language met with derision by almost everyone except the Lipovani communities of the Delta.

Romanian nouns have three genders—masculine, feminine and neuter. Adjectives (usually placed after the word they describe) and pronouns always "agree" with the gender of the noun. "Mai" and "cel mai" are generally used to make comparatives and superlatives: eg. ieftin (cheap); mai ieftin (cheaper); celmai ieftin (the cheapest). In Romanian, articles are not always needed: the indefinite article "a" comes before the noun and is un for masculine and neuter words, "o" for feminine ones; the definite article "the" is added to the end of the noun: -a for feminine words, -ul or -le for masculine or neuter ones. The plural forms of nouns are slightly more complicated, but tend to end in -i or -le. Verbs

---

1 T. Burford, & N. Longley, *The Rough Guide to Romania,* London: Dorling Kindersley Ltd., 2011.

2 An ethnic German people who are native to or have ancestral roots in the cultural and linguistic region of Swabia, which is now mostly divided between the modern states of Baden-Württemberg and Bavaria in southwest Germany [Source: Wikipedia].

are conjugated, so do not require pronouns such as "I" or "you", although these may be added for emphasis.

Pronunciation is likewise fairly straightforward. Words are usually, but not always, stressed on the syllable before last, and all letters are pronounced except for the terminal "-i". However, certain letters change their sounds when combined with other ones. When speaking, Romanians tend to slur words together.

Traditional Beliefs and Folklore

Romanians remain superstitious to this day. They maintain a certain reverence to nature and spirits alongside their devotion to religious saints. As strong believers in the supernatural, they continue to practice rituals to appease deities that their ancestors honoured, such as the gods of the sun and planets and to ward off evil beings, like witches and vampires.

Strigoi[1]

In Romania, a lot of superstitions revolve around vampires. They are called strigoi from the Roman term "strix" which can mean a screech owl, a demon or a witch.

There are different types of strigoi. Strigoi vii are witches who turn into vampires after death. At night, they can send out their souls to see other witches or Strigoi morts. The strigoi morts are dead bodies revived to suck out the blood of their family members and livestock. Among those who are doomed with the fate of being a vampire are children born with a caul or a tail, those born out of wedlock, people who died an unnatural death, those who died before baptism, or the seventh child of children of the same gender (like the seventh of nine sisters). A pregnant woman should eat salt and avoid being seen by vampires or witches, or her baby could become a strigoi as well. The most common cause of vampirism is being bitten by a strigoi.

---

1 In Romanian mythology, strigoi are the troubled spirits of the dead rising from the grave. Some strigoi can be living people with certain magical properties [Source: Wikipedia].

Dracula[1] and Vampires[2]

Truth, legends and fiction swirl around the figure of Dracula like a cloak and perceptions of him differ sharply. In Romania today, schoolbooks and historians extol him as a patriot and a champion of order in lawless times while the outside world knows him as the vampire count of 1,000 cinematic fantasies derived from Bram Stoker[3]'s novel of 1897 — a spoof-figure or a ghoul.

While vampires feature in native folklore, Romanians make no associations between them and the historical figure of Dracula, the Walachian prince Vlad III[4], known in his homeland as Vlad Tepes — Vlad the Impaler. During his lifetime (1431 – 1476) Vlad achieved renown beyond Walachia's borders as a successful fighter against the Turks and a ruthless ruler; his reputation for cruelty spread throughout Europe via the newly invented printing presses and the word of his political enemies — notably the Transylvanian Saxons. At this time, Vlad was not known as a vampire, although some charged that he was in league with the Devil, or (almost as bad) that he had converted to Catholicism.

Vampires

Horrible though his deeds were, Vlad was not accused of vampirism during his lifetime. However, vampires were an integral part of folklore in Eastern and Southeastern Europe, known as vámpír in Hungarian and strigoi in Romanian.

---

1 Count Dracula is the title character of Bram Stoker's 1897 gothic horror novel *Dracula*. He is considered to be both the prototypical and the archetypal vampire in subsequent works of fiction [Source: Wikipedia].

2 T. Burford & N. Longley, *The Rough Guide to Romania*, London: Dorling Kindersley Ltd, 2011.

3 Irish author, best known today for his 1897 Gothic novel *Dracula*. During his lifetime, he was better known as the personal assistant of actor Henry Irving and business manager of the Lyceum Theatre in London, which Irving owned [Source: Wikipedia].

4 Known as Vlad the Impaler or Vlad Dracula, was voivode of Walachia three times between 1448 and his death. He was the second son of Vlad Dracul, who became the ruler of Walachia in 1436 [Source: Wikipedia].

Details of their habits and characteristics vary from place to place, but in their essentials are fairly similar. A vampire is an undead corpse, animated by its spirit and with a body that fails to decay, no matter how long in the grave. Vampirism can be contagious, or people might occasionally be born as vampires, bearing stigmata such as a dark-coloured spot on the head or a rudimentary tail. However, a vampire is usually created when a person dies and the soul is unable to enter heaven or hell. The reason may be that the person has died in a "state of sin" — by suicide, for example, or holding heretical beliefs — or because the soul has been prevented from leaving the body. Hanging was a form of death dreaded by Romanians, who believed that tying the neck "forces the soul down outward"; while the Orthodox custom of shrouding mirrors in the home of the deceased was intended to prevent the spirit from being "trapped" by seeing its reflection. As Catholicism and Orthodoxy competed for adherents in the wake of the Ottoman withdrawal from the Balkans, priests also claimed that the cemetery of the opposing church was unconsecrated land, thereby raising the fear of vampires rising from the grave.

Once created, a vampire is almost immortal and becomes a menace to the living. In Romanian folklore, vampires frequently return to their former homes at night, where they must be propitiated with offerings of food and drink and excluded by smearing garlic around the doors and windows. Should a newborn baby lie within, it must be guarded until it is christened, lest a vampire sneak in and transform it into another vampire. Two nights of the year are especially perilous: April 23, St. George's Day[1] (when, as Jonathan Harker was warned in Bram Stoker's novel, "all the evil things in the world will have full sway"), and

---

1 Also known as the Feast of Saint George, is the feast day of Saint George as celebrated by various Christian Churches and by the several nations, kingdoms, countries and cities of which Saint George is the patron saint.

Saint George's Day is celebrated on 23 April, the traditionally accepted date of the saint's death in Diocletianic Persecution of AD 303. For those Eastern Orthodox Churches which use the Julian calendar, this date currently falls on the day of 6 May of the Gregorian calendar. In the 19th Century, it was the 5th May [Source: Wikipedia].

November 29, the eve of St. Andrew's Day[1]. On that night, vampires rise with their coffins on their heads, lurk about their former homes, and then gather to fight each other with hempen whips at crossroads. Such places were considered to be unlucky, being infested by spirits called Iele (Man's enemies). In Gypsy folklore, vampires (mulé) also live at the exact moment of midday, when the sun casts no shadow. Gypsies must cease travelling at that time, for it is then that mulé control the roads, trees and everything else. Interestingly, Gypsies only fear their own mulé — the ghosts and vampires of gadjé (non-Gypsies) are of no account.

The greatest danger was presented by vampire epidemics, which began in the 17th century, perhaps due to the influence of Gypsy folklore. Although in horror films and Bram Stoker's novel, vampires must bite their victims and suck blood to cause contagion in Eastern European folklore, the vampire's look or touch can suffice. A classic account refers to the Austro-Hungarian village of Haidam in the 1720s. There, before witnesses, a man who has been dead for ten years returned as a vampire to his son's cottage, touched him on the shoulder and then departed. The man died the next morning. Alarmed by this report and others relating how long-dead villagers were returning to suck their children's blood, the local military commander ordered several graves to be exhumed, within which were found corpses showing no signs of decay. All were incinerated to ashes—one of the classic methods of exterminating vampires. Another epidemic occurred in the village of Medvegia near Belgrade, starting in 1727. A soldier claimed to have been attacked by a vampire while in Greece (where vampire legends also abound), and died upon his return home. Thereafter, many villagers swore they had seen him at night or had dreamt about him, and ten weeks later complained of inexplicable weakness. The body was exhumed, was found to have blood in its mouth, and so had a stake driven through its heart. Despite

---

1 A national holiday in Romania (since 2015). Saint Andrew is represented in the New Testament to be the disciple who introduced his brother, the Apostle Peter, to Jesus as the Messiah. He is the patron saint of Cyprus, Scotland, Greece, Romania, Russia, Ukraine, the Ecumenical Patriarchate of Constantinople, San Andres Island (Colombia), Saint Andrew (Barbados) and Tenerife [Source: Wikipedia].

this precaution, there was an outbreak of vampirism a few years later, and of the 14 corpses examined by a medical commission in 1732, 12 were found to be "unmistakably in the vampire condition" (undecayed).

This was the catalyst for an explosion of interest across Europe until Pope Benedict XIV[1] and the Austrian and Prussian governments declared vampirism a fraud and made it a crime to dig up dead bodies. But in 1899 Romanian peasants in Carasova dug up 30 corpses and tore them to pieces to stop a diphtheria epidemic, and in 1909 a Transylvanian castle was burned down by locals who believed that a vampire emanating from it was causing the deaths of their children. Only recently, in 1988, outside Nis in southern Serbia, a 13-year-old girl was killed by her family, who believed her to be a vampire.

Skeptics may dismiss vampires and vampirism entirely, but some of the related phenomena have rational or scientific explanations. The "return of the dead" can be explained by premature burial, which happened frequently in the past. Nor is the drinking of blood confined to legendary, supernatural creatures. Aside from the Maasai tribe of Kenya—whose diet contains cattle blood mixed with milk—numerous examples can be found in the annals of criminology and psychopathology.

Bram Stoker's Dracula

During the 18th century, numerous well-publicized incidents of vampirism sparked a vampire craze in Europe, with both lurid accounts and learned essays produced in quantity. The first respectable literary work on a vampire

---

1 Born Prospero Lorenzo Lambertini, served as the Pope of the Catholic Church from 17 August 1740 to his death in 1758. Perhaps one of the greatest scholars in Christendom, yet often overlooked, he promoted scientific learning, the baroque arts, reinvigoration of Thomism, and the study of the human form. Firmly established with great devotion and adherence to the Council of Trent and authentic Catholic teaching, Benedict removed changes previously made to the Breviary, sought peacefully to reverse growing secularism in certain European courts, invigorated ceremonies with great pomp, and throughout his life and his reign, published numerous theological treatises [Source: Wikipedia].

theme was Goethe[1]'s The Bride of Corinth[2] (1797), soon followed by Polidori[3]'s The Vampyre, which arose out of the same blood-curdling holiday on Lake Geneva in 1816 that produced Mary Shelley[4]'s Frankenstein[5].

These and other similar stories fired the imagination of Bram Stoker, an Anglo-Irish civil servant who became manager to the great actor Sir Henry Irving[6] in 1878 and wrote a few other novels, now being rediscovered. In 1890,

---

1 German writer and statesman. His works include epic and lyric poetry; prose and verse dramas; memoirs; an autobiography; literary and aesthetic criticism; treatises on botany, anatomy, and colour; and four novels. In addition, numerous literary and scientific fragments, more than 10,000 letters, and nearly 3,000 drawings by him exist[Source: Wikipedia].

2 A dark poem believed to have been based on the classic tale by Phlegon of Tralles of the maiden Philinnion. In Goesthe's version, a young woman dies of grief and returns from her coffin as one of the undead, and only in death and then undeath can she find freedom [in https://www.vampires.com/the-bride-of-corinth/].

3 John William Polidori (7 September 1795–24 August 1821) was an English writer and physician. He is known for his associations with the Romantic movement and credited by some as the creator of the vampire genre of fantasy fiction. His most successful work was the short story "*The Vampyre*" (1819), the first published modern vampire story [Source: Wikipedia].

4 English novelist, short story writer, dramatist, essayist, biographer, and travel writer, best known for her Gothic novel *Frankenstein* or *The Modern Prometheus* (1818). She also edited and promoted the works of her husband, the Romantic poet and philosopher Percy Bysshe Shelley [Source: Wikipedia].

5 A novel written by English author Mary Shelley (1797–1851) that tells the story of Victor Frankenstein, a young scientist who creates a grotesque but sapient creature in an unorthodox scientific experiment. Frankenstein is infused with elements of the Gothic novel and the Romantic movement. At the same time, it is an early example of science fiction. Since the novel's publication, the name "Frankenstein" has often been used to refer to the monster itself. This usage is sometimes considered erroneous, but usage commentators regard it as well-established and acceptable [Source: Wikipedia].

6 Born John Henry Brodribb, sometimes known as J. H. Irving, was an English stage actor in the Victorian era, known as an actor-manager because he took complete responsibility (supervision of sets, lighting, direction, casting, as well as playing the leading roles) for season after season at the Lyceum Theatre, establishing himself and his company as representative of English classical theatre. In 1895, he became the first actor to be awarded a knighthood, indicating full acceptance into the higher circles of British society. Irving is widely acknowledged to be one of the inspirations for Count Dracula, the title character of the 1897 novel *Dracula* whose author, Bram Stoker, was business manager of the theatre[Source: Wikipedia].

| 罗马尼亚概况 | *Survey of Romania* |

PICTURE: Bram Stoker's Dracula
SOURCE: https://www.amazon.com/Dracula-Wordsworth-Classics-Bram-Stoker/
dp/185326086X

he conceived the idea of a vampire novel; after detailed research in Whitby[1] Public Library and the Reading Room of the British Museum, the setting moved east to Transylvania, and Count Dracula was born. Stoker's fictional Count was possibly influenced by the "Jack the Ripper[2]" murders which happened a decade earlier in Whitechapel, where Stoker lived for a time while writing his book.

---

1 A seaside town, port and civil parish in the Borough of Scarborough and English county of North Yorkshire.

2 The best-known name for an unidentified serial killer generally believed to have been active in the largely impoverished areas in and around the Whitechapel district of London in 1888 [Source: Wikipedia].

Stoker delved deep into Romanian folklore, history and geography and the book is a masterpiece in its mixture of fantasy and precise settings.

Other books on the same theme followed, but it was the advent of cinema and the horror film that has ensured the fame of Dracula. The silent *Nosferatu*[1] (1922) is perhaps the greatest vampire film. The BBC's *Count Dracula* (1978) is the most faithful to Stoker's novel, while Coppola[2]'s camped-up *Bram Stoker's Dracula* (1992) confuses things by including the historic Vlad Tepes in a prelude. There is also a fine tradition of spoofs such as *Love at First Bite* (1979), which opens with the communists expelling Dracula from his castle.

Other Traditional Beliefs[3]

Actions

- Do not sew, use needles or scissors, bake bread or sow flax on a Wednesday or a Friday.
- Do not conclude any business concluded on a Friday or the goddess Venus will punish you.
- In the Romanian gipsy custom, one must pay homage to the Wodna Zena or "Water Woman" by spilling some drops of water intentionally on the ground after filling a jug or before offering anyone a drink.
- To avoid provoking the water-spirit, do not draw water against the current. If you need to draw water in the evening, blow on the brim of the jug three times and pour a few drops on the coals after fetching the water.

Food

- Wearing bulbs of garlic around the neck is a charm against the "evil eye." Likewise, wreaths of garlic in Romanian houses protect the family.

---

1 A 1922 German Expressionist horror film, directed by F. W. Murnau, starring Max Schreck as the vampire Count Orlok. The film, shot in 1921 and released in 1922, was an unauthorized adaptation of Bram Stoker's Dracula (1897) [Source: Wikipedia].

2 Francis Coppola, an American film director, producer, screenwriter and film composer.

3 World Trade Press & ProQuest (Firm), *Romania : Society & Culture,* World Trade Press, Petaluma, Calif, 2010.

- Throw salt on the threshold of a new house to ward off evil.
- At midnight on New Year's Eve, make sure that there is food on the table to ensure an abundance of food throughout the year.
- A woman should not leave any leftovers on her plate, or else she will have an ugly husband.
- If you eat the corners of a slice of bread, it will create a good relationship between you and your in-laws.
- If the soup is salty, it means that the chef is in love.
- If a person accepts an apple from someone and if the apple breaks when bitten, he/she should return the apple immediately or it will cause bad luck.

Pregnancy and Birth

- Sew talismans like cloves of garlic and branches of basil into the hem of a pregnant woman's clothes to ward off evil.
- The midwife should pass a knife through the neckline of the mother's blouse to ensure an easy and speedy birth.
- The shirt worn by the woman in labour should be sewn with red crosses on the breast area to assure an abundance of milk.
- On the third night after the birth, wise women or spirits come to the head of the baby's cradle to determine its destiny or fate. To assure good predictions, the midwife prepares a table for the wise women and serves three twisted breads and three glasses of wine for them.
- The diapers and swaddling clothes of the baby should be white and sewn from the shirt of the father to transmit his manly power to the fragile baby. This must be worn for two years.
- The baby should be swathed in a thick wool diaper with basil, garlic, and a red hair to protect it from the evil eye.
- The swaddling cloth must have a piece of red waistband, tied crosswise over the chest of the child to ward off evil spirits.

Gift Giving

In Romania, gift-giving, both business and personal, is widely accepted.

Presents need not be expensive to be appreciated by Romanians. On March 1, Romanians celebrate the coming of spring with Martisor[1]. Girls and women receive little gifts like plants, shells, flowers, animals, or tools. They are often accompanied by red and white ribbons, the red symbolizing life and the white standing for purity, and are supposed to bring good luck.

December 6 serves as another important day for giving gifts, as St. Nicholas[2] leaves small gifts in the shoes of good children. Gifts are also left under the tree on Christmas Eve to be exchanged on Christmas Day. During a Romanian wedding, guests shower sweets, nuts or corn and water on the bride and groom, wishing them prosperity as they make their departure. Romanian wedding guests normally give the couple money, and it is not uncommon for money envelopes to be provided at the wedding reception. Business gifts are common in Romania but are not exchanged in the initial meetings. Wait until the successful completion of a business deal before offering your Romanian colleague a present. Gifts like pens, lighters or little electronic items with your company logo on them all make appropriate gifts. Imported liquor also serves as a possibility.

All gifts should be nicely wrapped. Your Romanian friends may open the gift immediately, or they may put it aside to open later. Thank-you notes are not common in Romanian society. When invited to a Romanian's home, bring flowers, high-quality chocolates, or imported liquor to the hosts. Flowers should

---

1 A celebration at the beginning of spring, on March the 1st in Romania, Moldova, and all territories inhabited by Romanians and Moldovans. Alike, though not identical customs can be found in Bulgaria, while similar ones exist in Albania, and Italy [Source: Wikipedia].

2 Saint Nicholas is the spiritual patron of Greece, Russia and of many other cities in Eastern Europe. According to the Romanian tradition, St. Nicholas comes with gifts on the night between December 5 and December 6. He places the gifts in everyone's recently polished boots, except for those who have been naughty—they receive a whip or a stick instead, as punishment.The gifts are usually small and symbolic, often oranges or chocolate, or small useful items, leaving room for bigger presents on Christmas.The Romanian traditional belief also says that if it snows on December 6, St. Nicholas has shaken his beard, so winter can start [in https://www.romania-insider.com/st-nicholas-celebration-in-romania-official-start-of-holiday-season-and-gifts-in-boots/].

be wrapped and offered in odd numbers because Romanians use even numbers of flowers for funerals. Roses and carnations are usually well-received, but they should not be red. If your host has children, bring some sweets or little toys for them as well. There are also taboos in gift-giving. For example, avoid even numbers when giving multiple items. Also avoid the number 13 as it is considered unlucky.

Customs and Courtesies

The Romanians use the formal addresses of Domnul (sir) and Doamna (madam) when addressing one another, though young people use first names among themselves. Some Romanians will use first names with English-speaking (American, Canadian, British) business contacts, but you should use the formal forms of address until your host indicates to switch to first names. Use titles (Doctor, Professor etc.) where appropriate. A handshake is the normal greeting, and the usual courtesies are observed when visiting people's homes. Business etiquette requires that you offer a business card to each person present. At meals, it is usual to say "pofta buna" (bon appetit) before eating and "noroc" (cheers) before drinking.

Dress

Romanians usually wear conservative clothing. Older women wear skirts and dresses while younger women tend to wear slacks. Female office workers may also be found wearing tailored suits. Businessmen wear conservative suits. The younger males most commonly wear denim jeans, t-shirts, sports jackets and other western-style clothing. Elderly people wear dark, conservative colours. People mourning the deaths of family members wear black clothes from 6 weeks to a year.

Eating

The Romanian diet is characterized by distinctive ethnic specialities such as mititei (grilled meatballs), patricieni (grilled sausage) and mamaliga (corn meal mush). Lunch is the main meal, usually consisting of soup, meat, potatoes, bread and a vegetable. Pork is the preferred meat. Bread is typically eaten with every meal. Beer and wine are common beverages. In the past, food shortages were common; however, food is generally available now, but more expensive.

Gestures

Good eye contact is considered a sign of honesty. It is impolite for someone to converse with their hands in their pockets or with chewing gum in their mouths. Men remove their hats before entering buildings and churches, but not stores. Women cover their heads when entering a church.

Visiting

Romanians enjoy getting together for holidays, anniversaries, birthdays or just to socialize. Most social visits are arranged in advance. It is also customary to bring a small gift for hosts when visiting as well.

Greetings

Only between close friends or relatives are greetings made on a first-name basis; adults usually address younger children by their first names. One is expected to address a person by using his/her title (Doctor, Professor) before their surname. Greetings among adults usually consist of a handshake. Gentlemen used to kiss ladies' hands when greeting. Today, gentlemen shake ladies' hands and greet with Sâru Mânã (SEH-ru MIN-nah), which literally means "I kiss your hand." When greeting strangers, Romanians expect their greetings to be returned.

Chapter 5
Social Life

Romanians' lives are generally guided by the religious traditions to which they adhere. Thus, ethnic Romanians who follow the practices of Eastern Orthodoxy participate in elaborate customs and ceremonies during Holy Week and at Easter. The Hungarian and German minorities, who generally belong to the Roman Catholic and Protestant churches, put a greater emphasis on the celebration of Christmas. The Hungarian and German communities also have traditional folk dress for both men and women that distinguishes them from ethnic Romanians and that is worn on special occasions. Among the ethnic Romanians, the folk costume has been tenaciously retained in the rural areas, and virtually every county has its own variant of colour and style.

Romania's households have gradually improved their standard of living during the last couple of years, as their income increased and unemployment declined. Since

1991, a significant number of new homes have been constructed throughout the country. Much of the housing boom was propelled by the emergence of the real-estate market and the accumulation of wealth due to a free-market economy.[1]

Lifecycles[2]

Romania has a conservative and patriarchal society where family, ancestral traditions and the Romanian Orthodox Church are the foundations for the culture. The Church is the most trusted institution in Romanian society and a profound influence on the daily lives of many Romanians. Although its importance is declining in urban areas and among the younger generation, the social activities of most households in rural areas are still Church-related, and the religious ceremonies that mark most transitional stages in life continue to be important to all Romanians. Most Romanians also cherish the traditions of family celebrations and enjoy participating in the country's colourful festivals.

Birth

Romanian culture considers birth the emergence of a new biological life from the unknown to the known world and from non-existence to existence. Many customs relate to birth because of the belief that evil spirits, fear, weakness, and other unseen influences may accompany the birth and affect the entire family. Pregnant women in Romania, therefore, usually wear clothes ornamented with spiritual symbols (like red crosses) around their womb or breasts. This is believed to protect the fetus within, avert evil influences, and promote an abundance of milk for the soon-to-be-born baby. Expectant mothers avoid wearing blouses from back to front or with the neck in the back, as it is thought to affect normal birthing. They sew talismans made of cloves of garlic

---

1 https://www.britannica.com/place/Romania
2 World Trade Press & ProQuest (Firm), *Romania : Society & Culture,* World Trade Press, Petaluma, Calif, 2010.

and branches of basil into the hems of their blouses for protection.

Traditionally, Romanian mothers used the white shirt worn by their fathers at their wedding to stitch small shirts, swaddling clothes, and diapers for both boy and girl babies. Then they covered these thin diapers (full of fatherly power against wicked influences) with a thick woollen cloth enclosed with garlic, basil and a red hair. Sometimes, they also tied a piece of red waistband diagonally over an infant's chest. These practices were considered essential for protecting babies from the "evil eye."

Nearly all births in Romania take place in hospitals in the presence of a skilled medical attendant or a certified doctor, although some traditional families still prefer the assistance of midwives for delivery at homes. Statistics reveal that the average infant and maternal mortality rates have dropped dramatically over the last 15 years to 16 infant deaths per 1,000 live births and 25 maternal deaths per 100,000 live births.

The foremost ceremony for infants is the "First Bath", where the eldest paternal female relative, along with other women in the family, bathe the baby for the first time in clean water supplemented with flowers, honey, milk and money. This is believed to "purify" and "infuse" the baby in the family. The elder women then bless the baby for moral, spiritual and physical integrity, and hand the child over to the mother.

A baptism ceremony for newborns is also obligatory in this predominantly Christian country. This ritual includes christening the child in church, appointing godparents, and holding grand celebrations at the home of the baby's parents. Romanian babies are typically named after their godfathers, close family relatives or famous saints. Customarily, godparents bathe the baptized babies in a bath of water, money, rice, basil, symbolizing wealth, plenty of food and sweet life, respectively. Then, the godmother and the parents exchange an unstitched piece of cloth, used by the priest to wrap the child after completing all rites. Godparents in Romania also play vital roles in the child's future wedding ceremony.

A playful ritual marks the beginning of the baby's 7th month. Romanians place a book, a pencil and an egg in front of the baby, and if the baby picks up the book, it is supposed to signify that he or she will be an intellectual. If a pencil, then he or she will exhibit artistic skills. And if the baby chooses the egg, he or she will be materially successful.

Childhood

From early childhood, Romanian children are given special care, affection and attention by their parents and other elders. Corporal punishment in schools and in the family is, however, a common form of discipline.

In most Romanian households, parents are involved in their children's upbringing and development. Grandparents and extended families are the typical caretakers for infants when parents go to work. Statistics reveal that about one-third of preschool children are nurtured by their grandmothers at home, and extended families help provide childcare for most children after their morning playschool services.

Important childhood activities in Romania include going to school, playing games, and participating in summer camps. Romanians typically consider children the most important family members and some traditional families show particular favouritism to male children.

Romanians spend a lot of money to provide a high level of education for their children. Most children go to preschools or kindergartens between the ages of three and seven. The government provides free and compulsory elementary education between ages 7 and 18. The majority of Romanian children also go to vocational schools to learn the basic skills of working on farms or factories, or they go to training institutes to obtain advanced technical skills in the arts or teaching. Many students pursue secondary education up to the age of 18 and then go on to the university level.

Romanian children are generally not expected to contribute to the household income. The government restricts the employment of children below the age of 16. Despite the criminal penalties for breaking child labour laws, official statistics reveal that there is a growing presence of children as paid labourers in agricultural, low-skill and hazardous jobs.

Coming of Age

In Romania, the annual spring festival of Junii Brasovului (The Feast of the Youth) includes traditional events that are considered "initiation" rituals for young men. The festival has been celebrated in the city of Brasov for more than 400 years and typically ends the Sunday after Easter Sunday.

Young Romanian men between the ages 18 and 20 (Junii) come in large numbers from across the country to the week-long festival. They participate in several exciting tests and games to prove their maturity and bravery. These include throwing a mace high in the air and *aruncarea in tol*, a custom whereby about ten Junii toss a new Junii into the air on a blanket. Another interesting ritual known as the Junite (Woman of the Junii) involves young Romanian women colouring eggs in red. When each of the Junii receives his red egg, he customarily sprays perfume on the woman who gave it to him. Similar ceremonies are conducted throughout the week, usually followed by the men eating barbecue and drinking wine in the evenings.

Unmarried girls in Romania are considered a symbol of purity. They typically perform ceremonial rituals at Sinzienele or the Summer Solstice every year to symbolize the girls' pending adulthood, help predict their future spouses, and improve their chances of marrying their own lovers. The rituals include young girls preparing wreaths with flowers of Lady's Bedstraw to appease the spirits of wealth and crops, and cutting and watering the petals of a thistle flower for prosperity and joy.

Many children from poor families, rural areas, or those living on the streets start working between the ages of 6 and 14 to contribute to their family income. Surveys indicate that poor young girls are particularly susceptible to trafficking, prostitution, pornography and beggary in Romania.

Dating and Courtship

Romanian culture has a liberal and acceptant attitude toward dating and courtship. Young Romanian boys and girls start dating while in their teens. They usually meet each other at schools, social events, and through family and friends. Finding dating partners online has also caught on in recent years.

"The Maiden Fair" (also known as "The Girls' Retreat") is a traditional match-making festival held annually around July 20 at Gaina Mountain in Transylvania. Large numbers of unmarried Romanians from around the country come here to make their acquaintance with the opposite sex and to choose their potential marriage partners. The fair also provides a platform for these youngsters to play, dance, eat, drink and enjoy themselves.

The custom of arranged marriages still exists in rural Romanian communities, where parents arrange marriages through professional matchmakers. Some Romanian parents also visit "The Maiden Fair" to find a suitable marriage partner for their offspring. The girl's parents usually decorate a table with lavish food including roasted chicken and palinca (strong drinks) and "negotiate" with the boy's parents at the fair. If they reach an understanding, both parties decide upon the dowry and later approach family astrologers to determine the compatibility of the potential couples.

Romanian youngsters usually go on dates to movies or coffeehouses, to parties for dancing and drinking, to sporting events, or for long walks. Dating or courtship does not generally last very long and soon leads to marriage.

A desirable Romanian husband is expected to be dynamic, virile, humorous, intelligent, family-oriented and financially independent. The typical attributes sought in Romanian women include beauty, courtesy, homemaking abilities, loyalty and submissiveness.

Premarital sex is increasingly prevalent in the country. As of the late 1990s, about half of all young females aged 15 to 24 had been involved in sexual unions before their marriage. In addition, the percentage of single mothers and children born out of wedlock in Romania has been rising over the last decade despite the fact that the Romanian government has been promoting free birth control methods for teenage and unplanned pregnancies.

Abortion is completely legal in Romania and free of cost in cases where young students have become pregnant, the woman is unemployed, or the pregnancy is a result of rape. The law specifies that only specialized physicians in licensed facilities can perform abortions. Most Romanian families opt for abortions as the easiest method of birth control, although there is growing awareness about contraceptives and family planning devices.

Romanians are quite liberal about cross-cultural and inter-racial relationships. The importance of parental or familial approval of one's dating partner is almost obsolete in Romania. Young men and women from different ethnic groups (e.g., Romanians, Hungarians, Roma, Ukrainians) are allowed to associate with one another, and inter-ethnic married couples are commonplace. However, the same cannot be said about homosexuality. Although it is no longer illegal, attitudes toward the subject tend not to be broadminded and the gay community keeps a low profile.

Family and Parenting[1]

The family occupies a central position in Romanian society. A typical Romanian family unit consists of a father, a mother and their children. The extended family system where parents, children and grandparents live together in the same house is common among traditional rural communities. Most Romanian families have one or two children while the number is typically higher among the Roma people due to early marriages. The average family size in the country is three: two adults and one child.

Children are very important in Romanian family life. In fact, traditional beliefs about infertility often burden childless parents with a social stigma.

---

1 http://www.law.byu.edu/page/categories/marriage_family/past_conferences/oct2006/pb_chapters/13%20-%20Suian.pdf

Chapter 5　Social Life

Adoption, however, is widely accepted and on the rise in the country. In Romania, both parents have equal rights and duties toward the child, irrespective of whether it was born out of wedlock or not.

　　Traditional attitudes toward gender roles have not changed much. Men still continue to play a dominant role in rural settings. The senior-most male member (usually the father or husband) is the head as well as the primary breadwinner of the household. He makes the chief decisions for the family including organizing the finances of household, planning the children's upbringing and ensuring family welfare. In urban Romanian families, however, men and women tend to have equality in making decisions, contributing to family income and performing household activities. Working Romanian women are still expected to handle childrearing alongside their domestic chores and professional roles. Very few fathers opt for the paternal leave offered at the time of childbirth.

　　Favourite family activities in Romania usually revolve around sporting events. Romanians mostly play soccer, oina (a traditional Romanian game similar to baseball) and tennis, and enjoy windsurfing, scuba diving and other water sports. Other popular activities include going on outings to beaches, movies, theatres, restaurants, and watching television, walking, hiking, canoeing, cycling, exploring caves, and meeting friends on holidays and special occasions. Slaughtering a pig at dawn and preparing bacon and sausages is another common activity among Romanian families.

　　Romanian families generally share their lunch (the main meal of the day) together. However, due to the often hectic pace of family life, with both parents spending most of their waking life in the office and children at schools, this is not always possible, and meal sharing is reserved for weekends and holidays.

　　Long-lasting marriages are more common than divorces or separations in Romanian society. Statistics reveal that Romania has one of the lowest divorce rates in Europe (an average of 1.4%). Divorce occurs more frequently among young urban couples than among rural couples. Although Romanian parents have equal rights over children, mothers frequently receive the custody of children, and fathers are usually required to pay child support.

Romanian children typically take good care of their elderly parents and seldom send them to old age homes. In extended families, grandparents take care of newborns and instill family values in older children.

Work/Professional Life[1]

Most Romanians start work at the age of 16 or 17. The Romanian Constitution does not permit children under the age of 16 to be employed in any kind of work, although children between 15 and 16 can work under certain conditions.

The majority of the workforce in Romania is employed in factories. They work, on average, for eight or nine hours a day with a lunch break at noon. Work hours cannot exceed 48 hours per week, and Romanian workers are entitled to two days off per week, usually Saturday and Sunday. Government offices and banks operate from 8:00 a.m. to 4:00 p.m. Shops, businesses and markets are normally open between 8:30 a.m. and 5:30 p.m. and are closed at lunchtime. Most workplaces are open through Monday to Friday at normal time, except Saturday from 9:00 a.m. to 2:00 p.m. on Saturdays.

There has been a steady decline in the unemployment rate from 8.3% in 2002 to 5.0% in 2006. Unemployment among Romanian women used to be higher than for men in the 1990s, but it is now evenly distributed. Part of the reason for the decrease in unemployment is the increase in external migration and the decline in the overall population growth rate (0.12% in 2006).

Women in Romania constitute nearly half of the total workforce (46%), and they are not discouraged from pursuing any particular profession. Women have started competing head-to-head with men, and this is evident in their representation in the information technology sector where a good 13% of all women work. Women occupy nearly 26% of executive-level jobs. In spite of this, they remain under-represented in top decision-making posts.

Although Romanian women are legally entitled to equal pay for equal work,

---

1 M. Sanborne, *Nations in Transition: Romania*. New York: Facts On File, Inc, 2004.

they earn only about 76% as much as men. While the gap is closing overall, it is still higher in lower tiers of employment. The law on equal opportunities for women also prohibits sexual harassment and any sort of direct or indirect discrimination against women at their workplace.

Married women were encouraged to work outside the home during the Communist era in Romania and, to help them, the state ran day-care centers and crèches. Children continue to stay and play at these centers during the day while their parents go to work. Nursing mothers can also take breaks to breastfeed their children without any reduction in their pay.

The age of retirement, defined as the age at which a person is eligible to receive a state pension, is different for men and women in Romania. It is 65 years for men and 60 for women.

Old Age

Old people are highly revered in Romanian society for their wisdom, experience and commitment to preserving the past traditions of Romania. Life expectancy for men in Romania is 72 years and for women it is 68 years.

Romanian grandparents normally spend their time caring for their grandchildren while both parents go to work. They live with their own children. Only those aged people who do not have children or close relatives take refuge in nursing homes or charity centres. The state also provides various facilities for the elderly like day-care centres, old-age homes and elderly clubs. Old people with a very low income are entitled to free counselling and care from the state including medical services and assistance with cooking, cleaning and personal hygiene.

The State Direction of Individuals with Disabilities provides for the disabled elderly in Romania, and residential institutions give primary care and housing to the critically ill. Recently, the government has welcomed non-governmental organizations and private firms to supplement the state services for the elderly.

Death

Romanian culture views death as the beginning of a beautiful journey or a transition from one life to another. Romanians typically believe that there are a star and a tree that exists for every person. They believe that the falling of the star marks a person's death. Fir trees are considered the "tree of life," and a dry and rotting fir branch placed at the head of the grave symbolizes grief.

The Romanian Orthodox Church prohibits cremations, so the dead are generally buried according to Christian rituals. Only about 12% are cremated. Typical practices are to wash and deodorize the body, to put it into a wooden coffin, and to take it to the deceased person's home. Prayer services follow, and the family holds an all-night wake with a candle lit continuously. Mourning cries and traditional songs may go on for two to three days and nights after the death. It is customary for relatives and guests to participate during this period by paying homage to the deceased. After the funeral services at the church and the burial at the cemetery, mourners proceed to the deceased's home and share a meal there.

The mourning period may last for six weeks to one year. During this time, family members of the deceased wear black clothes and serve charity meals. Death remembrances in Romania often involve traditional plays such as partying, music and songs by teenagers and old women. It is believed that sometimes the soul does not leave the deceased's body but haunts and victimizes living people. Therefore, people make special food offerings every year on Saint George's Day (April 23) and Saint Andrew's Day (November 29), cover the mirrors in the deceased's home, and use garlic as preventive measures against vampirism.

Marriage in Romania[1]

In Romania, marriage was long considered a religious institution. Civil

---

1 Wardle, D. Lynn and A.S. Loveless, *Marriage and Quasi-Marital Relationships in Central and Eastern Europe* [in *The 2006 Vienna Colloquium on Marriage*, Printed in 2008].

marriage was not introduced in Romania until 1864. Even after the introduction of the civil marriage, the religious marriage was the more important of the two.

Romania had a long tradition of the church being the official institution responsible for issuing the marriage and birth certificates. The state could not afford to have sufficient offices in all small villages, and the church was therefore responsible for such matters.

The two versions of marriage coexisted up to 1948. Since then, the civil marriage became the only legal marriage. Religious marriage was not officially forbidden but discouraged and had to be preceded by a civil marriage. From the legal point of view, the religious marriage had no significance during the communist regime.

In practice during the communist regime, religious marriage continued to be performed after the civil marriage. Nobody could conceive of marriage without a religious ceremony. This same pattern of civil marriage followed by a religious ceremony has remained in place since the fall of the Ceausesc regime.

Today, the situation is the same. Only civil marriage is legally recognized and civil marriage must precede the religious marriage. In practical terms, civil marriage is today as it was in the past for most Romanian couples: a mere formality which preceded the religious marriage. What matters for the future spouses, for their families, for their friends and for the society is the religious marriage. The ceremony of the religious marriage, performed at the church, is the culminating moment when a new family is established.

A characteristic of Romanian society is that the majority of the population still lives in villages. In Romanian villages, the marriage was, is and will continue to be a concern not only for the future husband and wife, but for their two families and their relatives, and in a way a matter that concerns the whole village.

In the past, in Romania, as in other places, the marriage was, first of all, a matter between the families of the future husband and wife. The future spouses could oppose the marriage arrangements made by their families, but as a rule their role in arranging the marriage was very small. The situation is changed today. In most cases, the initiative of marriage are coming from the future husband and the future wife, but the role of their families is still very important. The families are supposed to be informed early on of the desire for marriage and agreement should come as a result of consultation between the two families. In most cases, the role of the two families in arranging the marriage is still very important, especially in the villages. It is not sufficient that the young couple inform their families and ask for their approval of the marriage. The idea of marriage is supposed to be thoroughly discussed and decided within the families. The media are still reporting cases of shock to parents when their children announce their imminent marriage without prior consultation and approval. This means that marriage is still a matter of long consideration, discussion, agreement and preparation.

Today, marriage in almost all the villages of Romania still means an event in which the whole population of the village takes part. In most cases, marriage today remains as the most important moment in the life of any human being. In the past, the marriage was arranged almost entirely by the families of the future spouses. In some cases, the future spouses were barely asked to their agreement. Their families decided for them.

The role of the families in arranging the marriage has diminished, but has not completely disappeared. Conceptions about marriage for the majority of the Romanian population go far beyond what most persons in Western Europe could imagine. The conception is based on the prescriptions from the *Bible*. In Romania, marriage is not primarily about self-esteem and personal fulfilment, nor is it just one lifestyle option among others. As in the *Bible*, there is a picture presenting the marriage as being rooted in the glory of God. In the mind of many Romanians, the man and the woman are made for each other and the institution of marriage is given to humanity as both opportunity and obligation.

These beliefs are so profound in the Romanian culture that very few people think to question them. Marriage is assumed by most Romanians like in the *Bible*, to be normative for human beings. The responsibilities, duties and joys of marriage are understood as matters of spiritual significance. From the perspective of the majority of Romanians, marriage must never be seen as a mere human invention—an option for those who choose to unite their lives—but an institution in which God's glory is displayed in the right ordering of the man and the woman, and in their glad reception of all that marriage means, gives, and requires. Several polls made in recent years showed that the great majority of young Romanians (between 92% and 96%) consider marriage and children as their most important goals and achievements in life.

As a civilized society, based on these realities and beliefs of the majority of the Romanian people, it is hard to imagine that Romania could ever accept the idea of same-sex marriage. For those for whom the family is the basis of the society and the love, affection, mutual support and upbringing of children are the most important functions of the family, the only conclusion is that where such families exist, you can say that you are in the presence of a civilized society.

The family is based primarily on a deep interpersonal relationship between husband and wife, sustained by affection and mutual understanding. To enable this, it receives abundant help from God in the sacrament of Matrimony, which brings with it a true vocation to holiness. Family is the place where children can experience more the harmony and affection between their parents, rather than disagreements and discord, since the love between father and mother is a source of great security for children and it teaches them the beauty of faithful and lasting love. The family is a necessary good for peoples, an indispensable foundation for society and a great and lifelong treasure for couples. It is a unique good for children, who are meant to be the fruit of the love, of the total and generous self-giving of their parents.

The Weakening and Marginalization of Marriage

In spite of these sound and happy realities concerning marriage, even in Romania, you can see, recently, the appearance of badly wrong ideas that marginalize or undermine marriage and the idea of marriage. These ideas are not only reflected in mass media, literature and the conversation found in the secular world but in some of the NGO platforms. Everybody in Romania is of the opinion that these decadent ideas are coming from the West. The seeds of undermining of marriage—or at least its reduction to something less than the biblical concept—are also evident in the way some Christians marry, and in the way others fail to marry. These seeds are very evident in the Romanian cities.

The winds from Westerns countries are bringing to Romania ideas that create confusion about marriage or even the idea that marriage is merely an option for those who "need" it. Ideas belonging to radical feminists which consider marriage as a patriarchal institution can already be found in Romania. In the post-revolution era, some of the Romanian marriages are also entered with a wrong motivation. Some young and poor girls look to marriage as a means to obtain social and material benefits. In a materialistic world, even marriage is sometimes cases determined by economic reasons.

There are also economic factors that contribute to the undermining of marriage. These economic factors are found mainly in the cities. The various challenges of present-day society, marked by the centrifugal forces and the wind of secularism and evil ideas generated especially in urban settings, making it necessary to strengthen the family and ensure that new families do not feel and remain alone.

A small family in the city can encounter difficult obstacles when it is isolated from relatives and friends. To sustain and help such new families, an important role could be played by the church. The ecclesiastical community has the responsibility of offering support, encouragement and spiritual nourishment which can strengthen the cohesiveness of the family, especially in times of trial or difficulty. Each parish has an important role to play, as do the various ecclesiastical associations, called to cooperate as networks of support and a helping hand for the growth of families in faith. These activities and new roles are something new for the orthodox churches in Romania.

Almost two million Romanians emigrated in the last 15 years for economic reasons. Most of these emigrants are young people and they are working in different countries in Western Europe. Many of them are illegal emigrants and being illegal emigrants they do not have the legal and economic conditions for marriage. Therefore, some of the young Romanian couples are entering into what is known as concubinage or cohabitation. Economic hardship, illegal situation, genuine love, external ideas are all the factors contributing to concubinage.

Many young people are searching for a soul mate in a marriage partner. They want an intimate and enduring relationship where they can share their deepest dreams and desires. But in a misguided effort to achieve this intimacy, they often enter into a cohabiting relationship. In so doing, they undermine their chances of attaining the very thing they most want. The secular liberal society does not teach, does not discuss and does not value notions like commitment and sacrifice. In schools, children are not taught to understand the importance of such values. There is too much emphasis on intellectual aspects of education and not enough on character and moral and religious values.

The Orthodox Church does not play its role to the fullest extent and does not explain to the young generation God's teachings concerning the marriage. Teenagers and young adults require continued catechesis on the meaning of "commitment" and "sacrifice". These notions should also be frequent topics of preaching on Sundays. There is a strong understanding among today's young people that erotic love and emotional happiness are the only reasons for marrying and staying married. God understands this quest for intimacy, which God himself has placed within the human heart. Sexual expression is a means of achieving marital intimacy, where the spouses are committed to each other and to the marital relationship. The Church has to consistently teach this truth. The rising numbers of extra-marital births is a clear indicator that Romania is also affected by evil factors and by decadence. In a global world, no country can escape bad behaviours entirely.

Divorce

Divorce was not imaginable due to several factors including religious norms and beliefs, moral customs and legal rules. Unfortunately, the number of divorces is growing in the cities even in Romania. The number of marital separations appears to be increasing as the first step to divorce. There are many reasons for this trend.

The first reason is this globalization process. Every day the media brings wrong ideas from the Western world about marriage and about the necessity to "modernize", about the rights of the women, about equality. The idea of modernization is understood among other things as implying satisfaction of all personal desires.

The second reason for the increase in the number of divorces is the rapid development of secularization and the widening separation between state activities and responsibilities vis-a-vis religious ones including marriage.

The third reason is the activity of feminist and homosexual NGOs and their international networks. Vocal, aggressive and anti-religious NGOs well organized at the national, regional and international levels continuously attack the family foundation. These organizations bring among their arguments the idea of human rights.

The fourth reason is the continuous revolution in family laws, now making divorce easy and quick, and in this way undermining the marital bond. The worst response to the growing number of divorces is to give in to this evil. Divorce should not be treated in a secular way only as a legal question, and above all divorce should be understood as a source of suffering for the couple, for the children and for all their loved ones. It is true that divorce is known today in any continent, but great disparities between the numbers of divorces in Western societies and the rest of the world still exist. The media in Romania had a full debate on divorce. It was the divorce of a minister followed by his marriage to his secretary 30 years younger than he. The Romanian public was outraged by this divorce. The scandal was bigger that the war in Iraq. The main question was how this man could remain minister after committing such an evident breach of the most elementary religious and moral norms. This public protest was good evidence that for the time being, at least, religious and moral values related to family are still powerful in Romania.

Social Conditions[1]

The transition to democracy and a free-market economy has remained a rough road for most Romanians. Most Romanians, like people all over the world, are preoccupied with day-to-day concerns: safe streets, decent housing, health care and feeding their families. By these basic yardsticks, the quality of life in Romania has shown no improvement, an actual regression or only a marginal advantage since the transition of power in the 1990s.

And public opinion surveys over the years have consistently shown that, aside from the wealthy and upper-middle-class elite, most Romanians are tired of a transition that never seems to end, or even go anywhere. Free elections and the chance to join NATO appear to have done little to concretely improve many people's lives, leaving both leftwing and rightwing governments to face a significant minority (particularly among the elderly) who are actually nostalgic for the Ceausescu era.

On paper, Romania has a comprehensive social welfare system. Government-funded and employer-funded insurance schemes provide for health care, sickness benefits, children's allowances, unemployment payments and pensions. But such benefits, even where they actually exist, were not adequate to cope with the huge price increases in basic goods and services that occurred throughout the 1990s as various governments ended many subsidies on everything from fuel to food.

Housing remains a major problem. Under Ceausescu, the government built high-rise apartment complexes for workers in urban areas. Most of these were shoddily built and have not aged well, but none of the post-Ceausescu governments has had the funds to replace them and the struggling free market in construction has not taken up the slack.

A 2002 report by the UN Economic Commission for Europe doesn't mince words: "Ten years of transition in Romania have not brought about an

---

1　Carey H.F., *Romania since 1989: Politics, Economics, and Society*, Lanham Lexington Books, Lanham. 2004.

improvement in average living conditions. In general, Romanians still live in cramped housing and only half have access to piped water . . . The quality of rural homes in particularly poor . . . a family of eight is more likely to live in a two-room flat than in a home with four rooms or more."

On a brighter note, the report noted that a new public housing construction program was begun in 2000 with international financing. Meanwhile, U.S.-based charity Habitat for Humanity has also done work in Romania. One project was building a new home in Beius for Adrian and Mihaela Tapos, both medical doctors who had previously lived with their four children in an apartment intended to temporarily house single doctors. With no running water or bathroom facilities, Mihaela recalls, life wasn't easy: "We had to carry the water from a pit well, and then pour it in the big 200-litre barrel in the loft", she said, "Water was pulled out of the well with a long wooden stick that had a metal pick at the end to hold the water handle. We did this for five years."

As in many other places, life in Romania is particularly hard for women, whatever their profession. Trafficking in women for the purpose of forced prostitution is a growing problem, both inside the country and internationally. The prosecution of rape is also difficult because it requires both a medical certificate and a witness, and a rapist can avoid punishment if he marries the victim.

Domestic violence is common, though many men fail to recognize it as a problem. The April 2000 issue of the Romanian edition of *Playboy* magazine included a "satirical" article explaining in graphic detail how to beat one's wife without leaving marks. International and domestic protests led to apologies by *Playboy*'s foreign editors and local publisher, and prompted a follow-up article on the costs of domestic violence.

The Health Crisis[1]

An even more telling example of the Ceausescu legacy is demonstrated by Romania's continuing health care crisis. By most statistical indicators, the

---

[1] https://www.oenb.at/dam/.../fsr7_transformationromania_tcm16-9508.pdf

situation has gotten steadily worse since the establishment of new government, a reflection of both the stagnant economy and "health hazards accumulated during the era under Ceausescu's ruling". These include environmental pollution, a shortage of medicines and unheated homes in winter.

In 1992, the nation's population actually decreased by 3,462, the first time that had happened in modern Romanian history outside of wartime, and a process that continued in the year that followed. The population declined an estimated 0.21% in 2002. Two major factors were increased emigration and the ending of Ceausescu's "pro-birth" policies, which had banned abortion and contraceptives. The end of those restrictions caused the ratio of abortions to births to explode: It was three to one in 1990 – 1991, one of the highest such rates in the world. The introduction of more progressive, Western family-planning practices lowered the ratio to just over one to one by 1998.

Life expectancy in Romania is among the lowest in Europe: 69.5 years in 2002 (74 for women; 67 for men), down from 71 in 1989. From 1991 to 2002 the death rate per 1,000 inhabitants rose from 10.9 to 12.3, while the birth rate fell from 11.9 to 10.8. The infant mortality rate (measuring the number of babies who die before their first birthday), after reaching 23.4 deaths per 1,000 infants in 1992, fell but remained high at 19 in 2002. This rate in Europe is second only to Albania's.

Various communicable diseases are also on the rise. Tuberculosis—known as the "squalor disease" because it is spread by unsanitary living conditions—climbed steadily from 64 people per 1,000 in 1990 to 116 in 1999. Contaminated drinking water has caused increasingly frequent epidemics of hepatitis A, while between 8% and 10% of Romanians are believed to carry the virus for hepatitis B, which, like AIDS, is spread by contaminated blood transfusions, syringes and unprotected sex.

As of 1999, the government had estimated that 7,000 cases of AIDS existed in Romania. Romania has more than 49,000 doctors (including 6,500 dentists), making for a ratio of one practising physisian for every 580 people—not an impressive statistic. Medical professionals are also seriously underpaid, prompting many to emigrate abroad. Other problems in the health care system include the poor physical state of the nation's hospitals, clinics and antiquated pharmaceutical industry.

Romania's government appears to have insufficient resources to confront the crisis. Health care costs took up 5% of the country's gross domestic product in 2000. Privatization plays a major role in the government's plans for health care reform, but so far the country's pharmacies are the only sector to have been extensively privatized.

Because doctors are so poorly paid, most patients (assuming they can afford it) accept that they must supplement their salaries with informal fees or gifts. "But the real bribes kick in when a Romanian goes to the hospital", according to one account. "There 'you need to bribe everyone', says one Romanian man who has just gone through the experience. To get a Caesarean operation for his pregnant wife, he had to pay a total of $200 for the surgeon, nurses, and food for one week. That sum of money is out of the reach of many average Romanians."

Finally, it is widely agreed that the persistence of pollution remains one of Romania's most serious public health problems. The issue is most commonly thought of in terms of how airborne particles and gases affect people's breathing in places like Zlatna, a town long infamous for its chronic air pollution from smelter emissions.

But in 2000, a singular event occurred in a different medium—water—that was so devastating some called it Europe's worst ecological disaster since the 1986 Chernobyl Nuclear Accident in Ukraine. On January 30 in Transylvania, heavy rains and snow caused a basin at the Aurul gold mine operation, which contained cyanide and other toxic substances used in extracting gold, to overflow into the Szamos River. An estimated 22 million gallons of deadly sludge flowed into Hungary's Tisza River in the two weeks that followed, and from there into the mighty Danube.

Up to 90% of the aquatic life in the worst-affected areas was killed, producing an estimated 220,000 pounds (100,000 kilograms) of dead fish. There were no immediate reported human casualties, and the flowing water eventually diluted the poisons to acceptable levels, but the long-term impact of the disaster remains unknown. The responsible party, Aurul, was a joint venture of the Romanian government and an Australian company, Esmeralda Exploration Ltd. In a telling comment on the state of affairs in Romania today, each side denied any responsibility and blamed the other.

Gender Equality[1]

Gender equality was not one of the top priorities of Romanian politicians after 1989. In 1997, the Romanian Parliament decided to create a sub-committee for the equality of opportunity for men and women. Soon after its creation, however, the sub-committee ceased any activity. It was reactivated in the year 2000, with a membership of five legislators: three men and two women. Since 2004, the sub-committee has been headed by a woman: Cristina Pocora. The subcommittee, along with members of regional and national non-governmental organizations helped draft the "Law for Equality of Opportunity among Men and Women", Law 202, which was passed in 2002.

This document outlawed gender-based discrimination and incriminated domestic violence and it emphasized equal access to education, health services, cultural activities, as well as the principle of equal pay for equal work. The law is very vague, however, when it comes to promoting women's role in public decision-making. Chapter four (articles 21 and 22), emphasizes the need for "equal participation" of women and men in decision-making, be it within local, regional or national institutions, non-governmental institutions or political parties.

Although the Romanian law recognizes the equality of chances between men and women, the tradition still places the woman on a lower position than the man. The World Economic Forum's statistics on equality of chances between men and women place Romania last in the European Union and 72nd

---

1 https://www.wikigender.org/countries/europe-and-central-asia/gender-equality-in-romania/

worldwide.

The Romanian law states that the equality between men and women means "taking in to consideration the different capacities, needs and aspirations of men and women and their equal treatment." However, a quick look at the country's Parliament reveals that only 12% of Romania's lawmakers are women. Only 53 of the 383 deputies and 12 out of the 167 senators were women as of 1 September 2015.

Moreover, although Romania's Government has a total of 44 ministers, only two of them are women. The situation is similar at the Constitutional Court, where only two of the Court's nine judges are women.

Differences also appear when it comes to job recruitment, as the attitude towards men is different from the attitude towards women.

The two categories are also treated differently when it comes to training and professional development, promotion, pay, parental leave effects on the person's professional future and sexual harassment.

According to researches carried out in the last 15 years, most of the persons harassed at work are women. Most of them are aged under 30, live in urban areas and have higher education. In most cases, the abusers have higher positions.

Half of the female workforce in Romania has low paid jobs such as administrative assistants, sellers, poorly skilled workers or unskilled workers. According to 2013 data from the National Statistics Institute, women continue to make 8% less money than men. Moreover, women in Romania often face rejection when applying for a job because of their age, no matter if they are considered to be too young or too old.

Although many women in Romania face discrimination at work or when trying to find a job, few of them get to claim these situations. However, the anti-discrimination coalition provides online legal advice, free of charge, to all those who have faced discrimination on www.antidiscriminare.ro.

Chapter 6
Government and Politics

Romania is a sovereign, independent, unitary and indivisible national state; the form of government is a Republic according to the Constitution of Romania, adopted in 1991 and modified in 2003. It is organized according to the principle of separation and balance of the legislative, executive and judicial powers. The legislative power is represented by the Parliament of Romania, with two chambers, comprising the Senate (176 members) and the Chamber of Deputies (308 members). 18 additional places in the Chamber of Deputies are reserved for the representatives of the national minorities. The executive power is represented by the Government, led by a Prime Minister, designated by the President of the state. According to the constitutional provisions and laws, the President of Romania, the Chamber of Deputies and the Senate are elected by universal, equal, direct, secret and free suffrage. The mandate of the Chamber of Deputies and Senate is on a term of 4 years, and since 2004, the mandate of the President of Romania is on a term of office of five years. At the same time, in case of the local elections, the mandate is on a term of four years. The judicial power in Romania is represented by courts of law, Public Ministry, Superior Council of Magistracy.[1]

Political Developments

The territory of Romania is organized administratively into communes[2], towns and counties. Some towns are declared municipalities according to the provisions of the law. The public administration in the territorial-administrative units shall be organized and shall function on the grounds of the principles of decentralization, local autonomy, deconcentration of public services, eligibility of the government authorities, legality and citizen consultation in solving local matters of particular interest. A package of laws on organization of administration, territorial planning and urbanism, finances, taxes, services for health, social security, education etc. has been enforced, regulating both the form of political decentralization of some public services and the form of territorial and administrative deconcentration by the Prefect institution. Decentralization as transfer of administrative and financial competence from the central government level to the local government level or private sector represents a system of managing local, commune, town or county interests through authorities freely elected by the citizens of the respective community.

Human communities or public services are self-governed under state control, according to the law. In Romania, territorial administrative decentralization is based on a community of public interests" of the citizens belonging to a territorial administrative unit, recognizing the local community and the right

---

1 H. F. Carey (Ed.), *Romania since 1989: Politics, Economics, and Society*, Lanham: Lexington Books, 2004.

2 The lowest level of administrative subdivision in Romania. There are 2,686 communes in Romania. The commune is the rural subdivision of a county. Urban areas, such as towns and cities within a county, are given the status of city or municipality [Source: Wikipedia].

Chapter 6　Government and Politics

to solve its problems and technical and financial decentralization of the public services, namely transferring the services from the center to local communities, aimed to meet social needs.

The decentralization process has also given expression to the beginning of a process to create and strengthen new forms of dialogue between central and local government, and represented by the Federation of Local Authorities in Romania (FALR), professional administrative corps or other associative structures of local government authorities (ACoR—Association of Communes in Romania, AOR—Association of Towns in Romania, AMR—Association of Municipalities in Romania, UNCJR—National Union of County Councils in Romania). On one hand, local autonomy refers to organization, functioning, competences and attributions as well as managing the resources that, according to the law, belong to commune, town, municipality or county. On the other hand, it represents the right and effective capacity of local government authorities to solve and manage, on their own behalf and under their responsibility, an important part of public affairs, for the interest of the local communities.

The constitution resembles in many ways the constitutions of 1866 and 1923. Like these, it provides for an elected Chamber of Deputies, a Senate and a centralized administration with heads of the 41 counties appointed by the minister of interior. The constitution protects private property and the freedom of political parties and established churches. The head of state is an elected president who must not be a member of a political party, and there is no place for the former royal dynasty. A significant change was in the role of elections. Since 1866, Romanian kings had appointed new governments that then managed elections so that they would provide the needed parliamentary support. The new constitution provides that the president appoints the prime minister and government only after elections have been held. Governments must secure the support of parliament for their confirmation and continued service. The president is elected for a renewable four-year term, chairs a security council, after an amendment in 2003 can call referenda, and can call for new elections if the government loses parliamentary support, but he cannot initiate legislative proposals or veto bills passed by both houses.

The three central bodies of the judiciary branch are the Constitutional Court, the Superior Council of Magistrates and the Supreme Court of Justice. The Constitutional Court, which may review the constitutionality of all laws of parliament, consists of nine judges who serve nine-year nonrenewable terms; the president, Chamber of Deputies and Senate each appoint three of its members. The two houses in joint session elect the members of the Superior Council of Magistrates to four-year terms, and the Council, in turn, proposes members of the Supreme Court of Justice for appointment by the president to renewable six-year terms. The Supreme Court is not only the final court of appeal but must also study and coordinate the activity of all other courts throughout the country.

The Romanian Parliament is today housed in the massive edifice begun before 1989 in a newly cleared area in southern Bucharest, formerly called the Palace of the People and now the Palace of Parliament. Deputies are elected to parliament for four-year terms by universal adult (age 18) suffrage based on proportional representation rather than personal mandates. The Chamber of Deputies has 343 members, of whom 15 are guaranteed seats for recognized ethnic minorities, and the Senate has 143 members. The government or one or another chamber may initiate legislation, and the chambers sitting in joint session may initiate votes of no confidence against individual members of the government, the government as a whole or the president. The number, names and popular support of political parties represented in parliament have repeatedly shifted.

The principal socialist party, which formed the government during the first and second Iliescu administrations in 1990 – 1996 and since 2000, emerged in 1990 under the name of National Salvation Front. After dissociating itself from the former Soviet Union and supporting the new constitution, the party now favours gradual economic reform. This is the party of Ion Iliescu, although the constitution stipulates that the president not be a member of a political party. Petre Roman, the son of a leading figure in the Communist Party, headed the government in 1990 – 1991. In September 1991, miners who had descended on Bucharest forced his resignation. His successors were two economists who had not been politically active, Teodor Stolojan and, after the elections of 1992, Nicolae Vacaroiu. The NSF divided in 1992, with Vacaroiu's faction becoming the Democratic National Salvation Front (DNSF) and a faction chaired by Petre Roman retaining the original name. The opposition NSF renamed itself Democratic Party – National Salvation Front (DP-NSF) a year later, and the DNSF became the Party of Social Democracy of Romania (PSDR). There is a small party called the Socialist Labor Party (SLP) and led by Ceausescu's one-time foreign minister, Ilie Verdet. After the 1992 elections, the government relied on parliamentary support from the SLP and the Romanian nationalists, described below. Later the DP-NSF simply became the DP.

The free market democratic parties originally centreed on the historical parties that dominated Romanian politics before 1938, the National Liberal Party (NLP) and the National Peasant Party (NPP). The NLP leadership proved ineffective and it split into many groups, however, the NPP, which later added Christian Democratic to its name (NPPCD) quickly became the standard-bearer of the opposition. The two principal leaders were Corneliu Coposu, a former secretary of Iuliu Maniu who spent seventeen years in prisons, and Ion Raţiu, a member of a distinguished Transylvanian political family who had been a leader of the emigration and boasted ties to Western financial and political circles. The government sometimes played on popular xenophobia in emphasizing the NPPCD's foreign connections, support for the restoration of the monarchy, and advocacy for the restoration of its former churches to the Greek Catholic Church. Urban intellectuals not sharing either of these vulnerabilities formed a separate group of the free-market democrats including the Party of the Civic Alliance (PCA). The NPPCD, NLP and PCA, along with several smaller parties, formed the coalition Democratic Convention of Romania (DCR) and supported the principles of the Timisoara Declaration. The DCR's presidential candidate Emil Constantinescu, the former rector of the University of Bucharest, lost the presidential elections in 1992 but won in 1996. Two members of the NPPCD served as prime ministers under President Constantinescu, Victor Ciorbea (1996–1998) and Radu Vasile (1998–1999), then were succeeded by the non-party National Bank Governor, Mugur Isǎrescu. The DP and the Hungarian Party also participated in these governments.

A week before the downfall of Nicolae Ceausescu on 22 December 1989, the spark for this result was given by demonstrations in Timişoara by citizens of various nationalities on behalf of a Hungarian Reformed cleric, Laszlo Tokes. The clergyman's courageous but not chauvinistic defence of human rights in Romania, in particular those of the Hungarian minority, attracted the support of Hungarian congregants, then of Romanian and German residents of this multiethnic city when he was threatened with demotion and transfer to another town. This act of solidarity and the Timisoara Declaration of March 1990 signified the hope that the revolution would usher in a new era of tolerance and fraternity in ethnic relations.

Laszlo Tokes became a member of the National Salvation Front during its phase as transitional governing council, but, like other leading non-communists, he soon left this body. On 25 December 1989, the Hungarian minority established its own political organization, the Democratic Alliance of Hungarians in Romania (DAHR). The DAHR participates in local and national elections and takes positions on countrywide issues, but defines itself as a federation rather than a political party, with autonomy for its territorial organizations and various associated organizations. The first leader of the alliance was Geza Domokos, the former director of *Kriterion*, the state publishing house for Romania's ethnic minorities while Tokes took the position of honorary president. As chief representative of the Hungarian minority, the DAHR has enjoyed the overwhelming support of Hungarian voters in the elections since 1990. As a supporter of free-market democracy and the opening toward the European Union (EU), the alliance joined forces with the DCR in the 1992 and 1996 elections and took a seat in the government during the Constantinescu administration. The policy of collaboration with Romanian democrats has had the support of Domokos, his successor since 1998, Bela

Marko, and, according to opinion polls, most Hungarians, but a minority led by Tokes favors a more militant stance.

There have been three main tendencies of Romanian ultra-nationalism since 1990: the Legionaries, chauvinists in Transylvania, and Bucharest-based xenophobes. The revived Legionary movement emerged in 1990 under the initial leadership of Marian Munteanu, a charismatic student leader. This movement claims to continue the traditions and platform of the interwar Legionaries and has eschewed collaboration with the other nationalist groups, but it has fragmented into various groups and failed to gain sufficient votes to take a seat in parliament. The Transylvanian group had its origins in the so-called cultural organization Romanian Hearth and civil servants eager to rally Romanians against a supposed Hungarian threat. After Romanian Hearth took a role in the bloody Hungarian Romanian clashes in Targu Mures in March 1990, the group organized into the Party of Romanian National Unity (PRNU) with the chief goal of opposing Hungarian interests. The PRNU entered parliament in 1992 but gained its greatest notoriety through the flag-waving and Hungarian-bating of former engineer Gheorghe Funar as mayor of Cluj, Transylvania's largest city, since 1992. The party subsequently elected him party leader but replaced him after disappointing results in the 1996 national elections.

The larger Bucharest-based organization is the Greater Romania Party (GRP). Its founder and still dominant personality is Corneliu Vadim Tudor, a poet and journalist who used the newspaper he founded, România Mare (*Greater Romania*), to build his base before establishing the party in 1991. The GRP mirrors the rhetoric of the PRNU equating Hungarian demands for cultural autonomy with territorial separatism but is anti-Semitic and glorifies leaders Marshal Ion Antonescu and Nicolae Ceausescu. The party included several military officers among its leaders, and for much of the 1990s enjoyed special access to official documents on its political enemies that Tudor used to smear them in the party newspaper. More than the SLP of Ilie Verdet, the GRP perpetuates the goals of the last years of Nicolae Ceausescu to concentrate state authority against all purported enemies in the name of national security and territorial integrity. The PRNU and GRP provided support for the minority government of Nicolae Vacaroiu after the elections of 1992.

After the failure of the NPPCD in its leadership of the coalition government in 1996–2000 in the elections of 2000, the party individually and the DCR as a coalition did not even meet the threshold for representation in parliament. The NLP successfully regrouped and emerged stronger in these elections, but the chief victors were the resurgent PDSR and GRP. Tudor won a surprising second place in the presidential election with his advocacy of radical measures against corruption and separatism, prompting alternative forces to throw their support to Iliescu in the second round. Under the second Iliescu administration, the GRP is the strongest opposition party by far but is isolated from the others, with whom it rarely collaborates. The PRNU also failed to enter the new parliament. With the initial tacit support of the fragmented free market democrats and the DAHR, the PSDR under Prime Minister Adrian Nastase[1] has moved further to the center. In 2001, the PSDR merged with the successor of the prewar socialist party and took its name, becoming the Social Democratic Party (SDP).

Romania's foreign policy has been reoriented toward the West. In his early years as national leader, Nicolae Ceausescu asserted a prominent diplomatic role for the country as intermediary between the blocs with the Israelis and Palestinians and the beneficiary of a special trade relationship with some Western countries. But the collapse of the economy in the 1980s brought an end to this role. The Soviet Union again became Romania's leading trade partner. In fact, Romania had never left Comecon, the Soviet trading network or the

---

1 Romanian former politician who was the Prime Minister of Romania from December 2000 to December 2004.

He competed in the 2004 presidential election as the Social Democratic Party (PSD) candidate, but was defeated by centre-right Justice and Truth (DA) Alliance candidate Traian Băsescu.

He was the President of the Chamber of Deputies from 21 December 2004 until 15 March 2006, when he resigned due to corruption charges. Sentenced to two years in prison in July 2012, he attempted suicide before beginning his term in the penitentiary. Released in March 2013, he was sentenced to four years in another case in January 2014, but released that August [Source: Wikipedia].

Warsaw Pact, and attended meetings of these organizations though participation was limited in some areas. In 1975, the United States granted Romania Most Favored Nation status in recognition of the country's special opposition. After rising criticism of Romania's human rights record at the time of the annual renewal of MFN in Congress, Ceausescu renounced it in 1988 in order to preempt its revocation.

Well-publicized human rights problems and delays in economic reform impeded Romania's desire to improve relations with the European Union after 1990. When President Iliescu travelled to Western countries, he was sometimes denied reception by other heads of state. The United States finally restored MFN in 1993 and made it permanent in 1996. Romania pursued an ambiguous policy toward Yugoslavia during its internal conflicts, mostly respecting but sometimes circumventing trade sanctions against that country. Treaties with Ukraine and Russia as well as Hungary have improved trade relations and clarified territorial issues with these countries. The relationship with Russia remains strained by Russia's retention of Romanian state reserves of gold, jewels and art valued at $5 billion, which were sent to allied Russia during World War I for safekeeping.

Romania has acceded to the Organization of Black Sea Economic Co-operation and the Central European Free Trade Association with the Visegrad countries. The country was formally invited to join NATO in 2002 and is engaged in the protracted process of accession to the European Union with a target date of 2007. The United States is currently considering a move of its military bases from Germany to Romania and Bulgaria that would establish a special strategic relationship with these countries. Romania's two major ongoing issues in foreign relations, however, remain contentious: EU accession and the Moldovan question.

Territorial Organization[1]

The communes, towns, municipalities and counties are territorial-administrative units, where local government authorities shall be organized and

---

1　https://www.gold.uclg.org/sites/default/files/Romania_0.pdf

function. At the country level, three hierarchical levels are identified: national, county and local. The county level is represented by the 42 counties of Romania including also Bucharest Municipality[1]. Each county has its residence at municipality level, representing the political, economic, social-cultural and scientific centre of the county. At each county level, the local government authority is exerted by a County Council[2], coordinating the activities of commune, town and municipality councils. The Government of Romania appoints a prefect for each county, inclusively for Bucharest Municipality, who are state representatives at local level. The Prefect directs the deconcentrated public services of ministries and other bodies of the central government in the territorial-administrative units. The local level comprises 2,851 communes, 216 towns and 103 municipalities. The communes, towns and municipalities have their own Local Council (deliberative authority) and a mayor (executive authority), elected after the poll organized on a term of four years.

Bucharest Municipality is organized on six territorial-administrative subdivisions, called sectors. Bucharest Municipality has a General Council of Bucharest Municipality and General Mayor of the capital and each sector has a local council and a mayor. In 1997, a new structuring of Romania into eight development regions has been proposed. The regions, which are not territorial-administrative units, are set up by gathering counties, aimed to develop European financial assistance programs within European Union regional development policies. Projects on creating metropolitan areas exist in most large cities in Romania. The metropolitan area is expressed by the association structures between territorial-administrative units, around Capital—Bucharest Metropolitan Area—or those around municipalities, county residence.

---

1 Romania's capital and largest city, as well as the most important industrial and commercial center of the country. With two million inhabitants in the city proper and more than 2.4 million in the urban area, Bucharest is one of the largest cities in Southeastern Europe. Bucharest is the 6th largest city in the European Union by population within city limits after London, Berlin, Madrid, Rome and Paris [Source: Wikitravel].

2 The county council is the public administration authority that coordinates the activities of all village and town councils in a county.

National Government

The Romanian government has made great strides with reform and capitalism, but still has major obstacles to overcome before becoming a full European partner. Struggling with poverty, dysfunctional politics, and incomplete economic reform all the time, Romania's authorities have demonstrated a sustained commitment to a reform agenda that is at the heart of reducing poverty and exclusion.

Executive Branch

The executive branch consists of a president, a prime minister and the council of ministers. Under the constitution, the president of Romania serves as chief of state, commander-in-chief of the armed forces, and also the head of the Supreme Council of National Defense. The president can serve two four-year terms. The prime minister is appointed and can be removed by the president in consultation with the governing party or coalition in parliament. Within 10 days of his appointment, the prime minister submits a proposed list of ministers and legislative program to parliament, which then meets in a joint session to give a vote of confidence in the government. If at least two attempts have been made to receive a vote of confidence in a government, and there has been no government for at least 60 days, the president may dismiss parliament in consultation with the presidents of both houses. Also, the president may dismiss and appoint a nominated minister without requiring a renewed vote of confidence. The parliament may only express votes of confidence or no confidence in the government and its program as a whole.

Legislative Branch

Romania's bicameral parliament consists of an upper house or Senate and the Chamber of Deputies. The Senate consists of 176 seats. Members are elected by direct popular vote on a proportional representation basis to serve four-year terms. The Chamber of Deputies has 308 seats. Both the Senate and the Chamber of Deputies must pass identical bills in order to enact laws. Members are elected by direct popular vote on a proportional representation basis to serve four-year terms. The electoral system is based on proportional representation and parties must surpass a 3% threshold to gain representation. The legal voting age is 18.

Judicial Branch

Supreme Court of Justice, the highest body in the judicial system, is responsible for civil, criminal, military and administrative activities. It is headed by the procurator-general who is responsible only to the Grand National Assembly. Under the Supreme Court are the Court of Appeal, 41 departmental county courts and lower courts. Court judges are appointed by the president from proposals made by the Higher Council of the Judiciary. The president of the Supreme Court is the senior judicial figure. The attorney general heads the Ministry of Justice. Judges are politically independent. Romania has a constitutional court. Military tribunals address internal and external security issues. The death penalty was abolished in December 1989 and is forbidden by the constitution.

Local Government

The local government structure in Romania has been in use for hundreds of years. There are two main tiers of local government. The judetes (counties) are the upper tier. There are 40 counties in Romania. The lower tier of local authority is made up of 2,686 communes (with populations up to 5,000), 280 orase (with populations between 5,000 and 20,000), and 86 municipii (larger cities with more than 20,000 people). Each unit of local government has its own administration, the right to own land and some local ruling authority. Local government elections are held every four years.

The Constitution of Romania stipulates the principle of political pluralism as a condition and guarantee of constitutional democracy, meaning that the fundamental law recognizes the importance of the political parties in free organization of society, in defining and expressing citizens' political will. The Romanian electoral system complies with the dimensions of European majority electoral system, that of proportional representation and it observes the principle of proportional representation, thus allowing the access of a greater number of political parties to the Parliament. The parliamentary elections are held on the basis of list ballot, being a proportional electoral system with closed list ballot.

The political parties and alliances, the organizations of minorities and independent candidates submitted in each constituency the lists of their own candidates. There are 42 constituencies (corresponding to the number of counties including Bucharest Municipality). Citizen participation in local governance is developing. The citizens acquire information about decision-making process, resources, management structures and planning. The statistics reveal that citizen participation in the meetings of the local councils is greater in the rural area than in the urban area. Legislation stipulates citizen participation to: A. organization and participation to public meetings; B. public debates, priority for good governance; C. public decision-making process; D. electoral actions, citizen's right to elect and to be elected as fundamental rights; E. right to legislative initiative represent the proof of democracy in Romania.

The vote is the means to express electorate's option, being a non-material relation between voter and voted. The texts of the articles of the Constitution of Romania reveal the characteristics of the vote: universal (all Romanian citizens who fulfil the conditions stipulated in the Constitution), equality (equality of rights for the Romanian citizens), free, direct and secret. They are also considered constitutional conditions of the vote, being completed by special laws, on the electoral action, such as: registering the citizens with "vote" right on a (permanent or special) electoral list and holding the voter's card.

The elections in Romania are held on three levels: A. local level (for local councils, county councils, city halls and General Council of Bucharest Municipality); B. general level (respectively for the Parliament of Romania) and, C. presidential level (for the office of President of Romania).

At the last elections, the electorate has proved a reorientation to the "useful vote", asserting a new significance of the "vote sanction"; the electorate has changed its attitude related to the vote, recording an increase of absenteeism, thus proving "a new type of civic competence".

The electoral management is exerted in electoral constituencies organized at the level of each commune, town, municipality and territorial-administrative subdivision for electing local councils and mayors, and an electoral constituency is formed for electing county councils at each county level. The electoral law stipulates that the number of the polling stations in a constituency is determined depending on the number of voters assigned to each polling station. The vote is exerted in polling stations, organized in localities, observing the representation norm, depending on the number of inhabitants. The local and county councils are elected on the ground of party lists according to the proportional representation system.

Central-Local Relationships

General issues

After 1990, Romania has undergone the process to redefine the role of central government related to local government, political and administrative competences delegated to local government, necessary sources as well as the performance of decentralization process and strengthening democratic local governance. In the governmental structure, the main body responsible of public administration is the concerned ministry with the related bodies (ex: Superior Council for Public Administration Reform, Coordinating Public Policies and Structural Adjustment, Central Unit for Public Administration Reform), namely the Ministry of Interior and Administrative Reform (MIRA). Within MIRA, there is a State Secretary for public administration reform. The Government, ministries and the other specialized bodies of central government transfer competences, currently exerted by local government authorities at county, commune or town level. The government authorities, by which local autonomy in communes and towns is achieved, are the elected Local Councils and elected Mayors in accordance with the law. The County Council is "the government authority coordinating the activity of commune and town councils", with a view to carrying out the public services of county interest. The local, county councils and General Council of Bucharest Municipality have rule-making functions and they are deliberative authorities on local level.

Supervision of local government

The institutional framework of the decentralization process ensures the development and operationalization of the adequate "infrastructure" and technical structure. It comprises the Ministry of Interior and Administrative Reform, the Ministry of Economy and Finance, specialized structures.

Concerning the constitutional regulations, the Constitution of 2003 adds the principle of public service deconcentration (article 120) to the principle of public service decentralization. Article 123 eliminates the confusion between the notions of decentralization and deconcentration, stipulating that the prefect is the representative of the Government on local level and directs the deconcentrated public services of ministries and other bodies of the central government in the territorial-administrative units.

At the central government level, there are regulating authorities — government authorities entitled to issue regulations, rules, procedures and standards in view of public service provision. They are in charge with public service financing, providing the funds necessary for public services in their own budget or the state budget. They may be regional operators of public services and authorities responsible for implementation in charge of service provision. The local council may be dissolved as such or by local referendum, action to administrative disputed claims court addressed by the mayor, vice mayor, secretary of the territorial-administrative unit or other interested person. The court analyses the situation, pronounces the judgment and communicates it to the prefect as irrevocable judgment. The mayor's mandate ceases as a result of a local referendum, organized at the request addressed to the prefect by the citizens of the commune, town or municipality.

Protection of Local Self-government Rights and Interest

In justice, the territorial-administrative units are represented as the case may be, by the mayor or president of the county council or a lawyer, empowered by the mayor, respectively the president of the county council or a legal adviser from the specialized apparatus of the mayor, respectively county council.

The local or county councillors, mayors, vice mayors, General Mayor of Bucharest Municipality, presidents and vice presidents of county councils, secretaries of territorial-administrative units shall be responsible as the case may be, administratively, civil or penal for the deeds committed in the exercising of their duties. The offences declared by the prefect, as public authority and representative of the Government on local level are subject to fines. The associative structures of local government authorities are: Association of Communes in Romania, Association of Towns in Romania, National Union of County Councils in Romania, other associative forms of general interest.

Local Finance and Management [1]

Local Government Incomes

Local government authorities have the competence to establish the levels for local taxes and charges, to elaborate and approve local budgets of communes,

---

1 https://www.loc.gov/resource/frdcstdy.romaniacountryst00bach_0/?st=gallery

towns, municipalities and counties under the limits and terms of law.

The revenues of local budgets comprise: A. own revenues from: taxes, charges, contributions, other payments, other revenues and shared amounts from the income tax; B. shared amounts from some revenues of the state budget; C. subsidies from state budget and other budgets; D. donations and sponsorships.

The share from GDP[1] designated to local budgets during 1998-2001 increased from 3.6% to 6.5%, and local public expenditure increased from 14% to 26%. From the state budget by the budgets of main credit directors as well as from other budgets, transfers may be awarded to local budgets in order to finance some development or social programs of national, county or local interest, which are approved annually in global form by the Law on state budget.

Further decentralization of some activities, the administration and financing by local government authorities of some public expenditure, as well as of other new public expenditure has determined an increase of local subsidies during 2003-2005 from 654.4 million lei[2] to 1102.1 million lei. In order to finance public expenditure provided also for balancing local budgets of territorial-administrative units in the law on state budget, shared amounts from some revenues of the state budget are approved. Thus, 80% from the amount designated to balancing local budgets is distributed by the decision of the Director of General Directorate for Public Finances according to a clear and transparent formula, and 20% by the decision of the County Council, exclusively to support the local development programs. The local, county councils and General Council of Bucharest Municipality may approve to contract or guarantee internal or external loans on short, medium or long term in order to achieve public investments of local interest as well to refinance the local public debt. The territorial-administrative units may benefit also of external loans, which are under state contract or guarantee in accordance with law.

---

1 Gross domestic product (GDP) is a monetary measure of the market value of all final goods and services produced in a period (quarterly or yearly) of time. Nominal GDP estimates are commonly used to determine the economic performance of a whole country or region, and to make international comparisons [Source: Wikipedia].

2 the currency of Romania. It is subdivided into 100 bani. The word "bani" is also used for "money" in the Romanian language [Source: Wikipedia].

Local Government Personnel and Management

The total number of public positions in the county councils, local councils and other local public authorities has recorded an increase from 40.69% in 2003 to 45.35% in 2006, reaching 58,282 civil servants in 2006. The increase is due especially to the efforts in view of decentralization, making administration more citizen-friendly and developing proximity services. The ratio between executing and leading public positions is nine to one, observing the maximum limit of 12% for leading public positions, stipulated in Law no. 188/1999 on Statute of Civil Servants.

The decrease of the number of public positions in the category of high civil servants is due to legislative changes—the public positions of director general and secretary of the county do not belong to that category. According to study level, the structure is as follows: executive civil servants with long-term higher education studies (44.80%), short-term higher education studies (3.72%), upper secondary studies (51.48%).

The degree of professionalization decreases in case of local councils and other local government authorities (only three of ten civil servants have higher education studies), due both to the lack of labour market with high qualification and lack of an attractive package of remuneration and rewarding the potential employees.

Concerning the increase of the capacity to prevent and resist corruption for civil servants, Law no. 7/2004 on the Conduct Code of Civil Servants was changed in 2007. Transparency International Romania[1] reveals a series of legislative developments with major impact on the "integrity at local government level" on allocation and management of local public finances, modification of

---

1 The Romanian chapter of Transparency International leading the fight against corruption and promoting integrity. Transparency International is an international non-governmental organization which is based in Berlin, Germany, and was founded in 1993. Its non-profit purpose is to take action to combat global corruption and prevent criminal activities arising from corruption. It publishes for example the Global Corruption Barometer and the Corruption Perceptions Index [Source: Wikipedia].

the law on local government and punishment of political migration. At the same time, the results of the Barometer[1] on 2007 reveal that both the services of public utilities and those issuing documents have obtained in 2007 higher rates than in the previous year, respectively 2.4 points and 2.9 points. Taking into account this perspective, Transparency International Romania draws attention to the fact that anti-corruption efforts should focus on genuine reform of the administrative system, as long as citizen perception on corruption is based on a large extent on personal experiences in the direct relation with the state institutions.

Political Parties[2]

The Romanian Parliament is bicameral. It comprises the Chamber of Deputies (Camera deputatilor) and the Senate (Senatul). The two assemblies are renewed every four years. The Romanian electoral law was modified on 20 July 2015. From now on, the lower chamber comprises 308 members (one MP for 73,000 people and 122 less than the number elected four years ago in 2012) appointed by proportional vote within 43 constituencies: 41 represent Romania's counties with 279 seats, one represents the capital, which has 29 seats and finally the last represents Romanians abroad and it has four seats.

To enter the Chamber of Deputies, all parties have to win at least 5% of the total votes cast nationally or 20% of all of the votes cast in at least four constituencies (8% for an alliance of two parties, 9% for an alliance of three parties and 10% for an alliance of four parties or more). A person who wins the support of at least 0.50% of the electorate in a constituency is allowed to stand alone for election.

Some seats in the Chamber of Deputies are reserved for the 19 national

---

1 The Global Corruption Barometer is the biggest ever survey tracking world-wide public opinion on corruption by Transparency International.

2 L. Stan & L.Turcescu, *Religion and Politics in Post-communist Romania*, New York: Oxford University Press, 2007.

minorities in the country. A national minority has the right to a parliamentary seat if the citizens' organization, which represents it, has a representative on the National Council of Minorities and if it wins at least 5% of the average number of votes cast to win a MPs seat. All voters (potential candidates) must be aged at least 23 if they want to take part in the parliamentary elections.

The Romanian Senate has 134 members. According to a new electoral law dated 20th July 2015, there is one Senator per 168,000 inhabitants. Two Senators represent the Romanians abroad. Nine political parties are represented in the present Romanian parliament.

Romania also elects its president by direct universal suffrage. The Head of State at present is Klaus Iohannis[1] who was elected for a five-year mandate on 16th November 2014 with 54.43% of the vote. He pulled ahead of the then Prime Minister Victor Ponta (PSD), who won 45.56% of the vote. The turnout at this election reached 64.1% as a whole.

Foreign Relations

General Relations

Romania is a member of numerous international organizations including the United Nations and many of its specialized and regional agencies, the International Bank for Reconstruction and Development, the International Monetary Fund and the World Trade Organization.

Romania is also a member of the European Bank for Reconstruction and Development, the Organization for Security and Cooperation in Europe, and the Council of Europe. In addition, Romania is an associate partner of the Western European Union and a member of the North Atlantic Treaty Organization's

---

1 The current President of Romania. He became leader of the National Liberal Party in 2014, after having served as leader of the Democratic Forum of Germans in Romania from 2001 to 2013. Iohannis was a physics teacher and a school inspector before entering full-time politics. [Source: Wikipedia].

Partnership for Peace program.

The government continued to make integration into Western institutions its chief foreign policy objective. Fundamental to this objective is Romanian membership in NATO and the European Union.

Relations with NATO and the European Union

Romania's top political priorities in the beginning of 21century included entry to NATO and the EU. Indeed, the issue of expansion of NATO was discussed and relevant Eastern European countries including Romania was formally invited to join NATO at its Prague Summit in November 2002. In March 2003, the Romanian foreign minister, along with the equivalent ministers of Bulgaria, Slovenia, Slovakia, Estonia, Latvia and Lithuania, went to Brussels to attend an accession ceremony. In Brussels, at NATO headquarters, NATO's existing members signed documents that would accept the new countries into the strategic alliance. The next step, which would extend over a period of a year, entailed ratification by national parliaments. Accession to NATO finally came to pass in March 2004.

Accession to the EU has posed even greater difficulty for Romania. Romania remains poor with low standards of living and among the highest inflation rates in Europe at 41%. Romania, as well as Bulgaria, is at the bottom of the list of contenders for accession. In 2000, the European Commission revoked Romania's visa-free travel to the EU after complaints of illegal immigration, and in December 2001, the ban on travel was lifted. However, the new government has implemented economic reforms and tightened border controls in 2001.

Currently, Romania's economy is growing, following deep recession since 1995. Yet despite evidence of economic recovery, Romania needs reform in almost every aspect of the economy and is far behind its eastern European counterparts in accession to the EU.

| 罗马尼亚概况 | *Survey of Romania* |

In 1997 and 1999, reports by the European Commission were issued; the latter report advocated conditional negotiations with Romania on accession. This was followed by an invitation to begin accession negotiations in mid-December 1999, at its Helsinki Summit. EU accession negotiations were started with Romania on 15 February 2000. Romania hoped to be considered for accession in 2007.

In 2005, the government of Romania was hoping to win support for reforms considered mandatory for European Union accession. If the reforms were not realized soon, then, it was believed that accession could be delayed for a year until 2008[1]. In September 2006, however, officials from the European Union announced that Romania would be admitted to the European bloc. Finally, Romania became the member of the European Union on 1 January 2007, along with Bulgaria.

---

[1] Meanwhile, at the close of 2005, the government was under international pressure when the Red Cross and Human Rights Watch reported that Romania was home to some of the United States CIA's "black sites"—the secret camps used by the United States intelligence agency to interrogate suspected al-Qaida members. The administration denied the claims. Nevertheless, officials of the European Commission said that there would be a comprehensive investigation on this matter. The investigation was to determine the veracity of the charges since such sites would be a violation of the European convention on human rights and the international convention against torture. If the sites are found, then Romania could be in breach of Article Six of the Treaty of Nice, which calls on all member states to uphold basic human rights.

In June 2007, the issue of clandestine prisons or "black sites" returned to the political purview when Dick Marty, an investigator for the Council of Europe, said that he had evidence to prove the United States' Central Intelligence Agency (CIA) directed clandestine prisons in Poland and Romania for the purpose of interrogating "war on terror" suspects. He noted that the secret prisons or "black sites" in Europe had been administered "directly and exclusively by the CIA".

Marty named Poland and Romania as host countries of these secret prisons. While the governments of both Poland and Romania denied hosting such "black sites", the CIA issued a statement noting, "The CIA's counter-terror operations have been lawful, effective, closely reviewed, and of benefit to many people including Europeans—by disrupting plots and saving lives." The United States President Bush acknowledged the existence of CIA prisons overseas but did not specify host countries.

Also in 2007, the European Commission drew attention to Romania's enduring corruption challenges by calling on the country to actively combat this issue.

Regional Relations

Relations with Hungary[1]

Romania has formed strong relations with Hungary, as Hungary played a key role in supporting Romania's bid to join the EU. Ethnic Hungarian party also took part in all the government coalitions between 1996 and 2009. In 1996, Romania and Hungary signed and ratified a basic bilateral treaty which settled outstanding disagreements, laying the foundation for closer, more cooperative relations.

Since the late 1990s, Romanian-Hungarian relations[2] have seen a constant improvement, with the last few years acknowledged as the best period in the history of relations between the two countries. The two countries have strengthened economic co-operation and joint actions aiming at improving energy security. With the first Romanian-Hungarian gas interconnector opening at the end of 2010, the two countries started jointly working on the AGRI project (gas transport from Azerbaijan via Georgia and the Black Sea to Romania and Hungary). The co-operation for the enlargement of the Schengen Area also forged closer bonds between the two countries with the implementation of the European Union Strategy for the Danube Region and the negotiations relating to the Multiannual Financial Framework of the European Union.

Amicable contacts between politicians from the two countries also contributed to emphasizing the willingness for cooperation between Romania and Hungary. It has become a tradtion for the politicians from the two countries to have annual informal meetings during the Hungarian culture festival in Baile Tusnad[3]. It is predictable that Hungary and Romania will remain close partners in many aspects of European politics and will not terminate their mutually beneficial cooperation.

---

1 https://en.wikipedia.org/wiki/Hungary%E2%80%93Romania_relations
2 https://www.osw.waw.pl/en/publikacje/analyses/2012-05-30/erosion-romanian-hungarian-partnership
3 A town in Harghita County, Romania

Relations with Moldova[1]

Moldova and Romania have gone through a highly complicated relationship since Moldova achieved independence in 1991 as most of Moldova used to be part of Romania during the Interwar period. The official language of Moldova is Romanian. Likewise, the peoples of the two countries share common traditions and folklore including a common name for the monetary unit—the *Leu*. There were previous signs that Romania and Moldova might unite after 1980s but they then quickly faded. However, in the second decade of the 21st century a growing unionist sentiment could be seen in both countries.

Relations with Russia[2]

Romania has long had tense relations with Russia due to complicated historical reasons. The question of energy plays a major part in Romania's relations with Russia due to Romanis's high domestic fossil fuel reserves. Due to its primary concern with the immediate neighborhood, Romania was supportive of pro-EU and pro-NATO measures in Georgia, and with forming a common Black Sea partnership within Europe.

As Romania's interests in Moldova's accession to the EU were incompatible with Russia's desire to maintain the frozen conflict in Transnistria, Romania continued to be dedicated to deepering ties with the US and NATO, as well as with its Black Sea partners, such as Georgia and Ukraine. Within the EU context, Romania's relationship with Russia is best portrayed as "below-radar supporter", where concerns are moderated by historical relations and local context.

According to a survey of Eurobarometer[3], 53% of Romanians view Russia

---

1 https://en.wikipedia.org/wiki/Moldova%E2%80%93Romania_relations
2 https://www.kremlinwatch.eu/countries-compared-states/romania/
3 Eurobarometer is a series of public opinion surveys conducted regularly on behalf of the European Commission since 1973 [Source: Wikipedia]

positively, while 41% have a negative view. Recently, however, nationalist tendencies have once again procured mainstream acquiescence, through social media channels and the voices of some opinion leaders. Some of these outlets have no overt pro-Kremlin inclination but "create a particularly fertile ground for pro-Kremlin media and serve as multipliers for narratives that promote the Kremlin's goal of weakening Romania's pro-Western sentiment."

Other Significant Relations

Relations with China[1]

On 5 October 2019, China and Romania have celebrated the 70th anniversary of the establishment of diplomatic relations. In the long history of Sino-Romanian relations, 5 October 1949 is a milestone of great significance. From that day on, the two countries opened their doors to each other in an all-round manner, ushering in a new journey that has led to great leaps in their bilateral relations.

Over the past 70 years, China-Romania relationship has made great strides. Despite the vicissitudes of the international situation, friendly cooperation has always been the dominant theme of their bilateral relations, which have been upgraded twice, resulting in a comprehensive partnership of friendship and cooperation. The two countries have maintained high-level exchanges, expanded cooperation and deepened common interests, forming an all-dimensional, multi-tiered and wide-ranging pattern of mutually beneficial cooperation.

Over the past 70 years, the economic cooperation between Romania and China has deepened. Bilateral trade has been growing steadily, and entered the "fast lane" in recent years. The trade volume has jumped from less than $300 million in 2000 to $6.68 billion in 2018, increasing almost 22 times, with an average annual growth rate of 18%. China has become Romania's largest trading partner in Asia. This achievement is particularly remarkable against

---

1 https://www.nineoclock.ro/2019/09/19/h-e-mrs-jiang-yu-ambassador-of-the-peoples-republic-of-china-to-romania-renewing-china-romania-friendship-and-opening-up-a-brighter-future/

the background of rising world trade protectionism. In recent years, Romania's wine, dairy products, honey and other high-quality agricultural products have found their way into China's markets across the oceans, enriching the "food basket" of the Chinese people. Chinese enterprises take an active part in the investment and construction of Romania's transportation infrastructure, new energy, high-tech and other fields. Chinese brands such as Huawei, ZTE, Lenovo and Xiaomi are increasingly popular among Romanian consumers. The vigorous development of bilateral pragmatic cooperation has brought tangible benefits to people of the two countries.

Over the past 70 years, friendship has been deeply rooted in the hearts of the two peoples. Both China and Romania have a long history and a splendid civilization, and the two peoples are keen to know more about each other. The two sides have promoted visa facilitation, bringing in nearly 10,000 Chinese tourists to Romania each year. The Romanian Culture Center in Beijing runs well. There are now over 100 sites in Romania where the Chinese language is taught, including four Confucius Institutes, and the Chinese Cultural Center will soon be officially inaugurated in Bucharest. The two countries have established 35 pairs of friendly provinces and cities, which ranks top in Central and Eastern European countries.

Relations with the United States[1]

The United States established diplomatic relations with Romania in 1880, following Romania's independence. The two countries severed diplomatic ties after Romania declared war on the United States in 1941; and re-established them in 1947. Recent years have seen a series of unequivocally pro-Western policies in Romania. The United States and Romania deepened relations by increasing cooperation on shared goals including economic and political development, deterrence and defense, and non-traditional threats such as transnational crime.

In 2011, the United States and Romania issued the "Joint Declaration on

---

1 https://www.state.gov/u-s-relations-with-romania/

Strategic Partnership for the 21st Century between the United States of America and Romania". The two countries identified key areas for enhanced cooperation, focusing on our political-military relationship, law-enforcement cooperation, trade and investment opportunities, and energy security. Romania and the United States are bound together through various ties in business, the arts, scholarship, and a host of other exchanges.

Romania's economy began a transition to capitalism after 1989. The country was committed to creating a legal framework consistent with a market economy and investment promotion. In 1992, the United States and Romania signed a bilateral investment treaty (BIT), which came into force in 1994. In 2003, prior to Romania's accession to the EU, the United States and Romania amended the BIT, which still remains in effect. Romania attracts U.S. investors who are interested in accessing the European market, with relatively low costs and a well-educated, tech-savvy population. In Romania, major U.S. firms operate in the energy, manufacturing, information technology and telecommunications, services, and consumer products sectors. Top Romanian exports to the United States include machinery, vehicle parts, steel and metallic items, and fertilizers.

Romania and the United States belong to a number of the same international organizations, including the United Nations, NATO, Euro-Atlantic Partnership Council, Organization for Security and Cooperation in Europe, International Monetary Fund, World Bank, and World Trade Organization, among others.

Relations with Israel[1]

Israel and Romania have very strong friendly relations, based on a long tradition of cooperation and historic bonds, as well as on common values and vision shared by the two peoples. The diplomatic relations between the two countries were established on 11 June 1948 when Romania recognized the State

---

1 https://www.nineoclock.ro/2016/05/12/israel-a-very-important-economic-and-cultural-partner-of-romania/

of Israel, immediately after its creation.

Over the years, Romania has become an important partner of Israel in Central and Eastern Europe, as the two countries share similar values and principles. Thus, the cooperation between Israel and Romania has grown stronger in many areas, such as political, commercial, economic, defense, and cultural relations. The closeness of ties between the two Governments is manifested through mutual visits of high-ranking officials and dignitaries, most notably in recent years.

Israel-Romania long-standing strategic and political cooperation is highlighted by the extensive exchanges of high-level visits. The significant number of agreements and protocols signed in those meetings covered a wide spectrum of fields, like defense, agriculture, health, labor, IT, telecommunication, education, culture and more. Furthermore, new areas of potential cooperation were identified, such as cyber security, energy, and applied research and development (R&D).

However, commercial links are the key factors in the development of their bilateral relations, with increasing interest from business communities on both sides. The rising number of economic forums that have taken place in recent years emphasizes the prospects for more trade and investment partnerships. In fact, in various sectors, Romania and Israel are complimentary to each other. Therefore, there are tremendous opportunities in combining the expertise, including by absorbing EU funds.

The bilateral agreement is reinforced on a regular basis by programs of bilateral relations in the field with cooperation protocols signed between the two countries. The documents contain stipulations which establish in detail the aspects of cooperation in the cultural and technical-scientific domains, as well as aspects of the Romanian-Israeli collaboration in domains such as the protection of the archeological patrimony, the interception of illegal trade with archeological vestiges and patrimony goods.

Chapter 7
Economy and Trade

Romania is one of the largest countries in Central and Eastern Europe. The nation is endowed with substantial natural resources including rich agricultural lands, diverse energy resources such as coal, oil, natural gas and an industrial base encompassing a wide range of manufacturing activities. Romania started the transition from 1990, but the transition was difficult because of 40 years of rigid central planning that took the economy to near-collapse. Further more, stop-go policies during the 1990s left Romania behind many other transition economies with mediocre growth, high inflation and low Foreign Direct Investment (FDI). Macroeconomic conditions improved after 2000 as a result of fiscal adjustment, enhanced financial performance of state-owned enterprises and privatization.

In 2019, Romania has a GDP of around $547 billion and a GDP per capita of $28,189. According to the World Bank, Romania is a high-income country with a mixed economy. According to Eurostat, Romania's GDP per capita was at 64% of the EU average in 2018, an increase from 41% in 2007 (the year of Romania's accession to the EU), making Romania one of the fastest-growing economies in the EU.[1]

Economic development[2]

The Romanian economy experienced rapid growth and transformation from 1947 to 1989. Industrial output grew at an annual rate of 12.9% from 1950 to 1977, thanks largely to heavy reinvestment of capital gained by the central control of prices and consumption. The agricultural sector declined from 74.1% of the working population in 1950 to 28.6% in 1982, while that of industry grew from 12% to 36.5% in the same period. There was a corresponding shift of population to the cities, the largest of which multiplied in size. The arduous process of collectivizing agricultural land was 90% completed by 1962. Collectivization favoured the mechanization of agriculture, but it still lagged behind the West because of low productivity and the disproportionate investment in the industrial sector. There was a downturn in the economy after 1976. A massive foreign debt led to rationing in 1981 and a dramatic decline in the standard of living in the following years that made it possible to retire the debt by 1989.

Economic development has been fitful since the fall of Ceausescu's ruling in 1989. Overall growth was negative in all sectors until recently, with high inflation and with unemployment hovering around 10%. The average retirement age, fifty for women and fifty-four for men, is one of the lowest in the world and serves to distort unemployment figures. Labor unrest, especially in the mining and heavy industry sector that stymied efforts to close unprofitable mines, produced on foreign television screens the horrifying sight of rioting miners on the streets of Bucharest, and helped, along with an unfavourable legal and

---

1 https://en.wikipedia.org/wiki/Romania

2 H. F. Carey (Ed.), *Romania since 1989: Politics, Economics, and Society,* Langham: Lexington books, 2004.

political environment, to discourage foreign investment. Only during a few years in the middle of the 1990s, then again beginning in 2000, did the economy show positive economic growth. The privatization of land ownership was 75% completed by 1995 and 97% by 1999. There has been some privatization in the services sector, but privatization of industrial firms has proceeded much more slowly.

Government sources attributed the recession after 1996 to the democratic coalition's efforts at economic restructuring. Corruption and the mismanagement of state enterprises was a continuing problem in the Democratic Convention as well as the administrations. The International Monetary Fund (IMF)[1], World Bank and European Union (EU)[2] signalled their dissatisfaction with reform efforts by repeatedly suspending financial support packages. By the turn of

---

1 an international organization headquartered in Washington, D.C., of "189 countries working to foster global monetary cooperation, secure financial stability, facilitate international trade, promote high employment and sustainable economic growth and reduce poverty around the world. Formed in 1944 at the Bretton Woods Conference, it came into formal existence in 1945 with 29 member countries and the goal of reconstructing the international payment system. It now plays a central role in the management of balance of payments difficulties and international financial crises. Countries contribute funds to a pool through a quota system from which countries experiencing balance of payments problems can borrow money. Through the fund, and other activities such as the gathering of statistics and analysis, surveillance of its members' economies and the demand for particular policies, the IMF works to improve the economies of its member countries. The organization's objectives stated in the Articles of Agreement are: to promote international monetary co-operation, international trade, high employment, exchange-rate stability, sustainable economic growth and making resources available to member countries in financial difficulty [Source: Wikipedia].

2 The European Union is a political and economic union of 28 member states that are located primarily in Europe. It has an area of 4,475,757 km² and an estimated population of about 513 million. The EU has developed an internal single market through a standardised system of laws that apply in all member states in those matters, and only those matters, where members have agreed to act asone. EU policies aim to ensure the free movement of people, goods, services and capital within the internal market, enact legislation in justice and home affairs and maintain common policies on trade, agriculture, fisheries and regional development. For travel within the Schengen Area, passport controls have been abolished. A monetary union was established in 1999 and came into full force in 2002 and is composed of 19 EU member states which use the Euro currency [Source: Wikipedia)].

the century, the level of marketization, foreign investment and standard of living compared unfavourably with almost all other East European countries. Incomplete reforms, due to the successful resistance of many vested interests, produced economic imbalances and negative growth in 1997–1999. Reforms became more serious in response to demands arising from the accession to the European Union and caused unemployment to reach 10%–11% (by various indices) in 2002. The new administration has been more successful in prosecuting balanced structural reform, leading to positive growth after it took office.

The privatization of agriculture, pursued by the governments of the first Iliescu administration, was a popular demand of the opposition National Peasant Party, which completed it once in power, but it failed to achieve the desired improvement in productivity. Agricultural employment rose by varying indices to 34% of the labour force (masking industrial unemployment) thanks to privatization but contributed only 13% of the gross domestic product in 2000. Many new landowners were unprepared for independent farming, and landholdings were often too small. Crops fluctuated wildly due to serious droughts in 2000, 2002 and 2003. Corn (maize) accounts for 40% of crop output in metric tons, and potatoes and wheat are each about 20%. The leader in meat production is pork, but its percentage of tonnage declined to below half of meat production in 2002 while poultry rose to 30%. Despite its large endowment of fertile black earth soil, Romania is a net importer of agricultural goods, and this trade imbalance has increased in recent years.

Mining of coal, salt, iron and other metals in Transylvania and the exploitation of petroleum in Walachia have historically been sources of wealth. Oil was exploited heavily in support of Nazi Germany during World War II, then subjected to a joint Soviet-Romanian company for a few years afterwards. Petrochemical industries were a centrepiece of Ceausescu's development strategy, but production peaked in 1976 and has declined since then as Romania became a net importer. Production rose slightly after 1990, buttressed by increased exploitation offshore in the Black Sea. Romania remains the largest producer in Eastern Europe and has substantial proven reserves. The largest producer is the state-run SNP Petrom SA. The company has an annual turnover of $2 billion and is the largest taxpayer in Romania. Many domestic and foreign interests are involved in reports of corruption at the company. Discussions about the company's privatization had reached a critical point as this article was completed in 2003. An Austro-Romanian company was privatized in 1998 under the name Rompetrol-OMV group and has a growing number of distribution points and two refineries. The Russian company Lukoil is increasingly active in Romania, having acquired a refinery in Ploieşti and many distribution points of its own. In response to price increases and reforms, there has been some increase in investment in this sector, the reopening of shut wells and exploration of new sectors in the Black Sea. Most refineries built during 1957-1989 are now considered obsolete, however. Natural gas reserves are also substantial, but production peaked in the 1980s and has declined by two-thirds since then.

Coal mining, concentrated in the Jiu Valley on the border between Transylvania and Walachia, has provided another major energy source but is plagued by hazardous work conditions that prompt labour unrest that is compensated by wage increases that then endanger the financial viability of enterprises. In 1977 and then again in the miners' marches on Bucharest in 1990–1999, these structural problems produced major social unrest that endangered the political establishment, although miners were less than 2% of the civilian labour force in 1999. The government did succeed in closing 209 mines and quarries in 1997–1999, assisted in part by loans from the World Bank. Romanian coal is mostly not of export quality.

More than half of Romania's electrical production (down from over 80% in the 1980s) is served by petroleum, gas and coal, both domestic and imported. There are thermal power plants in many parts of the country, but many are not operational due to damage caused by the declining quality of lignite fuel. The development of hydroelectric power began in the 1960s, with major stations at the Iron Gates on the Danube, Arges, and elsewhere in the Carpathians supplying 35% of electrical production in 1998. The construction of Romania's first and to date only nuclear power plant began at Cernavoda on the Danube with Canadian partnership in 1979. Due to repeated delays, the plant was not finally inaugurated until 1996, but by 1998 it accounted for an estimated 10% of Romania's energy production. A nuclear plant begun in Piatra Neamt in 1986 has never been completed. Overall energy production and consumption in Romania has stagnated along with the economy. The country is a net importer of primary energy but has become a net exporter of electrical energy in recent years.

Industry (manufacturing, mining, construction, and power) accounted for 36% of gross domestic product in 1998. Bucharest was the leader of the ten most industrialized counties, but half of them were in the lands formerly belonging to Hungary. The largest portion of the industry, accounting for 20% of the civilian labour force in 1999, was manufacturing in the metallurgical, mechanical engineering, chemical and timber-processing industries. Industrial production declined by an annual rate of 2% in the 1990s, hampered by energy shortages as well as mismanagement and labour unrest. Importation of machinery for engineering industries is a particular source of the current trade imbalance. Most of the progress toward privatization in the industrial section has come after 2000.

Among the better-known industrial firms are Dacia, which has produced cars in Pitesti (Arges County) with a license from Renault; Oltcit, which has produced cars in Craiova in a joint venture with Citroen since 1977 (the company was renamed Oltena in 1989); and the truck company in Brasov known since 1990 as Roman S.A. It had its origin as a manufacturer of railway rolling stock beginning in 1921, branched out to armaments, machine tools and mining equipment, and produced its first trucks in 1954. Beginning in 1971, it produced trucks with a diesel engine licensed by the Man Company of Germany; then it became a joint-stock company under its new name in 1990. Railroad cars and diesel locomotives have been a major industrial product and export item for decades, with plants in Arad, Bucharest, Caracal, and Craiova. They were heavily exported to the Soviet Union before the end of Ceausescu's ruling but have found fewer buyers since then. Romanian chemical (especially petrochemical) industries were heavily favoured but heavy polluters during 1947–1989 and have scaled back due to unprofitability and environmental concerns.

There has been more privatization in the services sector, which accounted for slightly over half of gross domestic product in 2000 and 31% of the civilian workforce in 1999. Romanian tourism has failed to flourish despite the splendour of the natural environment and controversial attempts to exploit the interest of visitors in places associated with Dracula, Vlad the Impaler. One-fifth of foreign visitors during the 1990s were from neighbouring Moldova. Economic activity in the service sector declined during the 1990s.

Transportation and communications are important factors in economic reform. The Romanian constitution stipulates that the transport infrastructure is the property of the state. This is not an unusual situation in Europe, but it does place limits on the flexibility of reforms and the infusion of market forces. A more unique constraint is the Carpathians, whose passes impose substantial detours on long-distance rail and road travellers. The Romanian Railways (Romanian: Căile Ferate Române, CFR) control the fourth-largest railway network in Europe. The company was reorganized in 1998, with the freight services now open to private companies and denied subsidies but passenger services still subsidized. Ten private operators had gained a 20% market share of rail traffic by 2003. Several major routes with international connections are electrified, but most of the network is not. Even the major interurban highways are below international standards. The determination of the rail-bed through Transylvania to Romania in the 19th century had major implications for the development of cities, and the same may be the case with decisions made in 2003–2004 concerning highway construction. Despite the plans of the European Union for a southern route between Arad and Timisoara that would circumvent Transylvania, the Romanian government reached an agreement with the party of the Hungarian minority for a highway to be built by the Bechtel Corporation through northern Transylvania. The intention to thereby better connect Transylvania with Bucharest and also with Hungary signified a new level of cooperation between the Romanian and Hungarian governments.

The completion of the Danube–Black Sea Canal in 1984, followed by the fall of the Iron Curtain[1], buttressed hopes for increased revenue for Romanian ports. Trade sanctions against Yugoslavia, then the closure of transport by American bombing, frustrated these hopes. The subsequent reopening of the Danube has yet to secure dramatic benefits for Romania. Most oil tankers are too large for the main channel of the Danube, let alone for the Danube-Black Sea Canal. The idea of a pipeline through Romania for crude oil shipped from the former Soviet Union to European markets had the double attraction of providing transit fees and even an opportunity for refining within Romania itself. The Romanian plan envisioned a pipeline from the port of Constanta, which has a refinery and can receive four tankers at the same time, to Trieste on the Adriatic, where it would link to existing pipelines connecting Austria, Germany and the Czech Republic. Romanian officials expressed optimism about the plan after talks with counterparts in Kazakhstan, Croatia and other countries, but many diplomatic and financial details still required resolution.

Press and communications have changed dramatically since 1989. The telecommunication infrastructure, as in other countries of the region, is in need of substantial modernization. Not atypically, the total number and per capita telephone lines have risen rather slowly, whereas the number of personal mobile phone subscribers has skyrocketed, but the market is still far from saturated. Personal and Institutional Internet use lags far behind Central European countries.

The freedom of the Romanian press has progressed unevenly. In dramatic contrast to the monotonous political press and more interesting but heavily censored cultural press of the Ceausescu period, private newspapers soon proliferated, some affiliated with political parties and others not. Censorship was a thing of the past, but the government attempted to limit access to supplies of newsprint for the opposition press. Soon this problem abated, and newspaper

---

1 On 19 August 1989, more than 600 East Germans, attending the "Pan-European Picnic" on the Hungarian border, broke through the Iron Curtain and fled into Austria. Hungarian border guards had threatened to shoot anyone crossing the border, but when the time came, they did not intervene and allowed the people to cross the border.

journalism critical of the government was important in public opinion before the elections of 1996. Today the daily newspapers with the largest circulation, an estimated 200,000, are *Adevarul* (*Truth*) and *Evenimentul zilei* (*Event of the Day*). Adevarul, formerly the organ of the NSF and its successors, is a sober independent paper while Evenimentul is a tabloid known for investigative journalism of official abuses. Despite the apparent freedom of print journalism, there are serious allegations of violence against journalists who reported corrupt activities of officials. In August 2003, a Romanian reporter won second place in Columbia University's Kurt Schork Awards[1] for investigative journalism for his reports on government corruption.

Broadcast journalism has freed itself with greater difficulty, as licenses and technical facilities were more subject to government control. A National Audiovisual Council, established in 1992, is the sole issuer of licenses and reportedly uses its authority in conjunction with government revenue offices to create difficulty for opposition broadcasters. Private radio stations appeared first, then later in the decade private television stations as well. The emancipation of book publishing has had mixed benefits. Publishing suffered from censorship but benefited from subsidies that supported literary authors and accepted scholarship. The end of subsidies and the establishment of many new private publishing houses, most notably *Humanitas*, has opened Romania to Western intellectual currents but also made the publication of many specialized scholarly

---

1 Kurt Schork (24 January 1947–24 May 2000) was an American reporter and war correspondent. He was killed in an ambush while on an assignment for Reuters in Sierra Leone together with cameraman Miguel Gil Moreno de Mora of Spain, who worked for Associated Press Television. The goal of the Kurt Schork Memorial Fund and Awards recognizes and assist freelance and local journalists who make a critical contribution to international understanding but whose work is often overlooked. The awards include two cash prizes of $5,000 each to provide some financial support to help the winners continue reporting a regional trade organization and free trade area consisting of four European states: Iceland, Liechtenstein, Norway and Switzerland. The organization operates in parallel with the European Union, and all four member states participate in the European Single Market and are part of the Schengen Area. They are not, however, party to the European Union Customs Union [Source: Wikipedia].

works more difficult.

Trade shifted toward the European Union after 1990. Romania formally associated with the EU and the European Free Trade Association (EFTA) in 1993, then the Central European Free Trade Association in 1997. Germany and Italy vied for the status of leading commercial partner for most of the 1990s, with the latter taking the lead in later years. France supplanted Russia as the third leading source of imports and was consistently the third leading export country. Among the more interesting trends in foreign trade were Hungary's rise to fifth leading country for imports and Turkey to fourth for exports. Romania is pursuing improved diplomatic and commercial relations with these aspirants to EU membership as a complement to its own accession efforts. In contrast to the last years of Ceausescu ruling, however, Romania had a serious foreign trade deficit. The country imported machinery and mineral fuels and exported clothing, transport equipment and chemical products. Substantial remittances from Romanian nationals working abroad redressed the deficit somewhat.

Credits from the IMF and World Bank, along with the creation of joint trading companies with Western companies in the 1970s, fueled Ceausescu's industrial ambitions but generated foreign debt and austerity later on. After the retirement of the foreign debt in 1989, Romania passed a law prohibiting the incurrence of foreign debt. This law was overturned after the end of Ceasescu's ruling. Romania now also saw foreign direct investment, but its success paled by comparison with former bloc members to the west. Western fast food outlets made their appearance, but the slowness of privatization for larger firms and labour unrest discouraged major investments. Support packages of the IMF, intended to support the ambitious privatization program of the democratic coalition after 1996, were suspended due to failure to reach the agreed targets. In consultation with the World Bank, in 2001 the prime minister announced a plan to privatize 63 state-owned enterprises. The second Iliescu administration has proven much more aggressive than the first one in pursuing privatization.

Chapter 7 Economy and Trade

The Romanian economy operated before 1990 without a convertible currency or true market. Domestically, prices were set by administrative fiat and served to subsidize favoured goods or accumulate capital for other ends. Foreign trade relied for the most part on bilateral agreements between states. A number of private banks arose after 1990, some of them engaging in pyramid schemes. The most infamous of these was the Caritas Bank. During the time of heavy inflation and unemployment in 1992–1994, an estimated 7 million Romanians and foreigners invested as much as $5 billion in Caritas and were guaranteed an eight-to-one return as long as they brought new investors into the scheme. As in post-communist Albania and Russia, the scheme fed on people's ignorance of capitalist finance and eagerness to improve their difficult situation.

The Romanian currency (singular leu, plural lei) has been freely traded since 1990, but due to poor budget balances, it has fallen steadily against the U.S. dollar until recently. The National Bank of Romania controls the currency. Its governor is a member of the cabinet and served simultaneously as prime minister in 1999–2000. An agreement with the World Bank in 1997 slated six other state-owned banks for privatization. In 2003, the European Bank for Reconstruction and Development (EBRD)[1] and the International Finance Corp (IFC)[2] acquired a 25% interest in the largest remaining one, the Romanian Commercial Bank, which controls one-third of the country's banking sector.

---

1 An international financial institution founded in 1991. As a multilateral developmental investment bank, the EBRD uses investment as a tool to build market economies. Initially focused on the countries of the former Eastern Bloc, it expanded to support development in more than 30 countries from central Europe to central Asia. Besides Europe, member countries of the EBRD are from all over the world. Headquartered in London, the EBRD is owned by 65 countries and two EU institutions. Despite its public sector shareholders, it invests mainly in private enterprises, together with commercial partners [Source: Wikipedia].

2 The International Finance Corporation (IFC) is an international financial institution that offers investment, advisory and asset-management services to encourage private-sector development in developing countries. The IFC is a member of the World Bank Group and is headquartered in Washington, D.C [Source: Wikipedia].

Has the economic well-being of Romanians improved since the end of Ceausescu's ruling? The severe rationing that preceded it is a thing of the past. Wages in many sectors remain low, and powerful trade unions in de facto collusion with state firms' officials looking out for their interests long-delayed privatization.

Women's health has improved. Ceausescu's Romania had enacted draconian sanctions against abortion and contraception including regular, mandatory gynaecological examinations in order to encourage population growth. The impact on the birthrate was only moderate and temporary; apparently Romanian doctors violated the law. International and Romanian women's groups were relieved to see the legalization of birth control after the end of Ceausescu's ruling. One consequence of pronatalist policies was that many unwanted children were deposited in orphanages. Their number (650 orphanages with 98,872 children in 1998) and the poor conditions in these institutions attracted foreign investigative journalists, whose television documentaries gained unwelcome notoriety for Romania. Some unscrupulous adoption agencies took advantage of compassionate foreigners eager to adopt unwanted Romanian children despite the cost and in ignorance of illnesses such as AIDS and hepatitis. In response, a strict prohibition on foreign adoptions was enacted, and measures were taken to improve conditions. Romania's high infant mortality rate was reduced by 16% from 1996 to 2000.

There has been improvement in the state of the environment. Legislation or government initiative shut down or rehabilitated some of the most serious industrial polluters, notably the chemical and metallurgical plants in Copşa Mica, Zlatna and Hunedoara in Transylvania. Concerns remain about the state of the fragile Danube Delta, where overharvesting of reeds for cellulose endangered wildlife habitats, and about the quality of water along the Black Sea coast. Concern for tourism as well as standards imposed by the European Union have served to encourage remedial measures. As elsewhere in Eastern Europe, emissions into the air per unit of energy produced remain above levels in the European Union. The EBRD is supporting efforts to increase energy efficiency and improve municipal water supplies. Emissions of greenhouse gases have declined significantly, and at the end of 2003, Romania joined other countries of the region in making commitments under the Kyoto Accords to further reduce them.

Romania and especially neighbouring Hungary, Yugoslavia and Ukraine experienced an environmental disaster in January-February 2000. On January 30, Aurul, a Romanian-Australian joint venture extracting non-ferrous metals from mining scrap, permitted cyanide and metal laced water to leach from a holding dam to a tributary of the Somes and Tisa (Hungarian: Tisza) Rivers near Baia Mare. From there the plume of water, estimated at close to 100,000 cubic meters, crossed the border into Hungary on February 1. More than 100,000 kilograms of fish and many birds and other animals were killed in the more heavily populated Hungarian portion of the affected area, and the water supply of the Hungarian city of Szolnok was endangered. Melted snow and heavy rains led to three more spills in the same region later during the same winter and spring. Romanian and Hungarian environmental groups publicized events on their websites and organized demonstrations. This raised the awareness of the international and Romanian press to later cases.

Difficulties with the water supply have caused outbreaks of hepatitis and malaria. There is comprehensive health insurance provided by the state, but serious corruption mars health care delivery. The 2002 census revealed a decline in the country's population of 4.2% or one million to 21,680,974 since the census of 1992 due to an excess of deaths over births and to emigration. The emigration of the Hungarian and especially German minority peaked in the years around 1989. Hungarian emigration is ongoing, and according to the census, the decline in the Hungarian population exceeded the growth in the Roma population.

The per capita gross national income of Romania in 2003 was half that of Hungary but triple that of Moldova. The World Bank ranks Romania a lower-middle-income country based on this figure, above low-income Moldova but

罗马尼亚概况 | *Survey of Romania* |

below upper-middle Hungary. The UN Technology Achievement Index ranks Hungary 22nd, Romania 35th, and does not rank Moldova. The same UN agency's Human Development Index, based on a correlation of life expectancy, literacy, and educational enrollment, ranked Romania 72nd out of 175 countries as a Medium Human Development country in 2001, below Hungary at 38th (high human development) but above Moldova (108th) in the same category. Romania's international ranking remained below that of 1985 but had improved slightly over 1990.

Recent Economic Development[1]

Because of its strong trade and financial linkages with the EU countries, Romania's economy was hit hard by the global economic crisis with falling exports, capital inflows and remittances. As a result, following several years of rapid growth, the economy started to slow in late 2008 and turned to a large contraction in 2009. Facing the difficult economic situation, the Romanian government had limited policy options to support the economy with its large fiscal deficit and tight funding conditions. Against this backdrop, in May 2009 the IMF approved a Stand-By Arrangement (SBA)[2] for Romania intended to cushion the effects of the sharp drop in capital inflows while addressing the country's external and fiscal imbalances and strengthening its financial sector. The government's policy performance under the SBA has remained broadly on track, with its fiscal policy geared toward restoring sound public finances over the medium term. Combine that with some improvement in the global and regional economic situation, Romania's economic growth was expected to

---

1 https://www.nordeatrade.com/fi/explore-new-market/romania/trade-profile

2 An economic program of the International Monetary Fund (IMF) involving financial aid to a member state in need of financial assistance, normally arising from a financial crisis. In return for aid, the economic program stipulates needed reforms in the recipient country aimed at bringing it back on a path of financial stability and economic sustainability. The SBA is a sub-set of IMF and World Bank programs aimed at Structural adjustment [Source: Wikipedia].

recover at a moderate rate in 2010. However, drastic austerity measures related to its arrangement with the IMF resulted in a further contraction in 2010. But the economy returned to positive growth in 2011 largely due to strong export performance. Under pressure from the IMF to substantially cut its deficit over the next two years, the Romanian government was in 2011 looking to privatizations to meet its goal and make needed investments in infrastructure.

In March 2011, Romania and the IMF/EC[1]/World Bank[2] signed a 24-month precautionary Standby Agreement, worth $4.9 billion, to promote compliance with fiscal targets, progress on structural reforms and financial sector stability. The package provides an important emergency buffer for the European Union's second-poorest economy. In March 2012, IMF mission chief Jeffrey Franks said the Romanian government had limited room to ease its austerity program by raising public sector wages or through minor tax cuts while maintaining its fiscal deficit target.

After two years of decline, economic growth had resumed by March 2012 and inflation had fallen to historical lows. However, the economic outlook for the year was being weighed down by the declining growth prospects in the euro area. Continued commitment to the economic reform agenda would be crucial to help withstand current uncertainties and increase potential growth.

Romania's economy was almost flat in 2012 but inflation remained stub-

---

1 The European Communities (EC), sometimes referred to as the European Community, were three international organizations that were governed by the same set of institutions. These were the European Coal and Steel Community(ECSC), the European Atomic Energy Community (EAEC or Euratom), and the European Economic Community (EEC); the latter of which was renamed the European Community (EC) in 1993 by the Maastricht Treaty, which formed the European Union [Source: Wikipedia].

2 An international financial institution that provides loans to countries of the world for capital programs. It comprises two institutions: the International Bank for Reconstruction and Development(IBRD), and the International Development Association (IDA). The World Bank is a component of the World Bank Group. The World Bank's stated official goal is the reduction of poverty. However, according to its Articles of Agreement, all its decisions must be guided by a commitment to the promotion of foreign investment and international trade and to the facilitation of capital investment [Source: Wikipedia].

bornly high by March 2013, mainly because of higher food prices following the bad harvest. It was expected to come down in the second half of 2013 to slightly above 3.5% by year-end. Still, Romania's central bank was being held back from cutting rates. In May 2013, the bank kept a record low 5.25% main interest rate on hold for a 9th consecutive meeting. However, it did warn of plans to decrease borrowing costs as inflation eased.

In March 2013, the IMF granted Romania a three-month extension of its Stand by Arrangement in an effort to promote the country's fiscal discipline, encourage progress on structural reforms and strengthen financial sector stability. Romania was trying to complete the $6.6 billion euro IMF agreement in June and although it had not yet drawn on the funds, the deal gave the leu currency a boost and helped keep government borrowing costs in check. Looking ahead, growth was expected to pick up for the year, mainly driven by domestic demand.

In September 2013, the Romanian authorities agreed to a $5.4 billion follow-on Standby Agreement with the IMF/EU on the condition it would continue with reforms, although Bucharest declared it would not draw funds the agreement. Overall, economic growth accelerated for the year, boosted by strong, industrial exports and robust agricultural harvest. In the 4th quarter alone, the economy expanded by 5.4% compared to the 2012 4th quarter. That marked the fastest economic growth since 2008. Inflation declined to a historical low annual rate of 1.6% in December 2013 and the current account deficit was substantially reduced. Still, progress on structural reforms was shaky. Growth in the first quarter of 2014 was estimated by the government to be about 3.2%.

In May 2014, Romanian government declared it planned to join the Eurozone at the beginning of 2019. Also in May 2014, Romania's central bank left its key interest rate at a record low of 3.5% after a rate-cutting cycle that lowered borrowing costs by 175 basis points. At the same time, it predicted lower inflation of 3.3% for 2014 and 2015 assuming volatile capital flows in emerging markets did not create risks for its outlook. The economy appeared to be bouncing back.

Chapter 7　Economy and Trade

Romania's economy grew by 5.8% in the first half of 2017, the fastest in the EU. Growth was led by private consumption (up 7.4% year-on-year [y-o-y]), fueled by a reduction in the standard value-added tax (VAT) rate from 24 to 20% in January 2016 and by minimum and public sector wage and pension increases. Investment growth was timid (up 1.1%), reflecting the poor performance of public investment mainly due to the drop in EU investment funding.

Inflation is on an upward trend, driven by the pickup in private consumption, but it remains within the boundaries of the Central Bank. Annual headline inflation moved into positive territory in February 2017 and reached 1.2% in August, as the base effect of the VAT cut dissipated. The National Bank of Romania (NBR) Board maintained the policy rate at 1.75% in August, amid early signs of corporate credit growth recovery (up 4.3% as of July 2017) and concerns over the outlook of the fiscal and income policy stance. Household credit grew by 6.6% y-o-y in July 2017, supported by the fiscal stimulus, labor market improvements, and low-interest rates.

The labour market strengthened further on the back of strong economic growth and fiscal relaxation. Real wages increased by 13.5% y-o-y as of July 2017, and unemployment increased marginally by 0.2% from an eight-year low value of 5% registered in June 2017. Nonetheless, the low employment rate of 61.2% in the first quarter of 2017 reflects persistent structural rigidities in the labour market.

Fiscal policy has remained pro-cyclical in 2017. The budget execution posted a deficit of 0.63% of GDP in July 2017, an increase of 0.4% compared to the same period last year. The widening of the deficit reflects an 11.4% increase in public expenditure and a lower-than-expected revenue collection (up 9%), particularly from VAT (down 4.6%). The increase in current spending was driven by hikes in employee compensation (up 20.3%) and social assistance spending (up 10.7%), while public investment spending contracted by 34.4%.

Agriculture[1]

Romania lies in the Southern-Eastern part of Europe, upon the crossroads of the main communication axes North-South and East-West. The total area of the country is 238,391 km^2 of which 93.6% rural areas and 48% of Romanian population represents rural population.

The rural area has the following features: A. Consists of 12,000 villages that house around 46.6% of entire Romania's population. B. 67% of the rural population is involved in agriculture, 17% work in the food industry and the other 16% practice non-agricultural activities. C. 30% of rural inhabitants work on subsistence and semi-subsistence exploitations of 1.17 ha and respectively of 3.3 ha, representing about 97% out of the total of 4.5 million agricultural exploitations. One of the major problems of the rural areas is that its population grows older.

In Romania, the agricultural sector represents a basic branch of the national economy, having significant economic and social importance and implications. The share of agriculture, forestry, fishery and hunting in Gross Domestic Product was about 9% in the year 2005. Romania has a wide range of soil types with high theoretical potential, about 60% of arable land having a good and medium fertility. The Romanian total agricultural area stands for 61.7% of the country's territory, and the arable land represents 63.9% of the total agricultural land. The surface of arable land per inhabitant is about 0.42 ha. Most of the agricultural land belongs to the private sector.

The forest covers about 6.38 million ha, representing 26.7% of the Romanian territory. The forest distribution is not uniform geographically, 58.5% of it is concentrated in the mountain region, and 34.8% is located in the hilly areas and 6.7% in the plain. Broadleaved are dominant in Romanian forests (69.3%) and the rest are coniferous. At the end of 2004, the ownership structure of forests presented itself as follows: A. Public ownership of state: 5.03 million ha

---

1 www.oecd.org/agriculture/agricultural-policies/37659465.pdf

Chapter 7 Economy and Trade

(78.9%), managed by the National Administration of Forests — Romsilva or local councils. B. Private forests (communities, churches, legal persons, individuals): 1.35 million ha (21.1%). Further to the legislation entered into force this year, the restitution of forests to former owners is continuing.

Farm Structure

The main challenge that Romania is facing nowadays is the existence of high number of subsistence and semi-subsistence peasant households featured by a small area size of 1.72 ha and respectively of 3.3 ha, with plots excessively scattered, with low financial resources and a low degree of agricultural machinery endowment. The majority of small farms have only marginal contacts with markets; most of these contacts are being limited to local markets, respectively direct sales from farm. The duality of farm structure is an important issue for the Ministry of Agriculture and Rural Development (MAFDR)'s policy. The policy is to convert the family small farms into commercial farms by land concentration and association means, thus becoming more efficient and increasing the living standards of the rural society. The producer groups are promoted by the ministry's policy, through its rural development objectives. Thus, MAFDR established one of its priorities to stimulate the family farms to convert in commercial farms in order to become more efficient and to increase the living standards for the rural society.

Labour Force

The population working in agriculture from the total active population has represented in the last two years around 34% of the total labour force (34.7% in 2003 and 35.7% in 2004). The share is due to the high number of agricultural exploitations—4.4 million representing 54% of total arable land, the rest of 44% arable land belonging to the commercial farms which represent approximately 23,000 agricultural holdings with specialized employees in the field (engineers and technicians in crop sciences and animal breeding). The goal of the ministry is to promote the development of commercial farms, producer groups and associations and cooperatives.

These aspects are going to be solved by the new approach of the Romanian Ministry of Agriculture, by leading the capitalization of the rural area by the means of investments incentives for the rural area and subsidies for agriculture in an efficient way. The value added will increase in rural area, especially by the promotion of balance of raw material production from vegetal and animal sectors, agro-food industry and biofuels industry, and by the means of economic diversification in the rural area.

Agricultural Production

The share in agriculture production is mainly represented by the animal and vegetal sectors, the agricultural services will be supported by increasing the number of the Small and Medium Size Enterprises in this sector. During the last two years, MAFRD has been promoting the organic farming program in order to increase the investments in agriculture and to improve the endowments in the field.

The Crop Production

The cereal sector has a high share, about 62%, because of the good soil quality for these plants and also of the national demand for these agricultural products. Also in Romania, the areas and the production of technical plants, sugar beat and oil crops are in line with the national tradition of crop cultivation. Because the costs are moderate regarding crop technology, the maize represents an easy plant to cultivate and with a law degree of mechanization on small parcels. In the commercial farms, the scale economy ensures the development of agricultural activities. This is the reason why Romanian Government through the Ministry of Agriculture is supporting a semi-subsistence farm to become a commercial farm, by completion the *Land Property Reform* and by encouraging the households to become a commercial farm — establishing the legal framework for granting the annuity allowance. The ministry intends to support the producer groups and the farmers association through the National Program for Rural Development 2007-2013. The Ministry intends to grant a direct support yearly in order to ensure the competitiveness of the domestic producers at the national and international level having in view the globalization process. In the same political line, the Ministry of Agriculture drew up the legislation for the improvement of the agricultural internal market and the promotion of the agricultural products export. The Ministry of Agriculture is promoting the development of energy and biomass crops, rape, maize in the light of future and current environmental strategic development. The industry of biofuels is welcomed in Romania, the foreign and national investments being encouraged. In the Rural Development Program, there are funds allocated for investments projects.

An important factor of agricultural development is the energy crops, such as rape seeds, oil plants, corn for the production of biofuels, biodiesel and for bio-ethanol, Romania promotes national and foreign investments in biofuels and alternative energy industry. The European strategy for alternative energies and Kyoto protocol[1] are in line with this incentive.

Livestock and Livestock Products

In the livestock sector, Romania elaborates a strategy for the improvement of animal breeding in order to increase the performance of the milk and meat sector. The absorption of the vegetal raw material and the breeding improvement will result in an increase of animal production for the agro-food industry. The synergy between those represents a real incentive for rural society development.

In the same line, the Romanian Government aims the financial support for

---

1 An international treaty which extends the 1992 United Nations Framework Convention on Climate Change (UNFCCC) that commits State Parties to reduce greenhouse gas emissions, based on the scientific consensus that (a) global warming is occurring and (b) it is extremely likely that human-made CO^2 emissions have predominantly caused it. The Kyoto Protocol was adopted in Kyoto, Japan, on 11 December 1997 and entered into force on 16 February, 2005. There are currently 192 parties (Canada withdrew effective December 2012) to the Protocol. [Source: Wikipedia].

balancing the animal and vegetal sector in order to ensure the absorption of the vegetal raw materials by the animal and food industry.

Food Industry

The food industry represents an important share in the whole Romanian industry and ensures the absorption of agricultural raw material and supplies the internal consumption with agro foods (bread and milling industry, vegetal alimentary oils milk and meat processing). The improvement of food industry in Romania is achieved by special investments programs, financed by the national budget and the EU budget such as National program for improvement of food industry performance through quality (for implementation of HCCP standards, quality management ISO 9001 and environment management ISO 14001), National Farmer Program and Special Accession Program for Agriculture and Rural Development (SAPARD) program — having, as the main aim, the support of the entrepreneurs investments and the modernization plans for small and medium size food processing plants, localized in the rural areas.

Industrial Development[1]

As a member of the European Union (Romania's most important trading partner), Romania has the 11th largest economy in the European Union by total nominal GDP and the 8th largest based on purchasing power parity[2] and is one of the fastest-growing markets in recent history with consistent annual GDP

---

1 https://ace-notebook.com/romanias-industrial-development-free-related-pdf.html

2 An economic theory that states that the exchange rate between two currencies is equal to the ratio of the currencies' respective purchasing power. Theories that invoke purchasing power parity assume that in some circumstances (for example, as a long-run tendency) it would cost exactly the same number of, for example, US dollars to buy euros and then to use the proceeds to buy a market basket of goods as it would cost to use those dollars directly in purchasing the market basket of goods. A fall in either currency's purchasing power would lead to a proportional decrease in that currency's valuation on the foreign exchange market. [Source: Wikipedia].

Chapter 7　Economy and Trade

growth rates above 6% (+8.4% for 2008).

Industrial development in Romania received about half of all investment during the 1951–1980 period. As officially measured, the average annual growth rate in gross industrial production between 1950 and 1980 was 12.3%, one of the highest in Eastern Europe. In 1993, however, industrial production was at only 47% of the 1989 level. The next year, industrial production increased by 3.3%. The economy lags significantly behind the majority of EU countries. In 2005, GDP per capita was 34.8% of the EU-25 average and around 55% of the new EU Member States average.

Romania's macroeconomic performance before crisis was favorable (more of 6% annual GDP average growth over the last six years) in spite of the worsening world economic outlook. GDP growth has been driven by high fixed investments and private consumption, fuelled by strong growth in credit to the private sector. The EU conferred functioning market economy status on Romania in October 2004 due to the significant progress made in the implementation of economic reforms.

The Romanian Government's fiscal policy was based on reorienting the taxation system to encourage growth, economic and social development and to reduce inflation. The economy has been able to rapidly capitalize on the opportunities. FDI has been attracted to the country by comparatively low wages, rising productivity as well as by the market size.

However, there remain serious deficiencies to overcome in order to boost Romania's economy.

Infrastructure

Romanian Inadequate road, rail, water and air transport facilities, and a lack of inter-connectivity, all of these inhibit growth. Its current economic competitiveness (including low productivity, outdated and obsolete production equipment and technologies, highly energy-intensive industry, underdeveloped entrepreneurship, a difficult business environment and inadequate business support infrastructure, poor access to finance and insufficient R&D[1] and ICT[2] investment) hamper business growth.

Human Capital

Limited adequacy of education and CVT[3] to meet the needs of a modern knowledge-based economy, low value placed on education and inequality of opportunity lead to social exclusion amongst vulnerable groups in Romania.

Administrative Capacity

Romanian public services are weak and provide low customer satisfaction. Lack of sufficient administrative capacity is reflected by poor management structures, insufficient skills of civil servants, inadequate inter-institutional cooperation, which ultimately lead to poor quality of the services delivered to the society, and thus jeopardize social and economic development.

Territorial Dimension

Following the industrial restructuring, regional disparities rapidly appeared

---

1 Research and Development (R&D), also known in Europe as Research and Technological Development (RTD), refers to innovative activities undertaken by corporations or governments in developing new services or products, or improving existing services or products. Research and development constitutes the first stage of development of a potential new service or product [Source: Wikipedia].

2 an another/extensional term for Information Technology (IT) which stresses the role of unified communications and the integration of telecommunications (telephone lines and wireless signals), computers as well as necessary enterprise software, middleware, storage, and audio-visual systems, which enable users to access, store, transmit and manipulate information [Source: Wikipedia].

3 A semiconductor intellectual property core which implements some steps of some video decompression algorithms. The scope is to calculate these on the SIP core rather than on the CPU. Intel Clear Video is paired with integrated graphics processors branded as Intel GMA [Source: Wikipedia].

Chapter 7 Economy and Trade

and they have continued to grow. Disparities between urban and rural are significant and increasing; this is particularly noticeable between Bucharest Ilfov[1] Region and the rest of the country. Both urban and rural areas are confronted with problems related to infrastructure (caused by underinvestment), local economic development and social environment.

After 1990, the developing of the industrial sector in the very confusing transition without practical and theoretical experience had to cross from communist economy to one of few models of capitalism. In 1995, industrial production increased by 9.4% in absolute volume and was 13% higher than the 1992 output. In 1996, industrial production increased by 9.9% with the largest increases coming in the processing industry (+12.5%) and machine and electronics (+27.3%). After the Russian collapse of 1997[2], however, the industrial growth rate for 1998 was -17%.

Industrial production picked up after Romania began to recover from its recession in 2000, and the industrial growth rate was 6.5% in 2001. Although industry continues to be a large sector of the economy (30% of GDP in 2000), it is outmoded and in need of serious modernization and restructuring. Key industries in 2002 included textiles and footwear, light machinery and automobile assembly, construction materials, metallurgy, chemicals, food processing, and petroleum refining. Romania produced 68,761 automobiles in 2001, a 12% decrease from 2000. It produced 759 heavy trucks in 2000, a 13% decrease from 1999. The country had ten oil refineries in 2002, with a capacity of 504,000 barrels per day.

---

1 The county that surrounds Bucharest, the capital of Romania. It used to be largely rural, but, after 1989 many of the county's villages and communes developed into high-income commuter towns, which act like suburbs or satellites of Bucharest [ource: Wikipedia].

2 The Russian financial crisis (also called Ruble crisis or the Russian Flu) hit Russia on 17 August 1998. It resulted in the Russian government and the Russian Central Bank devaluing the ruble and defaulting on its debt. The crisis had severe impacts on the economies of many neighboring countries. Meanwhile, James Cook, the senior vice president of The U.S. Russia Investment Fund, suggested the crisis had the positive effect of teaching Russian banks to diversify their assets [Source: Wikipedia].

Romania has been successful in developing dynamic telecommunications, aerospace and weapons sectors. Industry and construction accounted for 32% of GDP in 2003, a comparatively large share even without taking into account related services. The sector employed 26.4% of the workforce. With the manufacture of 245,000 vehicles in 2008, Romania was Europe's 12th largest producer of automobiles.

In 2004, Romania enjoyed one of the largest world market shares in machine tools (5.3%). Romanian-based companies such as Dacia Automotive, Petrom, Rompetrol and Bitdefender are well known throughout Southeast Europe. However, small and medium-sized manufacturing firms still form standby bulk of the manufacturing sector. These firms employ two-thirds of the Romanian workforce. Romania's industrial output was expected to advance 9% in 2007, while agriculture output is projected to grow 12%. Final consumption was also expected to increase by 11% overall—individual consumption by 14.4% and collective consumption by 10.4%. Domestic demand was expected to go up 12.7%. The growth of the industrial sector was the principal stimulus to economic development. In 2007, manufacturing industries accounted for approximately 35% of the gross domestic product and 29% of the workforce. Benefiting from strong domestic encouragement and foreign aid, Bucharest's industrialists introduced modern technologies into outmoded or newly built facilities at a rapid pace, increased the production of commodities—especially those for sale in foreign markets—and ploughed the proceeds back into further industrial expansion. As a result, the industry recovered from the decline of the 1990s and was expected to grow by 7.1% in 2008.

Romania is also perceived as a dynamic market for machine tools, especially in the backdrop of growth in the domestic automobile and mechanical engineering sectors. Romanian machine tool exports abroad have been growing at more than double-digit figure since 2002-2007. The exports comprised mainly machining centres, grinding, honing, lapping machines, gear cutting machines, lathes and milling machines, presses and other metal forming machine tools.

Much of the Romanian manufacturing industry consists of branch plants of EU firms, though there are some important domestic manufacturers, such as Dacia, Daewoo, Roman Brasov, Igero Bus. This has raised several concerns for Romanians. Branch plants provide mainly blue collar jobs, with research and executive positions confined to the EU. About half a million cars are produced each year in Romania. Ford bought Daewoo Romania company for €57 millions to produce Ford automobiles to a car production estimated to be over 300,000 by 2010. Ford will invest €675 million (US$923 million) in the former Daewoo car factory. Ford also said it would buy supplies from the Romanian market worth €1 billion (US$1.39 billion).

The Dacia Logan was the top-selling new car in Central and Eastern Europe in the first half of 2007 with 52,750 units sold, ahead of Skoda Fabia (41,227 units), Skoda Octavia (33,483 units), Opel Astra (16,442 units) and Ford Focus (14,909 units), shows a market survey of JATO Dynamics, the leading supplier of automotive market intelligence.

The Romanian automotive industry ranks sixth in Central and Eastern Europe, behind that of the Czech Republic, Poland, Slovakia, Ukraine and Hungary with a total car production of 242,000 units in 2007. The production is expected to rise to 350,000 units in 2008 and 850,000 units in 2010 when the Ford plant will be at maximum capacity. Dacia is expected to increase its production to 400,000 units in 2009 and 500,000 units by 2010.

In Romania, a wide range of automobiles, minivans, sport utility vehicles (Dacia Duster), buses and trucks are produced. In 2007, Romania exported US$3.7 billion worth of vehicles and components. The vehicle export was 120,000 units in 2007. Romania is the 11th largest arms supplier in the world. It mainly builds warships, vehicles and equipment for the Romanian army and for external demand.

Logistics and Industrial Market[1]

Romania has the potential to position itself as a strategic regional trade and

---

1 http://www.flandersinvestmentandtrade.com/export/sites/trade/files/market_studies/2016-Romania-Transport%20Infrastructure,%20Transportation%20and%20Logistics.pdf

logistics hub for Central and Eastern Europe due to its geo-strategical location at the crossroads of the main trade routes between Western Europe and Asia, between South Europe (the Mediterranean) and Northern Europe. The Danube-Black Sea Canal facilitates river and sea navigation and offers access to both the Black Sea and the North Sea through the Rhine-Main-Danube waterway, connecting the Port of Constanta and the Port of Rotterdam. Romania's trade-related infrastructure consists of roads, railways, inland waterway transport, ports, airports and warehousing & trans-loading facilities. The logistics and industrial market in Romania started to grow particularly after Romania's accession to the European Union (January 2007), due to market penetration of foreign investors in various production segments (mainly automotive), attracted by lower costs, and also due to some retail expansion (especially in Bucharest). The logistics sector slowed down during and after the crisis years, however since 2015 it has come under spotlight. Measures taken by the Romanian government concerning fiscal relaxation and incentives, along with the wage rise for the population have triggered a rebound in investments and an increase of private consumption, which have led to production/exports growth and retail expansion. Booming investments in manufacturing and retail, coupled with the presence of numerous automotive companies, have resulted in an increased demand for logistics facilities.

The most attractive locations for the industrial and logistics centres in Romania have been the three highways: A1 (Bucharest-Nadlac/West Romania), A2 (Bucharest-Constanta/South-East Romania) and A3 (Bucharest-Bors/North-West Romania), due to the good connections with the rest of Europe, however other regions in the country are being targeted as well. Romania currently has 73 industrial parks, placed under both private and public ownership, which offer access to utilities and particular benefits packages, however, it stands far behind its potential and also behind some other countries in Central and Eastern Europe.

Under the current business and economic development in Romania (output/

exports growth, consumption's rise, which translate into a constant GDP growth as well), the logistics sector is very promising. Companies active in logistics/distribution and retail sectors are looking for options to expand their operations, which implies also the need of new logistics spaces. Developers of industrial and logistics parks are exempted from land, building and urban planning taxes as well as for land destination changing. In 2015, the highest level of new supply of industrial and logistics spaces is noticeable since 2008, namely 164,000 sqm new delivery, an increased transactional activity, the net take-up being higher by 44% comparing to the previous year, and a deep decrease of vacancy rate, reaching 5%. The most dynamic occupiers were companies active in the retail sector (37%), followed by distribution & logistics (30%) and production sector (26%). The upward trend has been followed also in 2016 with more than 300,000 sqm new delivery expected, robust transactional activity and an overall tendency of decrease of vacancy rate. At the end of 2016, Romania's modern industrial and logistics stock amounted 2.3 million sqm. Bucharest dominates the country's industrial and logistics sector with a stock higher than 1 million sqm (45%), and it is popular due to its strategic location—225 km from the Port of Constanta, 850 km from Budapest, and at the junction of two Pan-European Corridors. The existing supply of industrial and logistics spaces outside Bucharest amounts to 1.29 million sqm, the largest regional markets being Timisoara/West Romania, Ploiesti and Pitesti/South Romania, Cluj/North-West Romania and Brasov/Center Romania.

The logistics market in Romania is divided between logistics and transport companies which build/rent warehouses to provide producers and importers with logistics solution (third-party logistics providers), logistics and industrial developers which build on-demand/buys and afterwards rent logistics space, retailers which have their own warehouses, and also many producers which have not externalized their logistics activities.

Logistics services are becoming more and more complex as they have to adapt to technological and economic changes. Logistics is not only about transport and storage, but also about optimizing the whole supply chain: warehousing, loading, handling and transport. Moreover, intermodal/multimodal starts playing a significant role. Logistics players on the Romanian market already take into consideration the newest market trends (e.g. dynamic evolution of e-commerce, preference for new concepts like "green logistics" or "sustainability") and provide with the best solutions and IT integration, making investments in mechanical handling equipment, fleet modernization, use of alternative fuel, new technology into warehousing operations (e.g. voicepicking), continuous training of personnel, putting in place programs aimed at growing their own pool of specialists, etc. According to the Logistics Performance Index (LPI), a benchmarking tool published by the World Bank every two years that ranks countries on a scale of one to five according to their logistics "friendliness", Romania went down from 3.26 in 2014 to 2.99 in 2016. In a ranking topped by Germany (4.23), Romania trailed most of its EU neighbours, such as the Czech Republic (3.67), Poland (3.43) and Hungary (3.43). Although Romania has witnessed some progress in infrastructure and customs department, its drop in the ranking is due to some regress in international shipments, logistics competence, tracking & tracing and most of all in timeliness as fewer shipments reached their destination within the scheduled or expected delivery time. Thus, logistics remains a key challenge of the trade competitiveness agenda for Romania. Effective logistics and trade facilitation are of paramount importance in order to respond to deadlines and control costs with regard to both exports and imports to and from the EU. The government recognizes the need for efficient transport and trade facilitation logistics for realizing Romania's potential as a regional logistics hub, which will also enhance intrar-egional exports and focusses on addressing the weaknesses in the sector. Despite these deficiencies, transport and logistics players on the Romanian market are quite positive and confess that the sector is becoming more and more attractive as Romania offers opportunities that other, more established markets, do not. Romania's transport and logistics industry is currently enjoying a smooth ride, as it is estimated to have been increasing by at least 10% in the last three years, mainly due to a more stable economic environment, a skilled labour force and a great positioning within Eastern Europe, having Constanta harbour as an asset. Moreover, Romania has the potential to grow ten times in the following years and become an international hub.

Tourism[1]

In Romania, the contribution of this branch to economic development in the period of economic growth was relatively more modest than world values. The period 2000-2008 represents for Romania the stage in which economy recorded growths at relatively high rates of GDP, imports, exports and investments, even though they had, as primordial support, demand, imports and exports under the conditions of unprecedented growth in the foreign indebtedness degree of Romania on short, medium and long term. Based on evaluating the share in the development of national economy, the following characteristics of the tourism branch in Romania may be highlighted:

A. Tourism share in domestic market output was 3.1% in 2008 against 3.0% in 2000 and 2.2% and 2.1% respectively in the total output of goods and services, which signifies a relatively important field for the sustainable economic growth of Romania, particularly if considering that this share is almost equal to, or exceeds the share of traditional sub-branches or of new ones of the manufacturing industry in Romania; it should be noted that this share was maintained quasi-constant for the analyzed period, which supports the hypothesis of relative constancy in time of the technical coefficients of the input-output model;

---

1 Tourism and Economic Development in Romania: Input-Output Analysis Perspective: revecon.ro/articles/2010-2/2010-2-1.pdf

| 罗马尼亚概况 | Survey of Romania |

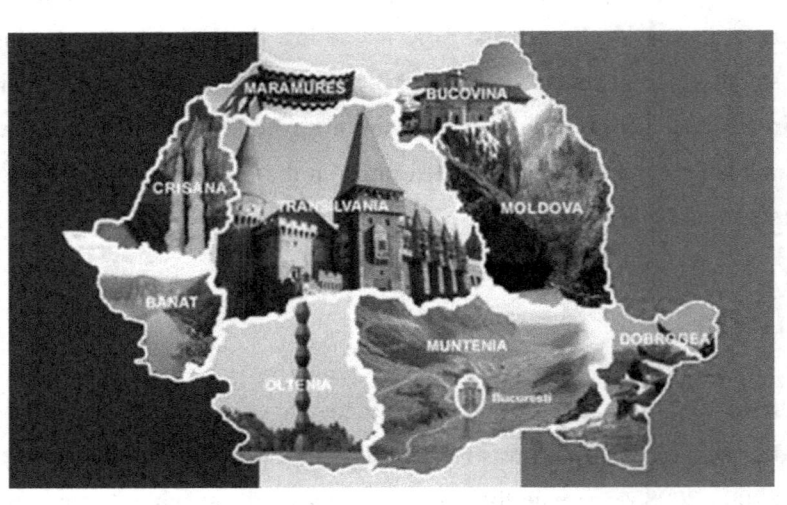

PICTURE: Romanian Tourism Map
SOURCE: http://www.business-review.eu/news/romanian-tourism-is-receiving-stronger-investments-105923

B. In total tourism output, the highest share is held by the "Restaurants" branch (51.7%) followed by "Hotels" (35.5%) in 2008, this hierarchy remaining unchanged against the year 2000; thus, tourism in relative terms brings more value added (1.45 times) by the contribution of "Restaurants" branch against the "Hotels" branch. This relationship is valid for the entire aggregate of the tourism branch for foreign tourists in Romania, the expenditures on hotels being still the most important factor for tourists' decision-marking;

C. The share of tourism in total intra-community imports in 2008 represents about 3.1% against 0.0% in 2000, which highlights the impact of Romania's accession to EU in the year 2007; the extra-community import of tourism recorded a higher share in total extra-community import, reaching 1.15%;

D. Both intra-community and extra-community imports in tourism had as original source the "Hotels" branch; With respect to the contribution of tourism to taxes (value added-tax), for the analyzed period, there is an increase of their share in total tax on product from 3.1% to 4.7% respectively which might signify also a relative increase in the taxation burden;

E. The consumption of tourism resources in total resources represents about 2.3% in 2008, on slight increase against 2000; The Tourism branch allocates a share of about 82% to final consumption from its total production which can be regarded as a preponderantly final branch, as for intermediate consumption allotted to the branch and for the other branches it is only 18%. This feature is very important because tourism represents a sector of the economy dependent on the development of demand of goods and services in infrastructure in a much larger proportion than intermediate consumption distributed to manufacturing and to other sectors of the national economy. Within final consumption, tourism has a share of about 5% from final consumption on total economy, a share on increase against the year 2000;

F. The share of tourism in total exports of goods and services was of about 2.1% from total exports in 2009, on increase against 2000, exports originating in close shares between the "Hotels" and "Restaurants" branches, 54% and 46% respectively under the conditions in which intra-community exports of the Tourism branch hold about 74.7% and the extra-community ones 25.3%.

Financial and Banking Industry

In the last 25 years, the banking system in Romania has come a long way to a market economy, with 40 banks, and private and foreign majority ownership. In 2014, 91.7% of total banks assets were held private, 81% were foreign ownership and the first five banks held 53.9%. Banks were affected by the financial crisis, 20% of employees were laid off and 19% of the territorial network was closed. Share of non-performing loans[1] increased

---

1 A loan on which the borrower is not making interest payments or repaying any principal. At what point the loan is classified as non-performing by the bank, and when it becomes bad debt, depends on local regulations.

nine times between 2008 and 2014, and the Romania National Bank issued a recommendation for banks to provisioned 90% of exposures of insolvent companies, but only four banks have complied with the recommendation. After 30 November 2014, other banks risk suspension of the right to collection of term deposits. The banking system in Romania shows, even in 2014, a low degree of financial intermediation, but development in the world economy shows that this can be an advantage, even if a decade ago was considered a weakness.

Until 1998, the Romanian commercial banking system was overwhelmingly state-owned. Credit institutions granted loans to a largely un-restructured real sector dominated by big, inefficient state-owned factories, subject to quasi-automatic refinancing by the Romanian central bank, which conducted an accommodative monetary policy. Inflation rates were very high. The Bucharest Stock Exchange was established in 1995, the over-the-counter market[1] (RASDAQ) in 1996. The latter traded shares were created in the wake of Romania's mass privatization program. The National Securities Commission was also set up in the mid-1990s.

Following early years of rapid expansion, stock values and turnover in both markets were badly affected by repercussions of the turmoil in Asian and Russian financial markets in 1997 and 1998[2]. Supervision, initially at a

---

1 An over-the-counter (OTC) market and an exchange market are the two basic ways of organizing financial markets. In an OTC market, dealers act as market makers by quoting prices at which they will buy and sell a security or currency [in https://www.investopedia.com/terms/o/otc.asp].

2 The Asian financial crisis, was a series of currency devaluations and other events that spread through many Asian markets beginning in the summer of 1997. The currency markets first failed in Thailand as the result of the government's decision to no longer peg the local currency to the U.S. dollar (USD). Currency declines spread rapidly throughout South Asia, in turn causing stock market declines, reduced import revenues and government upheaval. As a result of the devaluation of Thailand's baht, a large portion of East Asian currencies fell by as much as 38%. International stocks also declined as much as 60%. Luckily, the Asian financial crisis was stemmed somewhat by financial intervention from the International Monetary Fund and the World Bank. However, the market declines were also felt in the United States, Europe and Russia as the Asian economies slumped [in https://www.investopedia.com/terms/a/asian-financial-crisis.asp].

rudimentary stage, improved only slowly. After the election of a more strongly reform-minded government at end-1996, serious macroeconomic stabilization policies and structural reforms were initiated. The Romanian central tightened its hitherto lax banking supervision. The quasi-automatic central bank refinancing of loans was discontinued. A number of large state-owned credit institutions thereupon experienced serious financial difficulties and could only be kept afloat with sizeable public financial assistance.

In 2000, Romanian authorities embarked on prudent macroeconomic stabilization efforts. Some political instability was overcome by the election of a new government at the end of 2000, which sustained the stabilization and reform policies. The same year, the external economic situation, particularly in the EU, brightened and the decade long conflict in neighbouring former Yugoslavia drew to an end. Inflation and budget deficits slowly came down. With the strengthening of the economic upswing in 2001 and the following years, market participants gained more confidence and credit institutions expanded their activities speedily.

All in all, financial intermediation in Romania—notwithstanding expansionary tendencies—is still at a comparatively modest level. Provided that framework conditions do further adjust, there remains ample growth potential in the medium and long term, just as the growth and catching-up potential of the entire Romanian economy remains large and promising. With 22.4 million inhabitants and a territory of approximately the size of former West Germany, Romania is the second-largest EU accession country after Poland. If banking sector assets per capita in Romania reached the same level as they presently have in Poland, this would imply a medium-term expansion potential of close to 400%. Apart from the above-mentioned exposure to a possible marked depreciation of the domestic currency and the inherent credit risk, some of the most pertinent risks/problems for the Romanian financial and banking sector appear to be: A. the danger of a mismatch between increasingly medium-term loans and predominantly short-term deposits; B. insufficient risk analysis and management capacities at banks; C. the weakness, limited efficiency and transparency of capital market development and the modest level of supervision; D. the persisting lag in restructuring the real sector, particularly state-owned enterprises, sluggish privatization, weak corporate governance, loss-prone firms, lack of financial discipline; E. continuing limited contract enforcement capacities and de-facto recoverability of claims, inefficient and partly in transparent insolvency procedures, inadequate creditor protection; F. legal complexity and the generally weak rule of law, which may easily fall victim to government emergency decrees; G. despite some progress still unfavorable overall investment climate, still sprawling bureaucracy, pervasive corruption.

Foreign Trade

Romania is the 46th largest export economy in the world and the 38th most complex economy according to the Economic Complexity Index (ECI)[1]. In 2014, Romania exported $71.4B and imported $75.6B, resulting in a negative trade balance of $4.26 B. In 2014, the GDP of Romania was $199B and its GDP per capita was $20.3K.

Trade corresponds to more than 80% of Romania's GDP. The country is very dependent on imports. The global economic crisis has accentuated Romania's balance of payments deficit since 2009. In 2016, the trade deficit was situated around EUR 9.9 billion. This is also explained by the economic difficulties faced by Romania's main trade partners. The trade deficit is expected to persist, but Romania's trade balance in 2017 will depend on the dynamism of the Eurozone economies.

Romania's main export partners are Germany, Italy, France, Hungary and the UK. The country traditionally and mainly exports industrial products.

---

1 A holistic measure of the production characteristics of large economic systems, usually whole countries. As most of the measurements used in complexity economics, the goal of this index is to explain an economic system as a whole rather than the sum of its parts [Source: Wikipedia].

Romania's main suppliers are Germany, Italy, Hungary and France. Imports have been rising since 2011, due to an increase in consumption and the input needs of export-oriented industrial activity. The strongest growth was therefore recorded in the importation of consumer goods and electric and mechanical equipment.

Foreign Direct Investment

In 2016, Foreign Direct Investment (FDI) in Romania amounted to about EUR 4 billion, an increase of 36% compared to the previous year. Until 2020, Romania will receive EUR 40 billion of grants by the European Commission. In 2016, the former technocratic Government's fight against corruption accentuated the country's business-friendly image and attracted investors. Romania ranked 36th out of 190 economies in the 2017 Doing Business Report, issued by the World Bank.

The distribution of FID by sector shows a lead of the industrial sector (more than one-third of the total), with the metallurgy industry standing out. Other sectors have attracted investors such as banking and insurance, wholesale and retail, energy, construction and telecommunications. The regions that attract the most foreign capital are the following (in order of importance): Bucharest (more than 60% of the total), the centre and the south. Romania has numerous advantages: in addition to a large domestic market, the country has a strong industrial tradition, coupled with a cost of labour among the lowest in the EU. This has been the reason for the development of a significant industrial sector, particularly car making, but also services. The average growth figure of FDI in Romania is around 4% per year according to the "Invest in Romania" website.

The main investors in Romania are France, Austria, the Netherlands and Germany. The Czech company CEZ has invested over EUR one billion since 2011, in order to install a park of 240 wind turbines near the Black Sea.

Trade Relationship between Romania and China[1]

Romania and China established diplomatic relations 65 years ago and have a long track of fruitful economic, technologic, scientific and cultural exchanges and cooperation experiences all along with this time lapse. During the last few decades, Romania and China both have undergone major transformations, having, on the one hand, their economic fundamentals substantially changed, and, on the other hand, facing a new international environment, in which their positioning, relations, alliances and integration into the world economy are substantially different.

Trade flows in goods between Romania and China increased sharply in the last decade, reaching a record high in 2011 in spite of the economic crisis. Nevertheless, it decreased considerably during the subsequent period, mainly due to the diminishing value of imports. This trend of 2012-2013 is consistent with that recorded at the EU 28 level. However, Romania's trade with China represents only 0.6% of the EU-China trade. Romania has lost its competitive edge in many export fields, particularly those incorporating medium-complexity technologies, which explains in part the asymmetric bilateral trade structure. In spite of the increase of the trade in goods flows between Romania and China in the recent years as compared to the 2000-2005 time span, their values remain low as juxtaposed to other EU countries, due to the still underdeveloped connections between Romanian and Chinese companies.

Romania was a favourite destination for the early Chinese investments in Europe. Besides their history of friendship with China, Romania and the other CEE[2] economies, with their geographic placement, lower costs, cheaper but skilled and educated labor, make ideal locations for investments in export-oriented manufacturing, and that is why in the early 2000s the Chinese official plan for this region was to turn it into a manufacturing base for "made in

---

1 S. Pencea & I. M. Oehler-Sincai, *Romania, Strategic Partner in China-CEE Relations* [in *Global Economic Observer*, 3(1), 44, 2015].

2 Central and Eastern Europe (CEE)

Europe" Chinese goods. Among the targeted CEE countries, Romania was the first choice, followed by Poland, the Czech Republic and Hungary.

Five industrial fields in Romania (textiles, leather goods and luggage, TV sets, computers, telecommunications and electronic equipment), plus three services sectors were recommended for Chinese investments, revealing an option for a trade-substituting investment strategy aiming at avoiding import barriers and preserving/extending the existing market shares of Chinese exporters to Europe.

China is Romania's main Asian investing partner. It ranks the 5th among the foreign investors in Romania by the number of companies set up, but only the 18th by the amount invested, which is extremely far from the potential. Currently, there are over 11,000 Chinese companies registered in Romania, accounting for about 5% of the total number of businesses with foreign participation, but, presumably, just about one-third of them are still actually active.

Chapter 8
Transportation and Communications

Romania is located at a crossroads of European transport. Railways provide the main method of transportation for both freight and passengers in the country. Since the 1930s, diesel locomotives have been in service, and about one-third of the major lines have been electrified. Most of Romania's system of national roads have been brought up to modern standards.

The main lines of communication tend to focus on Bucharest and include many scenic routes. The country has maritime connections with many countries, and the port of Constanţa, which has undergone a major expansion, plays a large role in the national economy. Finally, the Danube River, supplemented since 1984 by the Danube-Black Sea Canal from Cernavoda to Constanta, is a major transportation route between the Black Sea, the Middle East, and Western Europe. In addition to local travel, international traffic has grown in significance,

Chapter 8 Transportation and Communications

and there are international airports in Constanta, Cluj-Napoca, Arad, Timisoara and Sibiu.[1]

Romania's telecommunications sector was privatized in 2003. Within five years, the fixed-line market expanded substantially, and there was an increase in Internet availability. Romania has significantly more cellular phone subscriptions than people, which marks an exponential increase from 2000, when about one-tenth of Romanians subscribed to cellular service.

Transport Infrastructure and Transportation[2]

Romania is not only a strategic point in Europe with a large market potential in terms of size and population, but also, as an EU member, a gateway

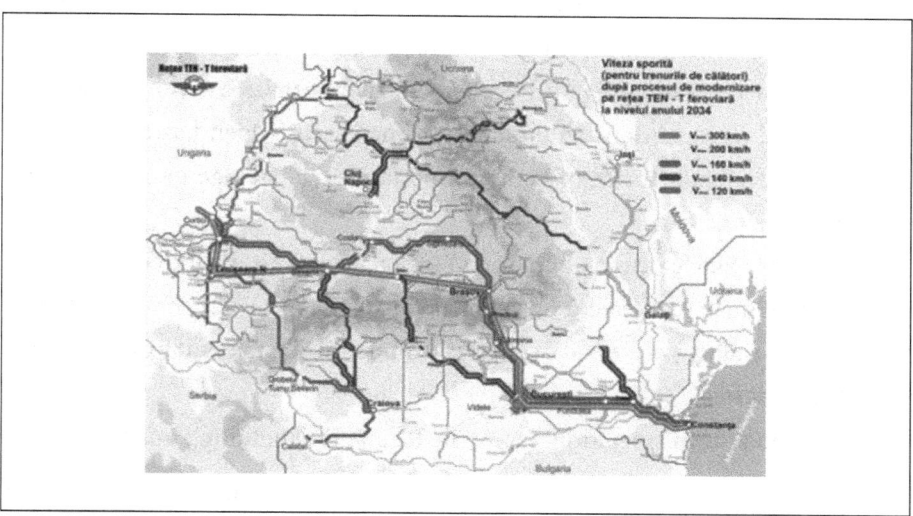

PICTURE: Romanian Railway Map
SOURCE: http://www.railwaypro.com/wp/with-the-new-master-plan-romania-goes-in-for-the-european-transport-policy/

---

1 https://www.britannica.com/place/Romania
2 https://info.publicintelligence.net/MCIA-RomaniaHandbook.pdf

to three major markets: the single EU, the CIS[1] and the Middle East at the junction of three Pan-European transportation corridors.

Romania enjoys a wide range of transportation options: road (86,080 km), rail (approximately 20.000 km in total, the 7th largest network in the EU, out of which 10,770 km in use), naval (32 ports on the Black Sea, mainly through Constanta port, and along Danube River 1075 km) and air (14 airports). However, the infrastructure is amongst the least developed in Europe. Although there have been some major transport investments, Romania continues to experience accessibility and connectivity constraints due to poor quality of infrastructure.

Despite the week infrastructure, the transportation market has registered growth in recent years due to the overall business development in Romania. Consumption has been on the rise, but also the production as companies have been in favour of regional production due to country's positioning, a more stable economic environment, more friendly fiscal environment and low costs (especially in the automotive sector, but other industries as well), therefore, both international and domestic trade have increased, which has resulted into an upward development rate of both transportation and storage in order to cope with the market demand.

Due to the high extension of the retail sector, determined by the consumption's rise, domestic trade registered growth amounting to LEI 199902.7 million (approx. EUR 44422.8 million) at the end of 2014 as per information released by the National Institute of Statistics.

The goods transportation sector in Romania (including road, railway,

---

1 Commonwealth of Independent States (CIS) was created in December 1991. In the adopted Declaration, the participants of the Commonwealth declared their interaction on the basis of sovereign equality. In September 1993, the Heads of the CIS States signed an Agreement on the creation of Economic Union to form common economic space grounded on free movement of goods, services, labour force, capital; to elaborate coordinated monetary, tax, price, customs, external economic policy; to bring together methods of regulating economic activity and create favourable conditions for the development of direct production relations. At present, the CIS includes Azerbaijan, Armenia, Belarus, Kazakhstan, Kyrgyzstan, Moldova, Russia, Tajikistan, Uzbekistan [http://www.cisstat.com/eng/cis.htm].

maritime, inland waterways and air transportation segments) reached 328.4 million tons of transported goods in 2015. The biggest percentage of the goods transportation sector in 2015 was represented by road freight transport (60.4%), followed by railway freight transport (16.8%), then by maritime freight transport (13.5%) & inland waterway transport (9.1%), while the lowest percentage was represented by air freight transport.

The modal choice of freight transport depends on various factors. In Romania, each mode of transport has its own advantages and disadvantages relating to price, speed, safety, weight and reliability. Transport by water is the lowest cost carrier, but also the slowest mode and operates shipments with lowest value while transport by air is the fastest, but the most expensive and operates shipments with highest value. Concerning freight weight, water transport facilitates the highest weight while air transport can operate only the lowest weight.

In between, there are the other two transport modes, road and rail, transport by road facilitating shipments with high value and low weight while transport by rail facilitates shipments with low value and high weight.

Road and rail transport, as intermodal, facilitates shipments with range of weight and value, rail being competitive with road over longer distances. Romania's transportation market reached 7 billion euros in terms of goods freighted and 2 billion euros in passenger transportation and it is in its 7th year of growth. Transport and storage, together with retail and wholesale trade, repair of motor vehicles and motorcycles, hotels and restaurants have been constantly developed and contributed 18% to the GDP formation, with an activity volume up 13.1%.

Development of sectors like e-commerce, retail, Fast-moring consumer goods[1], automotive and construction is expected to speed up and, as a consequence,

---

1 Fast-moving consumer goods (FMCG) or consumer packaged goods (CPG) are products that are sold quickly and at relatively low cost. Examples include non-durable goods such as packaged foods, beverages, toiletries, over-the-counter drugsand many other consumables. In contrast, durable goods or major appliances such as kitchen appliances are generally replaced over a period of several years. Though the profit margin made on FMCG products is relatively small (more so for retailers than the producers/suppliers), they are generally sold in large quantities; thus, the cumulative profit on such products can be substantial. FMCG is a classic case of low margin and high volume business [Source: Wikipedia].

transportation and storage would witness more development as well. Transport companies are expected to invest in trucks and storage facilities and, at the same time, to go global, expanding their activity towards Western Europe and Asia. However, building a strong infrastructure (a highway network inter-connected to the European transport corridors, a modern and more-efficient railway network, a better connection of the Constanta port with the hinterland, a better facilitation of traffic in the ports of Danube) would both give Romania the real possibility to become an international hub and would increase the efficiency of the local freight transporters.

Road

The road network in Romania is classified into different categories: national roads (motorways A, European roads E and main national roads DN), county roads DJ and communal roads DC. At the end of 2015, the road infrastructure had around 86,000 km, the motorway and the national road network accounting for just 20% of the entire network.

Out of the total national roads (A/E/DN), 35.2% (6,193 km) were European roads, 4.2% (747 km) motorways, 1.6% (281 km) lane traffic roads, 10.3% (1,807 km) lane traffic roads and 0.1% (22 km) lane traffic roads. From the point of view of the pavement, the structure of public roads network registered 37.9% modernized roads, 24.6% light cover roads and 37.5% stone and ground roads.

The road infrastructure is obviously underdeveloped and outdated, the level of motorway provision being very low comparing to the rest of Europe. The lack of highways along the main routes of transit makes traffic difficult, crowded, and with relatively low commercial speeds. At the same time, there are no express roads in Romania. Road safety and pollution are also reasons for concern.

Romania is still amongst the countries reporting the highest road fatality rates in EU with more than 90 dead per million inhabitants, while more than 13% of the greenhouse gas emissions come from the transport sector, 96%

Chapter 8 Transportation and Communications

of them being caused by road transport. Achievement of a high-performance infrastructure in order to ensure efficiency, durability, flexibility and maximum safety conditions of persons and goods is considered a top priority in the context of Romania's development plans. Road projects involving the development of new transport corridors (motorways and expressways) or extending existing roads (modernization projects) in order to increase the road connectivity between Romanian economic growth poles and to improve the travel conditions between regions are currently proposed by the Romanian Government for the next period.

Although the road infrastructure is poor, the transport by road, which is the predominant transportation mode in Romania, shows a slightly ascending trend in terms of freight volume, in 2015 totalling an amount of 199 million tons, representing 60.4% of the total freight transport.

Under the current business environment, with fast development rate in terms of production and consumption, road freight is expected to grow with an average 3.1% per year between 2016 and 2020, which is a quicker growth rate than the other freight modes. Over 1000 trucks run daily on the Romanian roads transporting to modern retail in order to cope with the market demand. However, the trucking sector in Romania is competitive from the entire Romanian fleet, a high percentage of trucks provides services to the European market.

According to market sources, a Romanian highway network interconnected to the European transport corridors could increase the efficiency of the local freight road transporters by up to 20%. Transilvania highway that will link the Centre and the Western regions of the country could lead to an expenditure decrease by 10-12% for the local freight transporters that perform international expeditions.

Railway

The total rail Romanian route network under exploitation amounts at about 11,000 km (the 7th largest in the EU), out of which about 8000 km (72%) is single track, while the average in the EU is 59%, and about 3000 km (27%) is double track. It comprises about 1000 stations, 200 tunnels and 4000 bridges. Only 37% of the rail network is electrified comparing to the EU average of 54%.

According to the National Institute of Statistics of Romania, at the end of 2015, the density of rails per 1,000 km territory was 45.2‰. Currently, only a small proportion of the total railway network is rehabilitated. Modernization of 35 railway stations is finalized while modernization of 47 railway stations is in preparation. The rail system in Romania is in an advanced state of disrepair due to a chronic lack of maintenance, which has led to low speeds, poor frequency and ineffective operations.

Despite a fully open market, the period between 1990 and 2010 was marked by strong declines (-80%) in terms of volume of rail transport both for passengers and goods. However, for the period 2010 and 2015, the market for rail stabilized, the transport by rail even showing a slight positive evolution. At the end of 2015, the volume of freight transport by rail amounted to 55 million tons, which represented 16.8% of the total freight transport (2nd place after road transport).

Under the current growing trend in exports (especially agricultural goods and heavy machinery) the rail freight will continue to see a good future. Moreover, Romania being a relatively large country, is suited to rail transport. Goods that have to be transported large distances could be transported more economically by rail than by road. For the coming period, Romania will focus on increasing the competitiveness of rail transport on the domestic market and the integration of the Romanian railway system in the Single European Railway Area. Therefore, some of the freight flows would be relocated from road to rail.

The high growth potential of transport by rail can be achieved only through sustained investments in infrastructure. Rail projects focused on upgrading the

Chapter 8   Transportation and Communications

rail infrastructure, in particular, the Trans-European Transport Network (TEN-T)[1] sections on the Romanian territory and the integration in the European network of high-speed rail transport, projects for connecting Bucharest with the largest industrial centres in the South of Romania, are to be carried out in the next programming periods (2015–2020 and 2020–2036): modernization of conventional railway lines, electrification, rehabilitation of bridges and tunnels, safety projects, development of cross-border railway lines together with acquisition of new rolling stock & locomotives. The TEN-T network covers about 20% of the total Romanian railway routes and accommodates about 50% of the total rail traffic by volume.

The rail passenger market and the rail private market have been open to private undertakings since 2004. In 2012, the passenger public operator (CFR Calatori)[2] had about 90% of the market, the rest being covered by private operators, while the freight public operator (CFR Marfa[3]) had a market share of 55%. The freight public operator was to be privatized by the end of 2016 at the request of International Monetary Fund, however, the Romanian Government postponed the process till the first term of 2018.

---

1   The Trans-European Transport Networks (TEN-T) are a planned set of road, rail, air and water transport networks in the European Union. The TEN-T networks are part of a wider system of Trans-European Networks (TENs) including a telecommunications network (eTEN) and a proposed energy network (TEN-E or Ten-Energy). The European Commission adopted the first action plans on trans-European networks in 1990. TEN-T envisages coordinated improvements to primary roads, railways, inland waterways, airports, seaports, inland ports and traffic management systems, providing integrated and intermodal long-distance, high-speed routes. A decision to adopt TEN-T was made by the European Parliament and Council in July 1996. The EU works to promote the networks by a combination of leadership, coordination, issuance of guidelines and funding aspects of development [Source: Wikipedia].

2   A state-owned Romanian rail passenger transport company founded in 1998 by the reorganization of the former CFR . In 2015, approximately 1,300 trains were put into circulation daily. CFR Calatori receives more than one billion Lei from the state budget annually in order to ensure the railway passenger transport activity. Transported passenger flows recorded an increase of 15.7% in 2014 (56,122,000 passengers) compared to 2013 [Source: Wikipedia].

3   The state-owned freight railway business of Romania. Formerly the freight division of Caile Ferate Romane (CFR), it was separated in 1998 to become a semi-independent business. [Source: Wikipedia].

Maritime and Inland Waterways

The maritime and inland waterway infrastructure comprises 32 river and seaports on the Black Sea, on the waterway navigable canals and along the Danube River together with the secondary navigable branches of the Danube. The maritime transport is provided by the direct access to the Black Sea through the three maritime ports: Constanta, Mangalia and Midia (the Port of Constanta being the main Romanian port among the first ten European ports).

The inland waterway transport, focused on the Danube river (1075 km along Romania), is provided through 29 inland waterway ports, the largest being the ports of Galati, Braila and Tulcea, located on the maritime section of the Danube. They are part of the TEN-T Network and a series of ports on the river Danube, the largest of which are Giurgiu, Oltenita and Droberta Turnu Severin. The navigable canals have been developed between the Danube and the Black Sea including the main canal, Danube-Black Sea Canal which ends in Constanta Sea Port and Poarta Alba-Midia Navodari Canal which links the main canal with the Midia Port.

The Danube-Black Sea Canal offers access to both the Black Sea and the North Sea through the Rhine-Main-Danube Trans-European Waterway, connecting the Port of Constanta and the Port of Rotterdam. One-third canal is Bega Canal and traverses Romania and Serbia, discharging through Tisa in the Danube River.

The Port of Constanta, located on the Western coast of the Black Sea, is the most important commercial sea and river port in Romania (3,926 ha, out of which 1,313 ha land & 2,613 ha water; 140 operating berths) and has a handling capacity of over 120 million tons/year. Its geo-strategic position, at the crossroads of the trade routes, is enhanced by connections with all transport modes: road, rail, inland waterway and air.

Although there have been performed some modernization works in the recent years, the Romanian port infrastructure like dams, berths, stone packing, port basins and port areas faces with an advanced state of physical degradation due to very old infrastructure in some ports, intensive and longtime exploitation, without realizing the maintenance and repairing works, and also no sufficient links with other transport modes. Regarding the waterway transport, there are many sectors with navigation bottlenecks in Romania generated by insufficient water depths during dry seasons, lock size or clearance under the bridge. According to the National Institute of Statistics, the volume of loaded and unloaded goods both in the maritime ports and inland ports has lately increased at the end of 2015 amounting to 44.5 million tons relating to maritime and 30 million tons related to inland. The vast majority of the goods transported by water in Romania are bulk goods. The Danube carries 3 types of traffic: domestic, transit and import/export at the end of 2015 totalling 13.2 million tons for domestic, 5.5 million tons for transit and 11.2 million tons for international.

Due to Romania's position relative to the Danube, the proportion of total inland freight in Romania transported by water is the second-highest in the EU. However, Romania compares unfavourably to Holland which has a similar position relative to the Rhine, the key difference between the countries being the lack of modern facilities in Romania. The Port of Constanta, the major maritime and river port in Romania, is the most developed and offers the widest range of facilities. The total traffic in the Port of Constanta was of 56.3 million tons in 2014, showing a slightly increasing trend, and was generated mostly by dry bulk and cereals (over 64%), followed by liquid bulk, and then by general cargo. Constanta handles over 70% of the total freight in the Romanian ports.

In addition, the Port of Constanta is a major regional container port (but not one of the top 20 container ports by volume in Europe), the modal share of containers leaving Constanta (excluding transiting) being estimated as currently: 56%—road, 41%—rail, 3%—barge. Constanta has a large hinterland and acts as a transhipment point for many goods, however, there is much potential to expand its throughput as long as the road, rail and water links are improved. Romania may play a leading role in connecting Central Asia and Central Europe through the Danube river and the Port of Constanta, which sum up an excellent transport system. Improvements of the infrastructure of both maritime and inland waterway would add benefits for the entire economy of Romania in an European context. Infrastructure projects focused especially on TEN-T ports are under preparation.

Air

Currently, the air infrastructure in Romania consists of 14 airports permanently open for traffic. They offer more than 130 direct flights to 76 destinations in 31 countries and also ensure a strong internal connection providing easy access to every region in the country. One airport is under construction, namely the one in Brasov (Center Romania) which, once finished, would enhance business development in the region. The most important airports are the ones in Bucharest (major international airport), Timisoara and Constanta (big international hub airports) and are operated by the Romanian government while the others are operated by local counties.

During the years, the air infrastructure in Romania has been involved in strategic programs for development, financed both from EU structural funds and domestic funds. Romania has significant infrastructure capacity given current air traffic demand, which has been witnessed significant growth year by year both for passengers and goods. At the end of 2015, according to the National Institute of Statistics, 34.3 thousand tons of goods were transported by air.

However, airports still need to be modernized and equipped in order to respond to international standards of safety and security. At the same time, upgrading of the air infrastructure, developing cargo handling facilities and extension to the runway, terminals, signalling systems and so on becomes top priority in order to cope with the upcoming demand. Expansion of manufacturing (especially manufacturing companies requiring complex or rapidly moving supply such as electronics and pharmaceuticals) coupled with the increase of higher-value consumer goods make freight transport by air an important mode of transport, fostering trade and commerce.

Moreover, the poor development of the highway infrastructure in Romania determine the big freighters to offer the solution to combine air freight with trucking. The modernization and development of the Romanian airports, with a special focus on improving the TEN-T connectivity of landlocked territories and the promotion of regional economic development are the main objectives for the next programming period in Romania. Further air infrastructure modernization projects are under preparation stage as proposed in the Master Plan General Transport.

Taking into consideration the amount of traffic and general airport activity, Bucharest is and remains the centre of the air freight market, Bucharest Henri Coanda airport being the most active airport and also home to the major carriers such as Tarom (Romanian Airline), British Airways, Lufthansa, Austrian Airlines. Recently, Romania has experienced significant market penetration from low-cost carriers (higher than 40%) including Wizz Air, Blue Air, Ryanair, however, Tarom continues to be the only carrier providing services to some ten destinations in the country in addition to multiple destinations overseas.

While Italy is number 1 as the country destination, followed by Germany, UK, Spain and France, Belgium has witnessed the most significant growth in weekly capacity, 65% or an additional 2,345 seats, due in part to Ryanair adding daily flights between Bucharest and Charleroi. Nonetheless, Blue Air has also contributed to the increase as it introduced twice-weekly flights from Bacau to Brussels.

Tips for Travelers[1]

A passport is required. Tourist visas for stays up to thirty days are not required. An exit visa must be obtained only in cases when the original passport used to enter the country was lost or stolen and a replacement passport has been issued by the appropriate embassy. For stays longer than thirty days, visas

---

1 www.un.org/esa/agenda21/natlinfo/wssd/romania.pdf

should be obtained from a Romanian embassy or consulate abroad. These should be extended at passport offices in Romania in the area of residence. Travellers can obtain visas and other information regarding entry requirements from the Romanian Embassy.

In an effort to prevent international child abduction, many governments have initiated procedures at entry/exit points. These often include requiring documentary evidence of relationship and permission for the child's travel from the parent(s) or legal guardian not present. Having such documentation on hand, even if not required, may facilitate entry/departure.

In addition to being subject to all Romanian laws affecting foreign citizens, dual nationals may also be subject to other laws that impose special obligations on Romanian citizens.

While most crimes in Romania are non-violent and non-confrontational, there has been an increase in the number of crimes in which the victim suffers personal harm. Crimes against tourists (robbery, mugging, pick-pocketing and confidence scams) are a growing problem in Romania. Organized groups of thieves and pickpockets operate in the train stations and on trains, subways, and buses in major cities. A number of thefts and assaults have occurred on overnight trains including thefts from passengers in closed compartments. Money exchange schemes targeting travellers have become increasingly common in Romania. Some of these scams have become rather sophisticated, involving individuals posing as plainclothes policemen, who approach the potential victim, flash a badge and ask for his/her passport and wallet. In many of these cases, the thieves succeed in obtaining passports, credit cards and other personal documents.

The loss or theft abroad of a passport should be reported immediately to the local police and the nearest appropriate embassy or consulate. Medical care in Romania is not up to Western standards, and basic medical supplies are limited, especially outside major cities.

When making a decision regarding health insurance, you should consider that many foreign doctors and hospitals require payment in cash prior to providing service and that a medical evacuation back to your country may cost be very expensive. Uninsured travellers who require medical care overseas often face extreme difficulties.

When consulting with your insurer prior to your trip, please ascertain whether payment will be made to the overseas healthcare provider or if you will be reimbursed later for expenses that you incur. Some insurance policies also include coverage for psychiatric treatment and for disposition of remains in the event of death.

Road conditions vary widely throughout Romania. While major streets in larger cities and major inter-city roads are in fair to good condition, most other roads are in poor repair, badly lit, narrow, and often do not have marked lanes. Many roads, particularly in rural areas, are also used by pedestrians, animals, people on bicycles, and horse-drawn carts that are extremely difficult to see, especially at night. Road travel can be particularly dangerous when roads are wet or covered with snow or ice. This is especially the case concerning mountain roads.

Romanian traffic laws are very strict. Any form of driver's license or permit can be confiscated by the traffic police for one to three months and payment of fines may be requested at the time of many infractions. Some examples are: failure to yield the right of way, failure to yield to pedestrians at crossroads, or not stopping at a red light or stop sign. Romanian traffic law provides for retention of licenses and possible imprisonment from one to five years for driving under the influence (alcohol level over 0.1% limit) or for causing an accident resulting in injury or death. In spite of these strict rules, however, many drivers in Romania often do not follow traffic laws or yield the right of way. Therefore, it is strongly recommended that defensive driving be practised while driving throughout Romania.

Wearing a seat belt is mandatory only in the front seats of a car. Children under 12 years of age cannot be transported on the front seat. Drivers must yield to pedestrians at all marked pedestrian crosswalks, but many of these are poorly marked and difficult to see. Unless otherwise marked with road signs, speed limits are as follows: inter-city traffic on highways, 120 km/hr for cars, 100 km/hr for motorcycles, 90 km/hr for vans. On all other roads: 90 km/hr for cars, 80 km/hr for motorcycles, and 70 km/hr for vans. Inner-city traffic: 50 km/hr. Speed limits for motor vehicles with trailers and for drivers with less than 1 years of driving experience are10 km/hr slower than those listed above.

Inter-city travel is generally done via trains and buses, which are relatively safe, inexpensive and reliable. However, travellers should be aware of pickpockets while on night trains or in train stations. Inter-city travel by taxi is much more expensive, and safety depends on the quality of the driver. Many older taxis are not equipped with seat belts. To avoid being overcharged, those using inner-city taxis should request the taxi by phone, make sure the taxi has an operational meter, or agree upon a price before entering the taxi.

Romania's customs authorities may enforce strict regulations concerning temporary importation into or export from Romania of items such as firearms, antiquities and medications. Romanian law allows foreigners to bring up to USD $10,000 in cash into Romania. No amount in excess of that declared upon entry may be taken out of Romania upon departure. Sums larger than $10,000 must be transferred through banks. No more than 1,000,000 Romanian Lei may be brought into or taken out of the country. Romania customs authorities encourage the use of an ATA (admission temporaire/temporary admission) carnet for the temporary admission of professional equipment, commercial samples, and/or goods for exhibitions and fair purposes.

While in a foreign country, you are subject to that country's laws and regulations. Persons violating Romanian laws, even unknowingly, may be expelled, arrested or imprisoned. Penalties for possession, use or trafficking in illegal drugs in Romania are strict, and convicted offenders can expect jail sentences and heavy fines.

Romania is largely a "cash only" economy. While an increasing number of businesses do accept credit cards, travellers are advised to use cash for goods and services rendered due to an increase in credit card fraud. Venders have been known to misuse credit card information by making illegal purchases on

Chapter 8   Transportation and Communications

individuals' accounts. There is an increasing number of ATM machines located throughout major cities. Travellers' checks are of limited use, but they may be used to exchange local currency at some exchange houses.

There is a significant population of stray dogs in and around Bucharest, and attacks on pedestrians and joggers are not uncommon. While there have not been any reported problems with rabies, travellers are advised to avoid all stray dogs.

Communications & media[1]

Romania has an outdated communications infrastructure that is gradually improving and it is starting to use new technologies such as cellular, satellite, and fibre-optics.

Broadcast Media

In 1992, the National Audiovisual Council of Romania was authorized to grant broadcasting audiovisual licenses to private stations. Between 1992 and 1999, 2,046 cables licenses, 217 television licenses, 341 radio broadcasting licenses, 14 satellite television station licenses and 9 satellite radio station broadcast licenses were granted. Radio and television stations broadcast in Romanian, Hungarian and German. Romania's government television station is Televiziunea Romana (TVR) with TVR International broadcasting satellite programming. Romania's major private television station is Soti TV. The government-sponsored radio station is Radiodifuziunea Romana. Public radio stations broadcast three radio programs on mediumwave and FM.

Since 1989, privately owned television broadcasts rapidly filled the needs of information-starved Romanians. Their Western counterparts absorbed many of these Romanian television stations because they lacked sufficient funding, up-to-date technology and professional expertise. The American-financed Central European Media Enterprises (CME) is Romania's first national commercial

---

1   https://en.wikipedia.org/wiki/Media_of_Romania

network and offers the nation PRO TV. PRO TV has been criticized for its bias in support of pro-NATO positions and reform-minded political parties. Privately owned and operated Antena 1 and Tele 7abc are attacked for their anti-Semitic reporting and nationalistic positions.

International funding of Romania's media runs the risk of shaping public opinion in conflict with national interests. Nevertheless, international investment in the media brings the Romanian people into the information world of the European Union nations.

Employees of the state-run television network TVR no longer hold secure jobs. State broadcast workers have experienced periods of wages not being paid and extensive layoffs.

In 2001, Romania had 50 privately-owned television stations and more than 100 privately owned radio stations. State television and radio cover more of the nation, particularly rural areas. Both the Romanian Broadcasting System and the Romanian Television Corporation, now independent and public-service oriented, jointly regulate state-run radio and television.

All private and public stations are under the jurisdiction of the National Audiovisual Council (NAC), which distributes broadcast licenses and regulates the airwaves.

There are about seven million households with TV sets in Romania. Television is still the most popular means of entertainment for Romanians, and it takes the lion's share of the advertising pie (about two-thirds) amounting to a total of 337 million euro in 2008. According to the Media Factbook 2009, the most popular TV shows among Romanians are football games, Romanian soap operas, prime time news, entertainment shows and international contests such as the Eurovision or big sporting events.

TV reaches most Romanians through cable networks that carry dozens of Romanian and international stations. The two main cable companies, sharing the market in almost equal chunks, are RCS & RDS and UPC.

However, analogue cable is in a slight decrease mainly due to the advancement of Direct to Home (DTH)[1], which has increased by more than 50% since 2007 according to the Media Factbook 2009.

Reception via analogue cable is at 66.8 %, DTH takes 22.6%, terrestrial accounts for 8.3% while 3.8% get their TV through digital cable with receiver. Both major cable operators offer digital reception through their own companies. Among the major players on the market is the national phone company Romtelecom with its Dolce service as well as a couple of other companies. Almost 50 TV stations distributed nationwide are registered under the National Study of TV Audience including general audience and specialized channels. There are also numerous local stations.

In the past few years, niche stations have started to bite into the audience of general-interest channels. On occasion, especially during important events such as a government crisis or election days, 24-hour news television can even gather the greatest number of viewers. There is a fierce competition between the two largest all-news TV stations, Realitatea TV (Realitatea-Catavencu) and Antena 3 (Intact). Sports channels have also grown more and more popular, and more and more numerous (at least seven are available to subscribers nationwide). There are also channels specializing in music, documentaries, women's interests, cartoons, films and reality shows.

Big local and international groups own some of the most successful TV and radio stations in Romania such as the American-based CME (owner of MediaPro International), Romanian companies Intact and Realitatea-Catavencu, the German group ProSiebenSat1. The Turkish group Dogan has also started a big investment program in 2007, although its channel Kanal D is presently trailing behind more successful stations.

The public television has come under criticism over the years for two main reasons. A. It is still politically controlled with its president and administrative council named on political criteria. B. It enjoys a hybrid 3-way financing system, which means it gets money from the state budget, from a special TV tax, and

---

1 A method of receiving satellite television by means of signals transmitted from direct-broadcast satellites [Source: Wikipedia].

also from advertising. The Parliament has come under a lot of pressure from the civil society to de-politicize public television, but it has not yet done so.

Print Media

The print media environment in Romania is rich and diverse if judged by the number of titles on the market. There is no available comprehensive data on the concrete effects of the economic crisis over the media yet, but evidence suggests there haven't been massive closures.

The most recent available statistics come from the National Institute of Statistics (NIS) which compiles data from 2007. According to NIS, in 2007 there were almost 300 publishers that published newspapers (159 dailies, plus newspapers appearing once or several times a week, and papers with no specific frequency) and over 350 publishers that published magazines.

The total yearly print run for dailies was 553.7 million, with an increase of almost 50 million, or 9.5% compared to the previous year. Non-dailies printed a total of more than 63.3 million copies, 25.5 million (or 67.5%) more than the previous year. The total yearly print runs for weekly newspapers was over 58 million in 2007, more than twice that of 2006.

The statistics institute recorded 1,515 magazine titles on the market in 2007. That is 126 more titles than in the previous year. The statistics take into account periodicals other than newspapers, from those appearing several times a week, to those appearing a few times a year, once a year or even at larger intervals, to those with no specific periodicity.

Just over 300 publications are audited by Romanian Audit Bureau of Circulation (BRAT). Members of BRAT usually enjoy more credibility and more advertising as print run and distribution figures are available for advertisers. Local newspapers audited by BRAT generally benefit from national ads, as the big advertisers looking to buy nationwide advertisements pay attention to the numbers.

As far as the publications distributed across the nation are concerned, the past few years have seen a decline in circulation for those dailies marketed as quality newspapers whereas the two national sports dailies have done relatively well, and the tabloids even better.

Austrian group Inform Media, which owns several local newspapers in cities from the region of Transylvania, closed down its free paper in Hunedoara three years after its launch.

Inform Media's written press operations in Transylvania now include three free dailies, five paid dailies (two of them in Hungarian), three free classified weeklies and two paid classified weeklies. Some of its free newspapers distribute more than 15,000 copies each day.

Unlike papers in Bucharest, local newspapers usually have not received any attention from big investors. That is one of the reasons why they are generally more vulnerable to pressure from local political and business circles, and from individuals who use the press to influence political/economic decisions and to win or keep public support. Among the chronic problems facing the local media are poor distribution networks and the lack of professional skills.

The global crisis and stiff competition from national newspapers have made the life of local publishers and journalists even harder. There are, however, successful local newspapers that strive to deliver quality products to their readers. In 2009, a number of quite prominent local publications closed. The Agenda media company in Timisoara shut down the print version of its local daily, *Agenda zilei*, and is now focusing on the regional weekly *Agenda*, its daily news website and its printing business. Publimedia, the publishing branch of MediaPro, closed its chain of six local weeklies after it had already shut down its daily newspaper in Cluj.

There is fierce competition in the business weeklies segment. There are two *The Economist*-style weeklies distributed nationwide, *Business Magazin* (around 11,000 copies sold each week), belonging to the MediaPro group, and *Money Express* (6,000), published by the Realitatea-Catavencu group. There are also two tabloid economic weeklies, *Saptamana financiara* (around 33,000), published by Intact, and Ringier's *Capital* (around 20,000 copies sold each week).

The glossy and magazine market was booming with more than a dozen women's magazines, a few men's magazines as well as publications dedicated to automobiles, computers, cooking, house and gardening and other niche products. There are many international franchises including *Elle, Esquire, Marie Claire, Men's Health, FHM, Playboy, GQ, Popcorn* or Harper's *Bazaar*. The fall in advertising has forced some publications to fold or to change their frequency, but most major titles enjoy steady print runs and some magazines have even picked up in circulation.

Telecommunications[1]

The telecom market has steadily increased over the last few years, to a value of 4.2 billion euro in 2008 (from 3.91 in 2007 and 1.96 in 2003), and mobile telephony was the main drive behind this growth according to a Romanian Telecom Market Overview by Roland Berger Strategy Consultants[2].

Mobile telephony accounted for two-thirds (66%) of the market in 2008, followed by fixed telephony (18%), and Internet and other data transmission services (16%).

According to experts, traditional voice services face growing competition

---

1 World Trade Press & ProQuest (Firm), *Romania : Communications*, World Trade Press, Petaluma, Calif, 2010.

2 A global strategy consulting firm headquartered in Munich, with 50 offices in 36 countries. The company was founded under the name Roland Berger Strategy Consultants in 1967 by Roland Berger. In 2011, the company's sales were roughly US$1.2 billion. The company, with around 2,400 employees worldwide, is an independent partnership wholly owned by its approximately 220 partners. Roland Berger operates as a generalist strategy consultancy and advises clients on management issues ranging from strategy development to performance improvement. Roland Berger advises in the fields of restructuring and marketing, with a focus on the automobile industry and the capital goods sector [Source: Wikipedia].

from alternative services such as Voice over IP (VoIP)¹. Prices have come down and the main provider, Romtelecom, the former state-owned monopoly, has to operate on the same market with other companies offering voice services since the deregulation of the voice market in 2003. Deregulation started to generate effects in 2005 when Romtelecom had started to lose lines to competitors. Owned by Greek company OTE, with the Romanian state a minority shareholder, Romtelecom now covers about 69% of the total number of fixed lines, or about 2.97 million lines as of September 2007 (losing one million since 2005).

Technically, though, Romtelecom has brought significant improvement to its network. Its fibre-optical network now spreads over 32,000 km according to Roland Berger. The company plans to invest 500 million euro in a next-generation network (NGN) ²allowing for integrated telecom services (voice, data and VPN³, Internet and video). In the past three years, it has already invested about 300 million in its infrastructure. Romtelecom now offers many households not only fixed telephony (digitized nationwide since 2007), but also digital television (through its Dolce brand) and high-speed Internet through ADSL (Asynchronous Digital Subscriber Line⁴) connections. Romtelecom and its sister

---

1 A methodology and group of technologies for the delivery of voice communications and multimedia sessions over Internet Protocol (IP) networks such as the Internet. [Source: Wikipedia].

2 A body of key architectural changes in telecommunication core and access networks. The general idea behind the NGN is that one network transports all information and services (voice, data and all sorts of media such as video) by encapsulating these into IP packets, similar to those used on the Internet. NGNs are commonly built around the Internet Protocol, and therefore the term all IP is also sometimes used to describe the transformation of formerly telephone-centric networks toward NGN [Source: Wikipedia].

3 A virtual private network (VPN) extends a private network across a public network and enables users to send and receive data across shared or public networks as if their computing devices were directly connected to the private network. Applications running across the VPN may therefore benefit from the functionality, security and management of the private network [Source: Wikipedia].

4 A type of digital subscriber line (DSL) technology, a data communications technology that enables faster data transmission over copper telephone lines than a conventional voiceband modem can provide [Source: Wikipedia].

company Cosmote also offer integrated fixed and mobile telephony services.

There are a total of 55 companies operating in the fixed telephony market as of mid-2008 in Romania, most offering both national and international call services according to the Romanian Telecom Market Overview by Roland Berger Strategy Consultants. More than 70 companies signed interconnection agreements with Romtelecom, but experts say only a few would have the resources and know-how to compete with Romtelecom at a significant level.

The largest CaTV[1] company, RCS & RDS, is now the leading competitor to Romtelecom in the fixed telephony market. Whith its landline telephony service, TEL had about 1.1 million subscribers in July 2008.

The other big player in the CaTV market and as one of the largest ISPs[2], UPC Romania, also offers voice services in addition to TV cable, data and Internet. In November 2008, its fixed telephony service using VoIP reached 120,600 subscribers.

Radiocom (formerly SNR), the national radio communications company, is also offering VoIP telephony and is working with the Ministry of Communications and Information Technology to implement the PLC (Power Line Communication[3]) technology in remote rural locations.

Three mobile phone companies, Vodafone, Orange and Zapp, are also offering fixed telephony services. Roland Berger appreciates that they target mostly households in rural and suburban areas with no access to wired networks.

One of the important regulatory decisions in the fixed and mobile phone market, bound to increase competition even further, is the portability of phone

---

1 Cable television is a system of delivering television programming for subscribers via radio frequency (RF) signals transmitted through coaxial cables, or in more recent systems, light pulses through fiber-optic cables [Source: Wikipedia].

2 An Internet service provider (ISP) is an organization that provides services accessing and using the Internet. Internet service providers may be organized in various forms such as commercial, community-owned, non-profit, or otherwise privately owned [Source: Wikipedia].

3 A communication method that uses electrical wiring to simultaneously carry both data and electric power. It is also known as power-line carrier, power-line digital subscriber line (PDSL), mains communication, power-line telecommunications or power-line networking (PLN) [Source: Wikipedia].

numbers. Starting in October 2008, customers in Romania are able to switch from one provider to another and keep their phone number.

Romtelecom also faces growing competition in the carrier services market, where companies such as Telecomunicatii CFR, Teletrans, Radiocom and RCS&RDS having made significant investments in infrastructure.

The main players in the mobile telephony market are Orange and Vodafone (both among the most profitable operators in Europe), followed by Cosmote and Zapp (now belonging to the Saudi Oger group). The total number of customers was 27.2 million in 2008, up from 22.9 million the previous year. The figures include prepaid services, which do not require a subscription contract. Many Romanians own more than one mobile line in order to minimize the cost of calling friends and family who have subscriptions to different providers.

SMS and MMS have become one of the most popular forms of communication. On average, a Romanian mobile-phone user sends one message every two days. These types of messages have also become an important advertising support.

For a while, Zapp had been the leading provider of mobile data and Internet services. However, especially after acquiring 3G licenses, giants Orange and Vodafone moved to offer comprehensive wireless packages.

RCS & RDS is a new player on the market, having launched its 3G voice service in 2007. The company is at present the only one offering the 4 Play package (TV, Internet, fixed telephony and mobile telephony). Its mobile phone brand, DigiMobil, has reached 1.2 million customers in the third quarter of 2008.

Romtelecom entered the mobile market in 2008 (although its sister company Cosmote was already a player). It is now building up its CDMA[1] network, which will allow it to offer not only mobile telephony but also push-to-talk and mobile internet services. Its mobile communication services are already available in a small area in Western Romania. The company said it would focus on mobile Internet services.

The mobile Internet growth has prompted many publishers to launch

---

1 It is an abbreviation of Code Division Multiple Access, which is a channel access method used by various radio communication technologies.

mobile versions of their publications. Hotspots[1] have also grown, from 760 in 2007, to 950 in December 2008, according to the Media Factbook 2009. However, most of them are located in the capital, Bucharest.

In March 2009, Romania was ranked among the top 10 countries in Europe (on 10th place) for the number of Internet users, with 7.4 million users, according to InternetWorldStats.com. However, in terms of Internet penetration, Romania was among the last countries on the continent, with 33.4%.

Much of this is due to the digital divide between cities and rural areas, where almost half of the country's population lives. In the market of Internet and data service providers, the competition is stiff. There were 1,200 active ISPs by the end of the third quarter of 2008 according to Roland Berger Strategy Consultants. With mobile operators and TV cable operators both venturing in new fields, users are targeted by attractive triple play offers — Internet, voice and cable TV from companies like UPC or RCS & RDS, or mobile telephony, fixed phones and broadband from Vodafone, Orange or Zapp.

As was the case with cable TV, the growth of high-speed Internet connection has been somewhat helped by communist-style urban planning. In the architecture of the big cities, entire neighbourhoods are occupied by apartment buildings several stories high, placed in close proximity, which makes it very easy to wire a big number of households with relatively low costs and effort. This is how a plethora of small companies started to offer cable services in the early 1990s before being swallowed by bigger and bigger players. A similar process has taken place with Internet connections. Families started to get Internet via the coaxial cable initially installed for TV, but also through UTP[2]/FTP[3] "neighbourhood networks", which have in turn started to become part of

---

1 A wireless network access point or area

2 A popular type of cable that consists of two unshielded wires twisted around each other. Due to its low cost, UTP cabling is used extensively for local-area networks (LANs) and telephone connections [https://www.webopedia.com/TERM/U/UTP.html].

3 FTP is an abbreviation of File Transfer Protocol, which is a standard network protocol used to transfer files between clients and servers over the Internet after logging in to an FTP server or using anonymous FTP [searchenterprisewan.techtarget.com › WAN protocols › Internet applications].

Chapter 8 Transportation and Communications

larger and larger networks.

These networks offer high-speed Internet, and have contributed to a high rate of piracy. For example, users are able to download movies through software like DC++ and torrents sites in a matter of minutes.

According to figures from the Roland Berger report on the telecoms industry, 3,730 of the total number of 6,300 Internet connections recorded in 2008 were broadband. Broadband connections first became more numerous than narrowband connections in 2006.

Digital Media

A few media companies have activities only in the new media segment. Internet Corp and iMedia are two examples. Both companies have successful sites dedicated to news, leisure, women's interests, the auto market etc. Most of the big players in the traditional media segment have also recently created special departments or companies dedicated to online and digital media.

Social media websites seem to be the most popular among Romanian Internet users. According to some estimates, social networking site by the name of Hi5.com has more than three million users in Romania while Facebook had almost 400,000 in October 2009. Trilulilu.ro, a video-sharing site modelled after YouTube, is also at the top with more than 2.2 million unique visitors in September 2009. Softpedia.com, an international website belonging to Romanian company SoftNews Net, attracted 2.1 million users from Romania on its forum in the same month. Another popular website is ejobs.ro.

Blogs have become one of the most popular means of expression in the past few years. However, very few of them attract significant audiences of at least thousands of users. According to a study published in September 2009, the impact of blogs is quite small, especially when compared to news sites. Most Internet users cannot name famous bloggers, and when they do, they usually give the names of TV stars who have also opened their own blogs.

The online medium has started to receive more attention from publishers around 2005 when advertising figures for the Internet and for mobiles began to grow. In 2008, the online advertising revenue was still only 3% of the total money invested in advertising, but it made for a 70% growth compared to the previous year according to the Media Factbook. Close to 16 million euro went into Internet advertising in 2008, compared to under nine million in 2007. Initiative estimates that online ad spend will have decreased 15%–20% in 2009, although the sector proved to be the least affected by the economic crisis.

Chapter 9
Education

Education in Romania is based on a free-tuition, egalitarian system. Access to free education is guaranteed by Article 32 in the Constitution of Romania. Education is regulated and enforced by the Ministry of National Education[1]. Each step has its own form of organization and is subject to different laws and directives. Since 1989, the Romanian educational system

---

[1] Political responsibility for the education system is in the hands of the Ministry of Education, whose name has changed regularly over the course of time. In the 1980s, the ministry was called the Ministry of Education and Training (Ministerul Educatiei si Invatamintului); in the 1990s, the Ministry of Education and Science (Ministerul Invatamintului si Stiintei), subsequently the Ministry of Education (Ministerul Invatamantului), then the Ministry of National Education (Ministerul Educatiei Nationale), the Ministry of Education, Research and Youth (Ministerul Educatiei, Cercetarii si Tineretului) and the Ministry of Education, Research and Innovation (Ministerul Educatiei, Cercetarii și Inovării), the Ministry of Education, Research, Youth and Sports (Ministerul Educatiei, Cercetarii, Tineretului și Sportului). Since December 2012, it has been called the Ministry of National Education.

has been through several reforms.

Kindergarten is optional under the age of six. Compulsory schooling usually starts at age 6, which is mandatory in order to enter the first grade. Schooling is compulsory until the 10th grade (which corresponds with the age of sixteen or seventeen). The school educational cycle ends in the 12th grade when students graduate the baccalaureate. Higher education is aligned with the European Higher Education Area. In addition to the formal system of education, to which was recently added the equivalent private system, there is also a system of tutoring, semi-legal and informal.

Romania ranks 5th in the all-time medal count at the International Mathematical Olympiad with 316 total medals, dating back to 1959. Romania has achieved the highest team score in the competition after China and Russia and right after the United States and Hungary.[1]

General Development[2]

After the fall of Nicolae Ceausescu in 1989, Romania became a parliamentary republic which entered a transition period whose goals included the realization of a free market economy and educational reforms.

In the 1990s, the education system was reformed and many educational laws were created. First of all, in 1990 there was the Interim Education Decree, a transitional law that set the period of compulsory education at seven years, once again allowed the existence of private institutions and urged a new accreditation system. In 1993, the Law on the Accreditation of Higher Education Institutions and the Recognition of Diploma was passed, followed by the Law on, including amendments that were implemented during this period. In 2004, a law (the Lege nr. 288/2004 Privind Organizarea Studiilor Universitare) was passed to reform

---

1 https://en.wikipedia.org/wiki/Education_in_Romania
2 https://www.epnuffic.nl/en/publications/find-a.../education-system-romania.pdf

higher education and adapted it to the Bologna Process[1] by dividing it into the three stages of Bachelor, Master and Doctor.

Romania has a unitary system of higher education, in which the same institution can provide both academic and professional programs. In March 2011, the Romanian Minister of Education, Research, Youth and Sports has announced a radical reform in higher education. The European University Association (EUA) has been asked to assist in this matter. The reform, which will affect the whole higher education field, implies that all universities will be categorized in three categories: A. research-intensive; B. teaching and research-oriented; C. mainly teaching institutions. During the first phase, all higher education institutions will be asked to self-evaluate and to propose the category they feel they should be placed in.

The official language of education is Romanian, although programs are also provided in Hungarian and German (for small minorities that speak these languages), and sometimes also in French and English.

Since 2003, compulsory education has been set at ten years (Forms I-X), for pupils up to 18 years of age. Compulsory education is free. Senior secondary and higher education are subsidized by public funding, although some institutions are able to pass on some costs to students such as examination or school fees. The academic year runs from September/October until June, covers 34 to 36 weeks and is divided into semesters of 17 to 18 weeks.

Early Childhood Education and Care[2]

In recent years, Early Childhood Education and Care (ECEC) received an

---

[1] A series of ministerial meetings and agreements between European countries to ensure comparability in the standards and quality of higher-education qualifications. The process has created the European Higher Education Area under the Lisbon Recognition Convention [Source: Wikipedia].

[2] http://www.europarl.europa.eu/RegData/etudes/etudes/join/2013/495867/IPOL-CULT_ET(2013)495867(ANN01)_EN.pdf

elevated attention from the Romanian Government. In 2011, a comprehensive legislation one gave the system a new shape, introducing measures that aim to promote and revitalize the national educational mechanism.

Structure of National ECEC Services

The early education of children not reaching the compulsory school age (that is, six/seven-years-old) is structured in a two-tiers manner: the period between zero and three years is known as the ante-preschool level (Romanian: nivelul antepreşcolar); while the period between 3 and 6 years is the pre-school phase (Romanian: învăţământul preşcolar).

The ante-preschool level focuses on the care of children from birth to the age of three years. Generally, new-born children are taken care of by their parents during the maternal leave (on average, 63 business days). After the termination of this period, children are taken care of in centres. Ante-preschool care is governed by Law 236 of 19 July 2007 which defines centres as units that offer specialized social services for the growth, care and early education of children until the age of three.

The pre-school phase is further divided into three levels, depending on the age of the children: lower group (three-four years), middle group (four-five years), and higher group (five-six years). Each group comprises of an average of 15 children.

ECEC Institutions

The Romanian ECEC system envisages three institutions that engage in the provision of early education: day care centres (Romanian: crèches), kindergarten (Romanian: grădiniţă) as well as daycare centres. The ante-preschool phase can be carried out in all three institutions while the pre-school phase is organized in kindergartens.

Day care centres are units of care for children between birth and three-years-old. In practice, children are brought to day care centres only at the age of three-months since that is the end of the average maternal leave for their parents. The main role of day care centres is to take care of the children by means of providing adequate food, medical and hygienic care, taking into consideration potential unique condition of each child. Education is not the focal role of day care centres per se. This is evidenced also by the care-takers there, who usually are medical and there professionals and seldom educators.

The kindergartens can operate with three different types of program: normal (on average: four hours/day), prolonged (on average: 11 hours/day) and weekly. Kindergartens are established by the county school inspectorates. Institutions providing ante-preschool and pre-school services must be established in accordance with the standards set out by the Ministry of National Education. Requests for establishment should be filed locally at the local administrative bodies. The official operating language in the pre-school institutions is Romanian, but other minority languages may also be used.

The children attending the ECEC facilities are supervised by educators or childcarers. Each children group in kindergartens has at least one educator, but in case of prolonged or weekly programs, multiple (usually two) educators engage with the children on a shifting basis.

The 2011 Law on National Education also introduced the so-called "preparatory class" (Romanian: clasa pregătitoare) which is a transitional year between kindergartens and primary school. The preparatory class is meant to serve as a hybrid program that is built on elements of kindergartens (e.g., games and tales) while familiarizing the child with the structure and working procedure of schools (schedules, structure, and so on).

Relevant Authorities

The Ministry of National Education is the key authority in the structuring and functioning of the ECEC services. Along with the Ministry, the local administrative authorities and inspectorates (organized locally) also play an important role as they are responsible for assuring the conditions necessary for the provision of ECEC services. The local authorities and inspectorates are also responsible for the hiring of educational staff in the various ECEC institutions. Payment of salaries is also done by the local authorities from a State budget allocated by the Government. Furthermore, the Ministry is also engaged with the coordination and monitoring of the national education system (including all forms of early childhood education and care) as well as setting the objectives of the separate levels of educational phases.

The local or municipal school inspectorates (in Romanian: Inspectoratul Școlar Județean/Municipal) operate with the function to oversee and supervise the operation of the educational institutions (both public and private) and their activities. The local school inspectorates are headed by an inspector general, and comprise of a managing board and an advisory council. The advisory council incorporates various actors such as directors of educational units, prominent teaching staff and representatives of parents and religious communities.

The local county administrations also play a crucial role in education. The local city hall is responsible, in cooperation with the local school inspectorates, for the establishment of ante-preschool and pre-school facilities. Its responsibility lies in the financial support and infrastructural coordination needed for these facilities.

Funding

Funding is made a State obligation under Article 104(1)-(2) of the Law on National Education of 2011. This provision provides that the basic financing relating to a number of expenses (e.g., salaries, educational materials and maintenance) must be allocated from the State budget. The local administrative body (generally, the city hall of the municipality) will be responsible for the distributing of the State budget accorded for the educational institutions.

On a yearly basis, a Government degree outlines the methodology and the structure in which the financing is conducted as well as the budget according to the local administrative bodies. The accordance of the budget is made on the basis of a standard cost per pre-school pupil. This standard cost is a result of a complex calculation involving numerous factors such as the capacity of the pre-school institute, whether it is situated in a rural or an urban environment, as well as anticipated costs. Government Decree 72 of 27 February 2013 sets out the current standard cost, which for the academic year of 2013 is set to €548 per child. Based on a similar structure, the ante-preschool education is financed through a State budget as well as other income sources such as parental contributions, donations or through sponsors.

One of the main developments introduced by the 2011 Law on National Education was the approval of a so-called "social coupon". The purpose of this social coupon is to provide governmental support for early childhood education and is accorded on the basis of family income.

Primary Education[1]

In 2001/2002, approximately 47.5% of Romanian population aged 29 or under were in education. At the beginning of the school year 2002/2003, 2,171,147 young people (representing 93.6% of the compulsory education age group) were enrolled in compulsory education. The official language of instruction is Romanian but, for all levels, teaching is also given in the language of linguistic minorities (Hungarian, German, Serbian, Ukrainian, Czech, Croatian, Turkish, Romanes).

In the 2004-2005 school year, 54% of the primary education units and 20% of the secondary education units were in the multi-grade situation. At the same year level, 177,560 pupils learning in multi-grade classes were enrolled in grades I-IV and 24,117 in grades V-VIII. In most of the multi-grade schools, teaching language is Romanian, but in 733 schools are using Hungarian in the teaching-learning process, 16 schools use German and 28 other languages (Slovak, Serbian, Romanes). The geographical distribution of these schools corresponds

---

1 http://scholarworks.umass.edu/anthro_res_rpt24/

to the areas where the population of Hungarian or German nationality is important (particularly in the counties from centre and west parts of Romania).

Regulations

Textbooks for public primary education are provided free of charge. Children who were seven years old by the beginning of the school year 2002/2003 were enrolled in the first grade of primary education by the local educational authorities. However, upon the written request of the parents or legally appointed guardians, children that were seven years old by the end of the year 2003 could also be enrolled in the first grade of primary education if their general development was consistent with the general requirements. Starting with the school year 2003/2004, the school entry age was lowered to six and consequently the Education Law (Law 84/1995) now stipulates that children who are six years old by the beginning of the school year are enrolled in the first grade of primary education by the local educational authorities.

Upon the written request of the parents or legally appointed guardians, children that are six years old by the end of the year can also be enrolled in the first grade of primary education if their general development is consistent with the general requirements. Public primary schools are established by the County School Inspectorates with the agreement of the Ministry of National Education and are financed from the state budget and the local budgets (county—for special education only, town, and commune). Economic agents, individuals and entities with legal personality can also establish primary schools with the agreement of the County School Inspectorates and according to the provisions of the law. Public primary education is organized in independent units (primary schools) or within schools covering all grades from I to VIII, which was the compulsory education sequence until the school year 2003/2004.

In rural areas, independent public primary schools are organized mostly in the villages where the number of pupils is too low to organize grades from V to VIII. In these cases, schooling of the pupils after primary education is ensured in the commune that has the village in its jurisdiction. Transition from primary to gimnaziu is only conditioned by the completion of the first four grades. The number of places offered in the 5th grade is overall at least at the level of 4th-grade graduates in each locality or in neighbouring localities in the rural areas. Children in primary education benefit of free medical and psychological assistance in schools' or other public medical and psychological units.

During the pre-primary and primary education, children can be re-oriented to or from the special education. The teachers and the school psychologist working with the children make the proposition and the commissions of experts make the decision, subject to the agreement of the parents or legally appointed guardian. The Ministry of National Education can approve the organization of courses for individuals older than 14 that did not complete primary education ("second chance" education). As a general rule, compulsory education (including primary education) is organized in day-classes. However, for individuals exceeding with more than two years the normal age of the grade, education within the compulsory sequence can be provided in other forms—evening classes, part-time education, distance learning—according to the rules established by the Ministry of National Education.

Geographical Accessibility

In general, the territorial distribution of schools providing primary education meets the population needs. In urban areas, most residential districts have at least one public school providing primary education, many of them within walking distance from the pupils' homes. If parents wish to enrol their child to a different school that the one existing in the neighbourhood, it is their responsibility to ensure transportation of the child. Multi-grade education is a reality based on economic and geographic necessity and is specific to rural areas. Multi-grade schools activity is very often associated with education activities organized in shifts. In the rural area, the primary schools' network is well developed. For instance, in any village there is at least one school providing primary education.

In some cases, owing to the geographical conditions (villages in the mountains and in the Danube Delta), distance between pupils' houses and the schools can be rather long. The Ministry of National Education provides transportation means (minivans) mostly for pupils that are attending gimnaziu education in zone-centre schools — local public administration authorities (commune) covering for the transportation costs.

In addition to the central-level measures, it has been reported that local public administration authorities, in some cases with the support of individuals, NGOs, charity foundations, etc., are currently ensuring in some areas transportation of the pupils attending primary education. However, in order to improve school attendance and enrolment ratios in primary education in the rural areas, further efforts are required towards supporting school transportation, mostly from the part of local public administration authorities, as reinforced by the Education Law (Law 84/1995).

Teaching Methods and Materials

Although the multi-grade situations exist, no corresponding multi-grade teaching methodology exits. The teaching methods used in the single-grade teaching are more or less applied in the multi-grade situation. However, an effective multi-grade teaching methodology would be necessarily entirely different, more complex and more effective than the single grade teaching methodology since the later ignores student variations. The teaching methods applied in primary education are chosen so as to meet the finalities of the educational level, the frame and reference objectives of every subject. The teacher is fully responsible for choosing the methods, taking the structure of the class into consideration, the teaching aids available in the school and following the methodological guidelines provided by the National Curriculum and the teachers' guides for each subject. For most of the subjects, a given class works with the same teacher all the way through primary education; foreign languages, religion and, in some cases, music and physical education are taught by other teachers.

During a given lesson, class management is entirely the responsibility of the teacher. In consequence, teachers can decide per se to organize the activities with all the pupils, in smaller groups or individually—depending on the specific objectives of the lesson and the level of the pupils. Separated group teaching-learning activities, with groups comprising at least ten pupils, can only be organized either within the school-based curriculum or within extracurricular activities. Individualized teaching-learning activities can be organized only during after-school activities and parents usually support the necessary costs.

Printed teaching aids can be acquired by the schools' libraries or recommended by the teacher and acquired by the pupils. Teaching through ICT[1] is rather at a low level due to lack of both hardware and trained human resources. Pre-primary education teachers and primary education teachers are trained in pedagogical high school (upper secondary education). Primary education teachers specialized in a subject like foreign languages, music and sports are trained in university colleges (short-term education), providing courses which last two years (for graduates of pedagogical high schools) or three years (for graduates of other high schools). Lower and upper secondary school teachers are trained in long-term higher education, four to five years, depending on the subject they will teach. Higher education teachers must hold a graduation diploma of long-term higher education as well as a diploma of doctoral studies.

---

1 An another/extensional term for information technology (IT) which stresses the role of unified communications and the integration of telecommunications (telephone lines and wireless signals), computers as well as necessary enterprise software, middleware, storage, and audio-visual systems, which enable users to access, store, transmit, and manipulate information [Source: Wikipedia].

| 罗马尼亚概况 | *Survey of Romania* |

Secondary Education[1]

Secondary education in Romania is made up of secondary schools, which house students from the 5th through the 8th grade, and high schools that educate students from the 9th form through the 12th grade. In each level of education, students graduate or pass with the passing of an "ability" or "leaving" examination. The first form of secondary school is lower secondary school and it is compulsory. Upper secondary school is not compulsory.

Lower Secondary School

The secondary school is typically found in schools that run through the 8th form or the 12th grade (The Educational System in Romania 2001). The ability examination for secondary schools is formed from a methodology produced by the Ministry of National Education. Students are assessed regularly in their classrooms by examination. At the end of the 8th grade, students are given an ability exam. Students are tested in Romanian language and literature, mathematics, Romanian history and Romanian geography. Students that do not pass the ability exam do not continue their studies in high school, but they can be given a grades certificate upon request. 8th grade graduates or vocational school graduates who earn an ability certificate can sign up to continue their education in high school.

High School

Entry into high school requires passing an admissions exam. High school education is offered from the 9th to 12th gradess during day school or from the 9th through 13th grades in night school or distance education (The Educational

---

1 http://education.stateuniversity.com/pages/1258/Romania-SECONDARY-EDUCATION.html

System in Romania 2001). There is an age limit of 16 for students who enter day school, but the night high school is open to any student who graduates the 8th grade. Restrictions are tighter for "normal schools" and theological seminaries that require an age limit of 16, a test average of seven points or higher on the ability exam, and a record of good behavior. Romanians who have studied abroad can take the high school admissions exam after they pass the "difference exams" offered and established by the Ministry of National Education.

There are three primary options for upper secondary schooling (Romanian Educational System 2000). The first is an academic option that consists of lyceu (four-year or five-year high schools). The second option is vocational school (scoala professional), that consists of two-year, three-year, or four-year options. Finally, there are apprentice schools that have one-year, two-year, or three-year programs. These schools are all typically taught in Romanian, but national minorities may form schools that teach in their own language (e.g., German or Hungarian).

Public secondary school tuition is free and so are the textbooks (Romanian Educational System, 2000). As of 1999, there were almost 1,300 high schools, of which most were public. There has been an increase in recent years in the number of private schools since the fall of Ceausescu.

High school curricula are generally focused in three areas, but this may vary by the type of upper secondary school. These orientations are: A. theoretical training (e.g., hard sciences and humanities); B. technological training (e.g., technical, services, and natural resources and environment); C. aptitude based (e.g., sports, artistic, military and theological).

Upper secondary school is based primarily on examination, but access to education at this level is an important consideration of government. Access is considered fairly tough for rural students. In the 1998/1999 school year, of the total number of 1,315 upper secondary institutions, 84.5% were located in urban areas, and about 93.7% of the total number of pupils were enrolled in these institutions.

The education participation rates in upper secondary schools of the average 15- to 19-years-old, are about 65%. One of the reasons for such low participation rates is the presence of admission exams. An additional reason may be the lack of such schools in rural areas.

Admission exams are required for entry into high school and also determine the type of high school which a student can enter. It's a written exam and covers Romanian language and literature (for all applicants), maternal language and literature (for national minority applicants), and mathematics (for all applicants). Those who wish to enter bilingual or special schools such as sports, marine studies, forestry, technical drawing for decorating, normal schools, and orthodox seminaries must pass special tests. These special tests are taken before the general admissions exams. If rejected by a low score on a special test, a student may still take the admissions exam to enter other high schools.

Upon passing the admissions exam or special exams, students may attend a wide variety of high schools. Two important types of high schools are theoretical high schools with concentrations on the sciences or humanities, and industrial schools, which prepare students in engineering and other industrial work. Other high schools include agricultural, forestry, economics, informatics, metallurgical, normal, arts, sports, military, the High School of the Ministry of Internal Affairs, and orthodox theological seminaries.

In order to graduate from high school, a student must pass a series of "leaving" exams. In all high schools, a student must pass the written exam and colloquy in Romanian language and literature. After graduation, a student can apply for work according to their education or can continue their education at the post-high school or higher educational level.

Post-high school education is more specialized and is organized by the Ministry of National Education. These schools are created by the initiative of the Ministry or upon the request of companies or other institutions. Admission to post-high schools consists of an admission exam, which can be taken whether a student is a high school graduate or not. The only exception is admission to medical school, which requires passage of the high school leaving exam. Post-high school is typically one to three years in length and is completed by passing a leaving exam. The exam can usually be taken two more times within three years of the last courses.

Postsecondary schools are divided into two types: post-high schools and foreman schools. Each type provides advanced training for an educated, vocational workforce. Foreman schools are more like "on the job" training for jobs in industry and technology. The post-high schools provide more specialized training in technological work as well as non-technological careers. Post-high school provides education in technics and services such as environmental and resource jobs, assistants in administration and personnel for banks.

Special Education

Special education exists for children with deficiencies and disabilities in order to prepare and integrate them into society. There is a special education network that exists at all levels of schools including preprimary, primary, lower secondary, upper secondary and postsecondary schools.

The program's goal is for public school attendance of every child with learning or development problems along with "making available the necessary psychopedagogical and specialized assistance". The program is aimed at integrating children into society. The program works to make communities aware of special education students so that they can be placed. In the 1999/2000 school year, eight counties were included in the integration program and in 2000/2001 the program was to be operational throughout Romania. The Ministry of National Education is cooperating in this program with UNICEF[1].

Higher Education[2]

In Romania higher education is provided by universities, institutes, study academies, schools of higher education, and other similar establishments,

---

1 A United Nations (UN) program headquartered in New York City that provides humanitarian and developmental assistance to children and mothers in developing countries. It is a member of the United Nations Development Group (Source: Wikipedia)

2 https://www.k12academics.com/Higher%20Education%20Worldwide/higher-education-romania

collectively referred to as higher education institutions (HEIs) or universities. HEIs can be state-owned or private; they are non-profit, apolitical in nature and focused on the public interest. Romania has a central government office that authorizes and approves educational institutions. The Ministry of National Education of Romania is the national institution to which all higher education institutions look for guidance and report to. There are 56 accredited public institutions, and 41 private ones (as of 2016). Universities are divided into three tiers: A. Universities focusing on education; B. Universities focusing on education and scientific research, and universities focusing on education and art; C. Universities with an advanced research and education focus.

Based on this classification, the Ministry of National Education of Romania has published a detailed ranking of Romanian universities. Some of the most prominent Romanian universities are also the oldest modern Romanian universities: University of Iași (Alexandru Ioan Cuza University) (1860), University of Bucharest (1864), University of Cluj (Babeș-Bolyai University) (1919).

Romania follows the Bologna scheme and most of its tertiary level programs are made of three cycles: a three-year bachelor's degree, followed by a two-year master's degree, and a three-year doctor's degree. However, some programs take longer to complete, for example those in engineering fields (four-year programs), or some bachelor's and master's degree are combined into a unique six-year programs (medicine, and architecture). Master's programs are a prerequisite for admission to PhD programs. Vocational education is handled by post-secondary schools with programs lasting two years.

The entire system is based on the European Credit Transfer and Accumulation System (ECTS). Since multiple-major programs are not available at Romanian universities, a student wishing to specialize in several areas of study is allowed to simultaneously attend several universities as a full-time student. Accreditation and diploma certification is in the hands of the National Center for Diploma Certification and Equivalency, and ARACIS, the Romanian Agency for Quality Assurance in Higher Education, both coordinated by the Ministry of

National Education of Romania.

In 2016, 531,586 students were enrolled in Romanian's 97 universities, in all three cycles, of which 464,642 were in public institutions. 76.3% of the students were enrolled in the first cycle (bachelor level), 20.1% in the second cycle (master level) and 3.6% in the third cycle (doctoral studies).

Romanian universities have historically been classified among the best in Eastern Europe and have attracted international students, especially in the fields of medicine and technology. Foreign students accounted for 27,510 (5.1% of enrollment, as of 2016).

Universities have full autonomy, in stark contrast from the pre-university segment. Each university is free to decide everything from their management to the organization of classes. Furthermore, many universities devolve this autonomy further down, to each department.

The Ministry of National Education of Romania established the National Authority for Scientific Research (Authoritatea Națională pentru Cercetare Științifică). This agency emerged from specific requirements designed to promote the development of a knowledge-based society. As in the other Eastern European countries, the Romanian higher education system has witnessed major transformations after 1990, in order to adapt its national educational framework to the European Union.

Admission

The admission process is left to the Universities, and, as of 2007, there is no integrated admission scheme. Some universities will give an "admission exam" in a high-school subject that corresponds best to the training offered by the university. Others, however, due to the lack of relevance of the system have begun implementing a different scheme, based on essays, interviews and performance assessments. This was done because in most cases tests, especially multiple choice ones, offered just a superficial assessment and a limited outlook of the students' actual performance.

International Programs[1]

Romanian Ministry of National Education, through the Public, Cultural and Scientific Diplomacy Directorate, cooperates with the Romanian Ministry of Foreign Affairs to facilitate educational exchanges and ensure foreign citizens the possibility to study in Romania. Foreign citizens can study in Romania on their own expenses at Romanian state universities or private Romanian universities in Romanian, with a supplementary preparatory year for learning the language (if the candidate does not speak Romanian already), or in foreign languages (if the respective university offers this option. Foreign citizens can also study in Romania on scholarships offered by the Romanian state on bilateral programs. The scholarships are offered by the Romanian state in keeping with bilateral treaties in force or with unilateral offers made by Romania to other states. They are managed by the Ministry of National Education, through the General Department for International and European Relations, based on proposals from the relevant authorities of the candidate's country of origin.

Cooperation between Romania and China in Educational Field[2]

The education departments of China and Romania have signed a series of agreements on educational cooperation over a long period of time, and the major agreements are those concerning the exchanges of educational delegations, students, teachers and experiences, and the direct cooperation between institutions of higher learning. In April 1998, the education ministries of the two countries signed the agreement on educational exchanges and cooperation for the period from 1998 to 2001. In pursuance of the agreement, each side at present provides the other with 22 scholarships. In July 1995, the Chinese State Education Commission and the Romanian Ministry of Education signed the agreement on the mutual recognition of record of schooling, diplomas and

---

1 https://www.mae.ro/en/node/2176
2 http://www.chinaembassy.org.ro/rom/zlgx/t66052.htm

certificates of higher education. From 1952-1999, China accepted 239 Romanian students in all.

With the bilateral relations between Romania and China deepened over the years, and the introduction of "Belt and Road" Initiative, the enthusiasm of learning Chinese and understanding China has increased in Romania[1]. In 2013, the Ministry of National Education of Romania approved the application by the Confucius Institute at the University of Bucharest and officially issued the confirmation to incorporate Chinese language into the latest list of foreign language courses in primary and secondary schools. This marks the official status of Chinese language in Romania's national education system and a new milestone in the development of Chinese language teaching in primary and secondary schools in the country.

Attaching great significance to Chinese teaching at basic education institutions, the Confucius Institutes in Romania have established a number of Chinese teaching sites in primary and secondary schools. With the hope to stimulate students' passion for Chinese learning and standardize Chinese language teaching, the Confucius Institutes launched the application to incorporate Chinese language as a course in primary and secondary schools.

It is reported that the Confucius Institute at the University of Bucharest has also planned to apply to the Ministry of National Education of Romania to accept HSK[2] grades into local high school and college entrance exams and achieve the integration between Chinese learning and exams and enrollment, which will be conducive to stimulating students' learning enthusiasm and promoting the learning and popularization of the Chinese language through institutional construction[3].

In the year of 2017, "Chinese Ambassador Scholarship" was launched at the Chinese Embassy in Romania whose main goal is to encourage Romanian

---

1 http://english.hanban.org/article/2016-06/29/content_649225.htm

2 HSK (Hanyu Shuiping Kaoshi) or the Chinese Proficiency Test is an international standardized exam which tests and rates Chinese language proficiency. It assesses non-native Chinese speakers' abilities in using the Chinese language in their daily, academic and professional lives.

3 http://english.hanban.org/article/2016-06/29/content_649225.htm

students to learn Chinese and to warmly welcome as many young people as possible to join the Chinese Language connoisseurs and to become successors and heirs of the friendship between China and Romania. The establishment of the Chinese Ambassador Scholarship fully demonstrates the importance attached by the Chinese Embassy to the Chinese teaching, as well as the strong support of Chinese enterprises and Chinese business associations in Romania for the Chinese teaching. Nowadays, Chinese learning enjoys great popularity in Romania, where over 8,000 people are studying Chinese in four Confucius institutes, eight Confucius classrooms and over 100 Chinese teaching points. Chinese learning opens a door for Romanians who study it to a wider world and they will strive to be the messengers of friendship between the two countries.

Besides establishing Confucius Institutes in Romania, the educational cooperation between China and Romina can be witnessed in other aspects. For example, The ECUST Sibiu Sino-European International Business School, jointly established by East China University of Science and Technology (ECUST) and Lucian Blaga University of Sibiu, was unveiled on 23 October 2018 in Sibiu, a city in central Romania, which is the first business school jointly established by China and Romania. ECUST will cooperate in running the new business school based on the concept of mutual cooperation, joint construction and consensus building. It is believed that the newly established business school will provide Romanian students with a platform to understand Chinese business culture, and strengthen exchanges between the two countries in higher education and culture[1].

---

1 http://www.china-ceec.org/eng/sbhz_1/t1606290.htm

Chapter 10
Religion

All persons in Romania have the right to belong to or adopt a religion, to manifest this individually or collectively, in public or private, by specific practices and rituals, including religious education, and the freedom to keep or change their faith. All persons have the right to be part of a religious community (religion or religious association) that is a legal entity or one that is not (religious group).

The Romanian state treats recognized religions as legal private or public entities. They are equal before the law and public authorities, organizing themselves and functioning autonomously, according to their own statutes, canonical code and regulations, abiding by the Constitution and the laws of the country. The Romanian state affirms its neutrality in terms of religions/faiths, in the sense that it does not favour one over another, but has a relationship of cooperation and social partnership with the recognized religions/faiths. Religious associations do not automatically receive the public utility status but may enjoy certain facilities or tax exemptions[1].

---

1 M. L. Ricketts, *The History of Religions in Romania* [in *Religion* (2002), 32(1), PP.71-85].

| 罗马尼亚概况 | Survey of Romania |

PICTURE: Metropolitan Cathedral in Lasi
SOURCE: https://book.lufthansa.com/lh/dyn/air-lh/revenue/viewFlights

Romanian Orthodox Church[1]

Although Byzantine Rite Christianity[2] has a bimillenial tradition and history in the Romanian space, developing according to canonical obedience

---

1 http://www.culte.gov.ro/library/files/noutati/state_and_religions_in_romania_(2015).pdf

2 An autocephalous Orthodox Church in full communion with other Eastern Orthodox Christian Churches and ranked seventh in order of precedence. Since 1925, the Church's Primate bears the title of Patriarch. Its jurisdiction covers the territories of Romania and Moldova, with additional dioceses for Romanians living in nearby Serbia and Hungary, as well as for diaspora communities in Central and Western Europe, North America and Oceania. Currently it is the only self-governing Church within Orthodoxy to have a Romance language for its principal and native tongue. The majority of Romania's population (16,367,267, or 85.9% of those for whom data were available according to the 2011 census data), as well as some 720,000 Moldovans, belong to the Romanian Orthodox Church. The Romanian Orthodox Church is the second-largest in size behind the Russian Orthodox Church [Source: Wikipedia].

to the Ecumenical Patriarchy of Constantinople[1], the Romanian Orthodox Church was institutionally consecrated with the establishment of the Holy Synod[2] and implicitly with the union of the Hungaro-Walachian and Moldavian Bishoprics in 1872. In subsequent years, the Romanian Orthodox Church became autocephaly (1885) and was raised to the rank of Patriarchy (1925). Since 30 September 2007, the Romanian Orthodox Church is under the guidance of Patriarch Daniel Ciobotea[3], who holds the title of Archbishop of Bucharest, Metropolitan of Muntenia and Dobrogea, Locum tenens of the throne of Caesarea Cappadociae, and Patriarch of the Romanian Orthodox Church.

The Romanian Orthodox Church is governed by the Holy Synod, presided over by the Patriarch and made up of three acting bishops. The central deliberative body of the Romanian Orthodox Church for all administrative, social, cultural, economic and patrimonial issues is the National Church Assembly, made up of three representatives of each bishopric (one clergyman and two lay persons), appointed by the bishopric assemblies for a period of four years. The central executive body of the National Church Assembly is made up of twelve members of the National Church Assembly (one clergyman and one lay person representing each bishopric in the country, appointed for a period of four years). The members of the Holy Synod may participate by deliberative

---

1 Constantinople was the capital of the Byzantine Empire and, following its fall in 1453, of the Ottoman Empire until 1930, when it was renamed Istanbul as part of Mustafa Kemal Atatürk's Turkish national reforms. Strategically located between the Golden Horn and the Sea of Marmara at the point where Europe meets Asia, Constantinople was extremely important as the successor to ancient Rome and the largest and wealthiest city in Europe throughout the Middle Ages, it was known as the "Queen of Cities" [in http://www.newworldencyclopedia.org/entry/Constantinople].

2 The Holy Synod is the ecclesiastical governing body for a church. It is presided over by a primate of a specific ecclesiastical area and consists, as members, of all the bishops to whom the primate is accountable [https://orthodoxwiki.org/Holy_Synod].

3 Born Dan Ilie Ciobot, is the Patriarchof the Romanian Orthodox Church. The elections took place on 12 September 2007. Daniel won with a majority of 95 votes out of 161. He was officially enthroned on 30 September 2007 in the Patriarchal Cathedral in Bucharest. As such, his official title is "Archbishop of Bucharest, Metropolitan of Muntenia and Dobrogea, Locum tenens of the throne of Caesarea of Cappadocia, Patriarch of Romania" [Source: Wikipedia].

vote in the meetings of the National Church Assembly and the National Church Council.

The Romanian Orthodox Church has brotherly and ecumenical ties with almost all Christian churches in the world, especially other Orthodox Churches. It has had visit exchanges and bilateral contacts at the highest level, with its sister Orthodox Churches, the Oriental Orthodox Churches, the Roman Catholic Church, the Protestant Churches in Europe, and with churches in America, Asia, and other parts of the world. Furthermore, the Romanian Orthodox Church is active as part of European and international church organizations—as a member of the World (Ecumenical) Council of Churches[1], the European Conference of Churches, and of other Christian organizations involved in different activities (youth, women, and so on)—as well as in international bilateral dialog between the Orthodox Church and other great Christian families (Oriental Orthodox, Roman-Catholic, Old Catholic, Anglican, Lutheran, Reformed, and so on).

The units that make up the Romanian Orthodox Church are: parishes, monasteries, deaneries, vicarages, diocese (archdiocese and bishoprics) and the metropolitan church.

According to data from the 2011 census in Romania, 86.45% of total population declared themselves as belonging to the Romanian Orthodox Church, most of them ethnic Romanians (96.46%), followed by ethnic Roma (2.92%), ethnic Ukrainians (0.24%), ethnic Hungarians (0.16%) and other nationalities.

Within the country's borders and as part of Romania's Patriarchate, there are 14,809 churches in operation, and organized as follows: 1 Patriarchate Center, six metropolitan churches, ten archdiocese, 13 dioceses, 1 vicar, 177 deaneries, 11,409 parishes, 2,444 branches, 541 monasteries, 192 sketes[2] and 15

---

1 A global fellowship of churches seeking unity, a common witness and Christian service. It is the broadest and most inclusive among the many organized expressions of the modern ecumenical movement, a movement whose goal is Christian unity [https://www.oikoumene.org/].

2 A monastic community in Eastern Christianity that allows relative isolation for monks, but also allows for communal services and the safety of shared resources and protection [Source: Wikipedia].

metochions[1].

The Romanian Orthodox Church (Patriarchate, diocese, vicarage, deaneries, parishes, branches, monasteries and sketes) has 14,933 priests and deacons in its service, of which 14,313 priests and deacons (in parishes, monasteries, sketes, eparchy centers and deaneries) and 505 priests (in state and private budget institutions).

A total of 12,765 priests and deacons in parishes, monasteries, sketes, eparchy centres, and deaneries receive salary assistance from the state budget, and the number of clerics receiving their salaries from own funds is 1,548.

Training of religious staff of the Romanian Orthodox Church is available in 29 secondary theological seminaries, 11 schools of theology and 4 theology departments in other universities that are part of the state university education, with some 7,851 students registered. Over 6,800 educators teach Religion in public schools.

Ukrainian Orthodox Vicarage

The Ukrainian Orthodox Vicarage in Romania is an administrative church unit with special missionary-pastoral status, and its role is that of coordinating the spiritual life of Ukrainian Orthodox believers in Romania. Canonically, the vicarage is under the jurisdiction of the Romanian Orthodox Church Patriarchate, but it is administratively self-ruling.

According to the 2011 census, there are some 40,000 Ukrainian Orthodox believers, making up 0.24% of the total Orthodox believers; these are under the ecclesiastical jurisdiction of the Ukrainian Orthodox Vicarage, grouped in two deaneries.

---

1 An ecclesiastical embassy church within Eastern Orthodox tradition. It is usually from one autocephalous or autonomous church to another. The term is also used to refer to a parish representation (or dependency) of a monastery or a patriarch [Source: Wikipedia].

Serbian Orthodox Diocese of Timişoara[1]

The Serbian Orthodox Diocese of Timisoara includes the Orthodox Serbians in Romania, who are under the canonic jurisdiction of the Serbian Orthodox Church. As such, it functions as an autonomous recognized denomination.

According to the 2011 census, there are 18,076 ethnic Serbians living in Romania, of which 94.8% are Christian Orthodox, most of these (11,112 persons) having declared that they belong to the Serbian Orthodox Diocese of Timisoara, while the rest (some 6,000 persons) stated that they belong to the Romanian Orthodox Church.

The diocese's three deaneries in Timisoara, Arad[2] and Socol[3] (Caras-Severin County) oversee 55 parishes and five monasteries served by 46 priests and deacons. Written records on the existence of the diocese's monasteries which are included in the list of historic monuments in Romania, date from as far back as the 16th-18th centuries.

Roman Catholic Church

The Catholic Church is present in Romania with its Latin (Roman Catholic

---

1 Timişoara is the capital city of Timiş County and also the main social, economic and cultural centre in western Romania. The third most populous city in the country, with 319,279 inhabitants as of the 2011 census, Timişoara is the informal capital city of the historical region of Banat [Source: Wikipedia].

2 The capital city of Arad County, historically situated in the region of Crişana, and having recently extended on the left bank of the Mureş river, in Banat region of western Romania [Source: Wikipedia)].

3 A commune in Caraş-Severin County. In 2011, the population of the commune numbered 1,873 people and its population was ethnically mixed. It is composed of five villages: Baziaş, Câmpia, Pârneaura, Socol and Zlatiţa.

Sokol means "hawk" in Serbian. The commune is officially bilingual, with both Romanian and Serbian being used as working languages on public signage and in administration, education and justice [Source: Wikipedia].

Church), Byzantine (Romanian Church United with Rome), and Armenian rite (Armenian-Catholic Ordinariate). The Catholic Church is the world community of Christian believers, united through faith and the Sacraments, under the leadership and canonic dependence of the Pope in Rome (currently His Holiness Pope Francis[1]). The Sovereign Pontiff[2] periodically appoints a Papal Ambassador as Apostolic Nuncio[3]. Archbishop Francisco-Javier Lozano is currently accredited as the Apostolic Nuncio for Romania and the Republic of Moldova.

The Episcopal Conference[4] provides the leadership for all Catholic believers in Romania, bringing together all Roman Catholic and Greek Catholic Bishops. This Romanian Episcopal Conference, in its present form, dates back to 16 March 1991. The plenary meeting of the Conference takes place twice a year (in spring and fall), with periodic extraordinary sessions. The Romanian Episcopal Conference has two sub-sections: the Latin sub-section and the Council of Greek Catholic Hierarchs. Their Presidents and Vice Presidents are elected alternatively from each of the two Religions. The current President of the Romanian Episcopal Conference is the Gracious Cardinal Lucian Mureşan, Major Archbishop of the Romanian Church United with Rome, Greek Catholic; and the Vice President is His Eminence Father Ioan Robu, Archbishop and Metropolitan Priest of Bucharest.

---

1 The 266th and current Pope of the Catholic Church, a title he holds ex officio as Bishop of Rome, and sovereign of Vatican City. He chose Francis as his papal name in honor of Saint Francis of Assisi. Francis is the first Jesuit pope, the first from the Americas, the first from the Southern Hemisphere, and the first pope from outside Europe since the Syrian Gregory III, who reigned in the 8th century [Source: Wikipedia]

2 One of the official titles of the Pope. The term "pontiff" is derived from the Latin: pontifex, which literally means "bridge builder" (pons + facere) and which designated a member of the principal college of priests in ancient Rome [Source: Wikipedia].

3 The title for an ecclesiastical diplomat, being an envoy or permanent diplomatic representative of the Holy See to a state or international organization. A nuncio is appointed by and represents the Holy See, and is the head of the diplomatic mission, called an Apostolic Nunciature, which is the equivalent of an embassy [Source: Wikipedia].

4 An episcopal conference, sometimes called conference of bishops, is an official assembly of the bishops of the Catholic Church in a given territory [Source: Wikipedia].

The Roman Catholic Church in Romania currently has 870,774 believers, according to the 2011 census, of which 500,444 (57.47%) are ethnic Hungarians, 297,246 (34.16%) ethnic Romanians, 21,324 (2.43%) ethnic Germans, 20,281 (2.33%) ethnic Roma, 9,250 (1.06%) ethnic Slovaks and the remainder other nationalities.

The Romanian Church United with Rome, Greek Catholic

The Romanian Church United with Rome, Greek Catholic, was established in Transylvania at the end of the 17th century, a union of some Romanian Orthodox Christians and the Catholic Church. The Synod of Alba Iulia[1], convoked in 1697 by the Orthodox Metropolitan Atanasie Anghel[2], accepted four principles that allowed this denomination to become part of the canonic jurisdiction of the Holy See[3]: recognition of papal primacy, the existence of purgatory, the receiving of the Eucharist with Matzos and Filioque[4] (the

---

1 A city located on the Mureş River in Alba County, Transylvania, Romania, with a population of 63,536 as of 2011. Since the High Middle Ages, the city has been the seat of Transylvania's Roman Catholic diocese. Between 1541 and 1690, it was the capital of the Eastern Hungarian Kingdom and the latter Principality of Transylvania. Alba Iulia is historically important for Romanians, Hungarians and Transylvanian Saxons [Source: Wikipedia].

2 A Romanian Greek-Catholic bishop of Alba Iulia between 1698 and 1713. He was the successor to Teophilus Seremi in the seat of Mitropoliei Bălgradului (Alba-Iulia). Through his continued efforts, he perfected the union of the Romanian Transylvanians with the Catholic Church [Source: Wikipedia].

3 Also referred to as the See of Rome, is the ecclesiastical jurisdiction of the Catholic Church in Rome, the episcopal see of the Pope, and an independent sovereign entity. It serves as the central point of reference for the Catholic Church everywhere and the focal point of communion due to its position as the pre-eminent episcopal see of the universal church. Today, it is responsible for the governance of all Catholics, organised in their Particular Churches, Patriarchates and religious institutes [Source: Wikipedia].

4 A Latin term added to the original Niceno-Constantinopolitan Creed (NCC; commonly known as the Nicene Creed), and which has been the subject of great controversy between Eastern and Western Christianity. The Latin term Filioque describes the Holy Spirit in Christianity as proceeding from both the Father and the Son (and not from the Father only). In the Nicene Creed, it is translated by the English phrase "and [from] the Son" [Source: Wikipedia].

procession of the Holy Spirit from the Father and the Son). By accepting these conditions, the Romanians United with Rome were guaranteed the following: that they may retain the Byzantine rite, that they may celebrate the Orthodox holy days, that the Synod may elect the Bishops, and that clergy and believers would have equality of rights with those of the Catholic Church. The Romanian United Church has functioned as one of the two Romanian churches in Transylvania for two centuries. With the establishment of the new regime in 1948, the Greek Catholic Church was abolished by the Romanian government, and believers were forced to convert to Orthodoxy or the Latin Catholic rite. According to this decree, all its properties were taken over by the state, except its churches and parochial houses, which were transferred to the Romanian Orthodox Church. After December 1989, one of the first measures taken by the Romanian state was officially recognizing the Romanian Church United with Rome, Greek Catholic.

The 2011 census recorded 150,593 Greek Catholic believers, representing 0.8% of the population that declared this as their religious affiliation; of these, 124,563 (82.71%) are ethnic Romanians; 16,144 (10.72%) ethnic Hungarians, 6,511 (4.32%) ethnic Roma, 1,204 (0.8%) ethnic Ukrainians and the remainder other nationalities.

The Romanian Church United with Rome, Greek Catholic has five eparchies, with 5 vicarages, 75 deaneries, 763 parishes, 540 houses of worship, some 760 priests, and over 25 monastic orders and congregations under the canonic jurisdiction of 5 archbishoprics.

Armenian Catholic Ordinariate[1]

At the end of the 17th century, the Armenians of Transylvania converted to Catholicism. An eparchy was organized with a seat in the city of Gherla[2].

---

1 A pre- or pseudo-diocesean ecclesiastical structure, of geographical and/or personal nature, headed by an ordinary who is not necessarily a bishop [Source: Wikipedia].

2 A city in Cluj County, Romania (in the historical region of Transylvania). It is located 45 km from Cluj-Napoca on the Someșul Mic River, and has a population of 20,203 [Source: Wikipedia].

The situation of the Armenian Catholics was similar to that of the Romanian Greek Catholics, namely that the Armenians accepted basic principles of Catholicism, but also retained the traditional rite and celebrated services in Armenian.

By the Concordat with the Vatican, the Armenian Catholic ecclesiastical unit was recognized on 5 June 1930 as a self-governing eparchy, directed by an Apostolic administrator (a priest with the jurisdiction of an ordinarius, or titular bishop), with its seat in Gherla. After 1948 and the abandoning of the Concordat, the Armenian Catholic eparchy's status changed, and the ordinariate entered de facto (but not de jure) under the administration of the Roman Catholic Archbishopric of Alba Iulia. Only after 1991 was the auxiliary bishop of Alba Iulia appointed as Apostolic Administrator, ad nutum Sanctae Sedis (i.e. ad interim). Thus, the Armenian Catholic Ordinariate entered a personal union with the Roman-Catholic Archbishopric of Alba Iulia. This Ordinariate presently comprises four parishes: Gherla, Gheorghieni, Dumbraveni and Frumoasa, but the Armenian Catholic believers also live in other Transylvanian cities.

Armenian Apostolic Archbishopric[1]

The Armenian Apostolic Eparchy is under the jurisdiction of the Armenian Apostolic Church, whose spiritual centre is in Etchmiadzin[2] (in Armenia), the residence of the Catholicos Patriarch of all Armenians.

The Armenians settled in the Romanian space as far back as the 11th and 12th centuries, and Prince Alexander the Good[3] established a diocese for them

---

1 The rank, office, or jurisdiction of an archbishop [Source: Wikipedia].

2 The 4th-largest city in Armenia and the most populous town of Armavir Province, located about 18 km (11 mi) west of the capital Yerevan and 10 km (6 mi) north of the closed Turkish-Armenian border [Source: Wikipedia].

3 A Prince of Moldavia, reigning between 1400 and 1432, son of Roman I Muşat. He succeeded Iuga to the throne, and, as a ruler, initiated a series of reforms while consolidating the status of the Moldavian Principality [Source: Wikipedia].

in 1401 in Suceava[1]. In the modern era, the Armenian Church was recognized by the Law on Religions in 1928, and the Law for the establishment and operation of the Armenian Eparchy was passed in 1931.

In 1949, the organic and administrative statutes of the Armenian Eparchy of Romania were approved, which mentions the fact that this denomination was under the dogmatic and canonic authority of the Catholicos Patriarch of all Armenians of Etchmiadzin, but regulates, leads and self-administers all its activities, in conformity with Romanian legislation.

The Armenian Eparchy is run by an Archbishop or Bishop, assisted by a Diocesan Vicar. The central body of the Eparchy is the Diocesan Congress, and the higher executive body is the Diocesan Council. The latter has three committees: the spiritual church committee, the cultural committee, and the economic committee. The parochial leadership bodies are the Parochial Assembly, the Parochial Council (curator) and Parochial Committees.

There are ten parishes in the Armenian Eparchy of Romania, served by four priests, three deacons, two cantors, with 16 churches and six confessional cemeteries. The most important communities are in Bucharest and Constanta[2]. The other communities on the territory of this country are made up of 12-20 families. There are two monasteries in Suceava County, registered on the list of historical monuments in Zamca and Hagigadar. During the 2011 census, 393 Armenian believers were registered in a population of 2,017 ethnic Armenians.

Russian Old-Rite Christian Church of Romania

The Russian Old-Rite Christian Church of Romania was established by

---

1 The largest city and the seat of Suceava County, in the historical region of Bukovina, north-eastern Romania. The city was the capital of the Principality of Moldavia from 1388 to 1565. Nowadays, it is a significant economic urban center of the Romanian Nord-Est development region [Source: Wikipedia].

2 The oldest continuously inhabited city in Romania. It was founded around 600 B.C. The city is located in the Dobruja region of Romania, on the Black Sea coast. It is the capital of Constanța County and the largest city in the region [Source: Wikipedia].

the Russian Old Believers in the first part of the 18th century. They refused the liturgical reforms of Patriarch Nikon of Moscow (1652–1658); as a result of state persecutions to which they were subjected by the state, part of the Old Believers took refuge in the Romanian Countries, where they formed the Old Believers (Lipovan) community. The first Old Believer (Lipovan) communities in the Romanian space were documented in the Suceava villages of Lipoveni (1724) and Manolea (1743). In 1846, the Old-Rite Metropolis of Fantana Alba was established in northern Bukovina, under the leadership of Metropolitan Ambrozie. The event marked the aggregation of Old-Rite Christian communities in an autonomous church, which included all Old-Rite believers in Europe, America and Australia. Ambrozie's successors (Kirill, Arkadi, and so on) also held the title of Metropolitans, and were recognized as spiritual leaders of all Old-Rite Christian believers in the world, a status and recognition they have to this day.

On 28 June 1940, following the occupation of northern Bukovina by the Soviet Union, the Old-Rite Christian Metropolis moved from Fantana Alba to Braila, where it is still located today, with prerogatives of spiritual leadership over all co-religionist throughout the world. Old-Rite Russian Christians follow the traditional Orthodox ordinances, celebrate services in the Slavonic language following the Pre-Nikonian liturgical practices, and follow the unrevised Julian calendar.

According to the 2011 census, the Russian Old-Rite Christian Church of Romania has some 33,000 believers, of which 17,268 (53.03%) are Russian Old Believers (Lipovans), and 13,667 (42%) Romanians, organized in 48 parishes with 69 churches, 46 priests and 10 deacons, plus 10 parishes and 9 priests for the communities outside the borders, and 4 monasteries.

The Russian Christian Orthodox Old-Rite community does not have its own organized system of theological education, and priests are chosen from among believers considered apt to celebrate religious services, familiar with the

Slavonic language, the specific aspects of the Church and its canons. As of 2003, with the support of the Romanian Orthodox Church, a class for the Russian Christian Orthodox Old-Rite students has been established in the Orthodox Theological Seminary in Iasi.

Reformed Church of Romania[1]

The Christian Reformed faith, based on the theology of Jean Calvin, arrived in Transylvania in the 16th century and was organized and institutionally recognized in 1564-1580, with the establishment of the Reformed Bishopric of Ardeal. After 1918, the Reformed parishes in Banat, Crisana and Maramures left the jurisdiction of the Hungarian Reformed Church, forming a new Diocese with its seat in Oradea. According to the 2011 census, the Reformed Church of Romania has 600,932 believers, most of which (93.78%) are ethnic Hungarian, united in two eparchies.

The denomination's governing bodies are: A. The Synod, for the whole church, with responsibilities for church legislation and doctrine; B. The General Eparchy Assembly, for each eparchy; C. The Deanery Assembly, for each deanery; D. The Parish Assembly, for each parish. The executive bodies are: A. The Ruling Council (at the eparchy level); B. The Deanery Council (at the deanery level); C. The Presbytery (at the parish level).

Reformed priests are trained (in Hungarian) at the Protestant Theological Institute in Cluj-Napoca.

Evangelical Church of Augustan Confession in Romania

The Protestant Evangelical Faith has as its foundation the theology

---

1 C. Romocea, *Church and State: Religious Nationalism and State Identification in Post-communist Romania*, London: Bloomsbury Publishing, 2011.

of Martin Luther[1], and established itself in the Romanian space with an independent church at the initiative of Johannes Honterus (1498–1549), an inhabitant of Brasov. The Medias Synod in 1572 set the Augustan (Augsburg) Confession[2] as the official doctrine of this church, adopted by the princes of the Roman-German Empire in 1530. After the annexation of Transylvania to the Hungarian Kingdom in 1867, the Protestant Evangelical Church of the Confessio Augustana, established traditionally by Saxon believers, developed significant socio-cultural activities which were however greatly hampered later during the Ceausescu regime.

Prior to 1940, the total number of Evangelical Lutheran believers was 250,000, reunited in over 250 parishes. Following the War and subsequent developments, especially the successive waves of emigration, the number of believers dropped significantly, and the 2011 census recorded 5,399 believers (of which 53.6% ethnic Germans, 27.8% ethnic Romanians and 14.4% ethnic Hungarians).

The organizational structure of the Church includes: the local church, the district church and the general church. The local church (parish) is a legal entity and is governed by a General Assembly of Representatives of church communities and a Parish Council (presbyterium). It includes five church districts (deaneries): Brasov, Medias, Sebes, Sibiu and Sighisoara. The district governing bodies are: the District Church Congress and the District Consistory. The district is led by a Deacon.

The parishes together form the general Church. The governing bodies are: the General Church Congress and the Supreme Consistory. The General Church Congress is made up of some 50 members of the Supreme Consistory, Deacons,

---

1 A German professor of theology, composer, priest, monk and a seminal figure in the Protestant Reformation. Luther came to reject several teachings and practices of the Roman Catholic Church [Source: Wikipedia].

2 The primary confession of faith of the Lutheran Church and one of the most important documents of the Lutheran Reformation. The Augsburg Confession was written in both German and Latin and was presented by a number of German rulers and free-cities at the Diet of Augsburg on 25 June 1530 [Source: Wikipedia].

and Church district curators, clerical and lay delegations. This body is able to deal with the most important issues of the Church, including the choice of Bishop, of the General Curator, and of the members of the Supreme Consistory. The Head of the General Church is the Bishop. The Supreme Consistory is made up of one Bishop, one General Church Curator, one vicar bishop, three priests (at least two of parish priest rank) and six laymen. The Supreme Consistory administers all the problems of the Church and represents it with other religions, and with the state authorities.

Evangelical Lutheran Church of Romania

The Evangelical Lutheran Church has the same doctrine and history as the Protestant Evangelical Church of Augustan Confession, but its believers are traditionally ethnic Hungarians and Slovaks. After 1918, the Hungarian and Slovak Lutheran parishes in Greater Romania formed a distinct church from that of the Saxons, which continued to this day. According to the 2011 census, the Evangelical Lutheran Church of Romania has 20,168 believers (some 62% ethnic Hungarians, 16% ethnic Germans, 12% ethnic Slovaks and some 9.8% Romanians).

The Evangelical Lutheran Church is organized on the basis of a synodal-presbyterian system, with its Head, a Bishop, elected by the General Assembly of Parishes. Its supreme representative body is the Synod, whose members with voting rights are: the Episcopal and Deanery Presidia, the Supreme General Notary, the Secondary Curator and the Legal Counsellor of the circumscription. From among the three deaneries (Brasov, Cluj-Napoca and Nadlac), a further 30 persons are appointed from among the clergy and laypersons. The Synod usually meets every three years.

Between Synod sessions, executive authority is vested with the Episcopal Presbyterate, made up of the Bishop, the First Curator-General, the Deputy

Bishop, the Internal Mission Minister, the principal Episcopal Counsellor, Deans, President of the Theological Commission, the Cathehetical Minister, the Diaconal Minister and the media officer. The Episcopal Presbyteriate usually meets annually.

The Unitarian Church of Transylvania

The Unitarian Church was established by the Transylvanian theologian Ferenc Dávid (1519–1579) and was officially recognized by the Diet of Turda edict granting religious freedom to the major Religions in Transylvania in 1568.

The organization of this Church is based on the synodal-presbyterial principle, holding that laypersons have an important role, that leadership is collective, and that church units are autonomous. The central governing bodies are: the Synod, the Supreme Consistory and the Church Consistory.

The Synod is made up, ex officio, of the Bishop, two Curators-General, and other church and lay dignitaries, as well as delegates elected from the deaneries and parishes, a total of some 250 members. The Synod meets once every three years, and has the following principal attributes: the election of the Bishop, the ordination of priests, and the amendment of the Church's Constitution.

The Supreme Consistory is made up of elected and ex officio priests and laypersons; it meets annually in Cluj and has as its principal attribute the governance of the Church. Between Supreme Consistory sessions, the operative governance is provided by the Church Consistory, which meets every three months. The Church Presidency is made up of the Bishop, the Vicar, two Curators-General and the Public Affairs Director. A General Assembly of Deaneries and a General Parochial Assembly provide governance at the deanery and parish levels.

At present, the Unitarian Church has its central seat in Cluj-Napoca, and has 57,686 ethnic Hungarian believers according to the 2011 census. Significant communities of Unitarian believers can be found in the Counties of Cluj, Braşov, Covasna, Harghita and Mureş, organized in the 6 Deaneries of Cluj Turda, Mureş, Târnava, Cristuru Secuiesc, Trei Scaune-Alba de Sus and Odorheiul Secuiesc.

The Union of Baptist Christian Churches in Romania

Baptist Christians claim the traditions of the 15th – 16th century Anabaptist movements, especially the efforts of John Smith, who founded the first Baptist Church in Amsterdam in 1609. The first Baptist Church in Romania was established in 1856 in Bucharest, and Baptist believers organized under the name of the Union of Christian Baptist Communities in 1920. At present, the Christian Baptist denomination in Romania has some 1,800 churches in all regions of the country and 700 pastors.

According to the 2011 census, there were 112,850 Baptist believers, of which 80% ethnic Romanians, 11% Hungarians, 7.8% Roma and the rest of other ethnic backgrounds.

The church's governing bodies are the General Assembly, the Church Committee and the Church Pastor, who serves as Presbyter (elder), also called a Bishop (supervisor). The Union of Christian Baptist Churches of Romania (Baptist Union) is a national representative body of the Christian Baptist denomination in Romania. The Baptist Union expresses the spiritual and doctrinal unity of Baptist believers in Romania and represents the general interests of Baptist Churches and other component parts of the Christian Baptist Church in Romania.

Christian Church of the Gospel in Romania – Union of Christian Churches of the Gospel in Romania

The institutional organization of the Christian Community of the Gospel began in Bucharest in 1899. With state recognition as a religious association in 1933, the Christians of the Gospel were constrained by the Carol II regime to merge with the Christians of the Scripture, forming the Christian Church of the Gospel, with two branches: branch one (the actual Christians of the Gospel) and branch two (the current Romanian Evangelical Church). Later, in 1946 the Christian Church of the Gospel was recognized as a religion/faith, and the two branches split again after 1989.

As a result of the split of the two branches and the drop in the population, there were 49,393 members registered according to the 1992 census, and 42,495 members in the 2011 census (of which 86.6% ethnic Romanians, 7% ethnic Roma and 4.6% ethnic Hungarians).

The organizational structure of the Christian Church of the Gospel is local in communities with a maximum of 20 members (over 18). There are 678 such communities functioning throughout the country and led by presbyters (elder brothers).

The Union of Christian Churches of the Gospel is led by the National Council of Brothers. The university level Timotheus Theology Institute in Bucharest and five biblical schools are run by the Christian Church of the Gospel.

The Romanian Evangelical Church

The Romanian Evangelical Church was established around the Orthodox theologians Dumitru Cornilescu and Teodor Popescu in the 1920-1924 period. In 1926, guided by the latter, several hundred believers built the first church in Bucharest. At the request of the authorities, in order that they might be distinguished from other believers, the new Christian movement took the name of Christians of the Scripture in 1927, organized officially as an association. Churches were established in a very short time in Ploiesti, Campulung, Targoviste, Rucar, Buzau, Pitesti, Barlad and Brasov.

As a result of pressure from the political authorities, the Christians of the

Scripture united temporarily in 1939 with the Christians of the Gospel. After 1990, the Romanian Evangelical believers separated from the Christians of the Gospel, forming the Romanian Evangelical Church.

The leadership for the denomination is provided by the National Council of Brothers (maximum 21 members), the Executive Bureau (three members) and the General Assembly of Representatives. The National Council of Brothers carries out missionary activities, coordinates the activities of the denomination including administration and finances. The Executive Bureau of the denomination directly subordinates to the National Council of Brothers, runs the daily problems of the church and represents it with the public authorities and other institutions in the country and abroad. The General Assembly of representatives is the supreme forum that guides and controls the activities of the Romanian Evangelical Church and is its main deliberative and representative (one representative for each 50 believers) body.

According to the 2011 census, the number of persons, who declared that they belonged to the Romanian Evangelical Church, was 15,514 (0.08% of the population that declared themselves as belonging to a religion), mostly ethnic Romanians (67.65%), Germans (15%), Hungarians (9.62%) and Roma (5.61%).

Christian Pentecostal Church—Apostolic Church of God in Romania

The Christian Pentecostals take their name from one of their most important beliefs, according to which the Holy Spirit descends on believers who acquire the gift of speaking in tongues, like the Apostles on the Pentecost. Pentecostals first appeared in the United States at the beginning of the 20th century, and the first Romanian community was recorded in 1922 in Paulis in Arad County. According to the 2011 census, 362,314 persons declared themselves to be Pentecostal Union — Apostolic Church of God believers, or 1.92% of the total population. Most Pentecostals are ethnic Romanians (76.36%), followed by ethnic Roma (19.66%), Hungarians (1.77%) and Ukrainians (1.76%).

The organization of this denomination has as its basis a decentralized system respecting the local church autonomy. The denomination has a central and collective leadership, represented by a 33-member Church Council and an Executive Committee of 9 members, with a President as its head. These bodies are elected at a General Elective Assembly, the denomination's highest governing body, which meets once every 4 years. There are 9 regional communities that serve as intermediaries between the local churches and the central governing body, in Arad, Brașov, Bucharest, Cluj, Constanța, Maramures, Oltenia, Oradea, and Suceava, plus two territorial communities (functioning as regional Romanian communities) outside the borders in Italy and Spain. One or several pastors head a local church, depending on the number of believers with an elected committee at each church, whose members also include presbyters and deacons, subordinate to the pastor.

Pastoral training takes place at the university level at the Pentecostal Theology Institute in Bucharest and at several theological seminaries and post-secondary schools.

Seventh-Day Adventist Church in Romania

The Adventist movement initiated by the American pastor William Miller (1782-1849) and centreed on the Second Coming of Jesus Christ on Earth (lat. adventus = coming) has been present in Romania since 1870, but only gained recognition in 1950.

The central governing body of the Church is the Union of Conferences, with 6 subordinate units, known as Conferences (Muntenia, Moldavia, Oltenia, southern Transylvania, northern Transylvania and Banat). The current pastoral body of the Church is made up of some 340 pastors.

According to the results of the 2011 census, the number of believers, who declared themselves as belonging to the Adventist community, is 80,944, mostly ethnic Romanians (79.6%), Hungarians (9.86%), Roma (8.39%) and Ukrainians (1.6%).

Clerical personnel training is conducted in the university level Adventist Theology Institute in Cernica and in 3 seminary secondary schools.

Federation of Jewish Communities in Romania—Jewish Faith

The first Jewish communities settled in the Romanian space in the 16th and 17th centuries under the protection of Romanian Princes who offered them freedom of belief, recognition of rabbinical courts and specific educational institutions. Prince Constantin Brâncoveanu treated them like a guild, and the position of Chief Rabbi, Hahambashia, was instituted in Moldavia in 1719. The political emancipation of the Jews became a reality with the Constitution of 1923, and in 1936 the Jewish communities were unified under the name of the United Federation of Jewish Communities. Nevertheless, the end of the period between the two Wars and the Second World War years were marked by restrictions of citizen and religious rights and freedoms of the Jews, culminating in the Holocaust.

According to the statute of organization and functioning of the Jewish Faith, the confessional activity of the Jewish Minority in Romania is headed by the Federation of Jewish Communities, which includes all communities and towns in the country, with its seat in Bucharest. Of the 39 communities and towns, the most important were in Bucharest, Oradea, Cluj, Iași, Timișoara, Arad, Botoșani, Galați, Bacău, Târgu Mureș.

The local governing bodies are the General Assembly, the Governing Committee and the Censors Commission.

According to the 2011 census, the number of Jews in Romania was 3,211, of which 2,371 declared that they belong to the Jewish Faith.

| 罗马尼亚概况 | *Survey of Romania* |

Islam[1]

The beginning of Islam in Romania is linked to the arrival of the Pechenegs[2] and Cumans[3] in the 11th and 12th centuries, and especially to the Turco-Tatar conquest of the Khanate of the Golden Horde in the 13th century. However, it is only in the 14th and 15th century that the first stable Muslim communities appeared as a result of the instauration of Ottoman suzerainty over the Romanian Countries. With the takeover of Dobrogea[4] by the Romanian state in 1877–1878, Muslim believers were organized into four muftiates, dropping to a single one in 1943 with its seat in Constanța. Muslim believers were ethnic Turks, Tatars and Albanians, and their status as an officially recognized religion dates back to 1928.

The religious activities of the Muslim community are led by the Mufti, elected by secret ballot from among the Imams. A synodal body, known as the Sura Islam, meets periodically to resolve any administrative and organizational problems of the faith, and assists the Mufti. The community is the basic unit of the Muslim religion, which includes all Muslim believers in a locality, and is governed by a committee of 5, 7 or 9 members elected for a period of four years. At present, there are 78 Muslim communities throughout Constanta, Tulcea, Braila and Galati County, and in Bucharest. There are 82 Muslim houses of worship in Romania: the Carol I Royal Mosque in Constanta, plus 78 mosques and 3 mesgids. The Muslim religion also has the concession of 108 cemeteries.

---

1 L. Stanj & L. Turcescu, *Religion and Politics in Post-communist Romania*, New York: Oxford University Press, 2007.

2 A semi-nomadic Turkic people of the Central Asian steppes speaking the Pecheneg language which belonged to the Oghuz branch of Turkic language family [Source: Wikipedia].

3 A Turkic nomadic people comprising the western branch of the Cuman-Kipchak confederation. After the Mongol invasion (1237), many sought asylum in Hungary, as many Cumans had settled in Hungary, Bulgaria and Turkey before the invasion [Source: Wikipedia].

4 A historical region in Eastern Europe that has been divided since the 19th century between the territories of Bulgaria and Romania [Source: Wikipedia].

Chapter 10   Religion

According to the 2011 census, there are 64,337 Muslim believers in Romania, making up 0.34% of the population having declared their religious affiliation; most of these are ethnic Turks (41.81%), Tatars (31.18%), Romanians (9.76%), and a significant number of persons belonging to various ethnic groups not separately registered in the census (6,906 believers, or 10.76% of the Muslim population), of which 67.27% live in Constanta County, 14.04% in Bucharest, 5.11% in Tulcea County, and the remainder in various urban centres, such as Braila, Cluj-Napoca, Calarasi, Galati, Giurgiu, Drobeta-Turnu Severin, and Ilfov County.

Religious Associations

A religious association is a legal entity religious structure, made up of at least 300 members, Romanian citizens or residents, that form an association in order to express a religious belief. The procedure for obtaining this legal status involves the registration of the religious association in the religious associations registry, determined by the court registry in the territorial constituency where the association has its seat.

To become established as a religious association, it is necessary to obtain the advisory opinion of the State Secretariat for Religious Affairs, accompanied by the documentation set out by Art. 41, point (2), letters a-c, of Law no. 489/2006 and Order no. 15/12.03.2012, published in the Official Gazette no. 222 of 03.04.2012, concerning the procedure for obtaining the advisory opinion of the State Secretariat for Religious Affairs for the establishment of new religious associations or the reestablishment of existing associations.

Both associations established on the basis of Government Ordinance O.G. nr. 26/2000 on associations and foundations and newly-established associations may obtain advisory opinion.

Three days from the submission of the application and documents required by Art. 41, point (2), the judge appointed by the Court Chair will verify the legality of the religious group, and determine whether or not the group may be registered in the religious association registry. Once it is registered, the registration agreement is communicated ex officio to the local financial body in whose territory the religious association's seat is located, for tax purposes, with the religious association registry registration number.

According to the law, religious associations may be exempted from taxation for their religious activities, according to Law no. 571/2003 on the Fiscal Code, with its subsequent changes and amendments. Religious associations may establish legal entity subsidiaries in accordance with their statute.

Religious Associations and Foundations

Legal regulations in effect for associations and foundations that are entirely or partly religious are included in Government Ordinance no. 26/2000 regarding associations and foundations. The State Secretariat for Religious Affairs has given its approval for the establishment of over 1,000 associations and foundations, of which more than half are operating under the aegis of legally recognized religions in the country, with the approval of the State Secretariat of Religious Affairs, which allows these associations and foundations to acquire public utility status.

Chapter 11
Sports and Outdoor Activities

Romania has a long and prestigious history within sports and what better place to start than football. Like many countries in Europe, football is the most popular sport in Romania and they now boast a long list of internationally known players and former players.

Away from football, handball is also extremely popular in Romania and their national team has won the World Cup four times which is a record held with Sweden; the women's team has also won the competition once. At club level, Steaua and Dinamo have won a number of European competitions which has put the country firmly on the map. Basketball is also enjoyed, especially by the youth in Romania. The final popular team sport is Rugby Union which has had a place in Romania for over 80 years. Although their reputation may have fallen of late, they have still been at every single World Cup since its inception.

Romania has a long, successful history with the

Olympic Games after appearing in every event since 1952 and accumulating 283 medals (15th in the official rankings) which is a surprise given the size of the country. [1]

Team Sports[2]

Football[3]

Football is one of the most popular sports in Romania. The official figures provided by the National Institute of Statistics (2017) showed that out of the 8,348 registered sports units providing sports programs in 2015 in Romania, 2,885 provided football, which was more than one-third of the national total. This aspect was also backed up by a number of 132,922 football players registered in all these units, meaning more than half of the 273,926 athletes registered nationally.

Although football is one of the most popular and appreciated sporting activities in Romania, in 2014 only 0.5% of the population played professional or amateur football, which is well below the European average of 2.7% based on official statistical studies.

The official press release of the Romanian Football Federation, published after attending the event dedicated to boosting the public participation to the football phenomenon in East Europe (UEFA Grow Summit, 2017), shows that Romania reveals a significant increase in the number of people who play football. Thus the Romanian Football Federation report shows that had they already achieved in 2016 their objective set for 2020, to reach to a number of football players of at least 1.5% of the population.

In the future, it doesn't look as though anything can topple football as it has over 110,000 competitors, nearly 100,000 more than tennis in second. In

---

 1 https://en.wikipedia.org/wiki/Sport_in_Romania

 2 http://www.cesport.eu/en/Nd/i/more/What%E2%80%99s+the+most+popular+sport+in+Romania%3F/idn/3196

 3 https://en.wikipedia.org/wiki/Romania_national_football_team

addition to this, there are over 3,000 football clubs available and less than 200 tennis clubs. Football really is a nation's sport and this is something that simply will not change in the immediate future. The Romanian Premier Division draws in an average of 5,400 people per game with a national high of 1.6 million during the 2006/2007 season.

Handball

Handball is the second most popular sport in Romania, after football. The Romania national handball team has won the Handball IHF World Cup 4 times (in 1961, 1964, 1970 and 1974). The only other team to have matched this record is Sweden in 1999 and France in 2011. The Romania women's national handball team has won the Handball World Cup in 1962. Steaua, Dinamo and CSM București have also won several European titles over the years.

Romania has produced many great handball players, including Gheorghe Gruia, Alexandru Dedu, Vasile Stanga, Petre Ivanescu, Cornel Penu, Alexandru Buligan, Marian Dumitru and Cristian Gatu.

On the women's side, the top Romanians include: three times IHF World Player of the Year winner Cristina Neagu, Luminița Dinu, Mariana Tirca, Aurelia Bradeanu, Valentina Elisei and Cristina Varzaru.

Basketball

Basketball is a very popular sport among Romanian youth. Gheorghe Mureșan was the first Romanian to enter NBA, and he became known as the tallest man ever to play in that league. Other products of the Romanian basketball school are Constantin Popa, Virgil Stănescu and Toni Alexe. The most important basketball team in Romania is CSU Asesoft. CSU Asesoft won the Eurocup in 2005 and consecutive the National Basketball Championship since 2000. In 2016, Romania was chosen as a host for the 2017 FIBA Euro Basket.

Individual Sports[1]

When it comes to individual sports, gymnastics seems to lead the way and the sport is responsible for a large amount of Romania's 283 medals at the Olympic Games over the years. Of course, the Romanian gymnast, Nadia Comaneci, will always be remembered for scoring the first-ever perfect 10 at the 1976 Games. Tennis has also been strong in the nation having been to three Davis Cup finals and having Ilie Nastase who won a number of Grand Slams throughout his career. Boxing rounds off the top three individual sports and has been extremely popular with TV broadcasting over the years. Romania also has its traditional sport of Oina which is a game similar to baseball.

Gymnastics

Romania holds a long tradition in artistic gymnastics, especially in the ladies competition. Gymnastics is responsible for the majority of Romania's Olympic, gold, silver, and bronze medals. The most famous Romanian gymnast is Nadia Comaneci, who was the first gymnast to ever score a perfect 10 at the Olympic Games during the 1976 Summer Olympics. She also won three gold medals, one silver and one bronze, all at the age of fourteen. Her success continued in the 1980 Summer Olympics, where she was awarded two gold medals and two silver medals. At the 1976 Olympic Games, Teodora Ungureanu did very well too, but did not receive as much fame as Nadia. Other famous gymnasts include: Daniela Silivas, Ecaterina Szabo, Lavinia Milosovici, Gina Gogean, Simona Amanar, Andreea Raducan, Maria Olaru, Catalina Ponor and Sandra Izbasa. Top Romanian men's gymnasts include: Marius Urzica and Marian Dragulescu.

Tennis

Ilie Nastase, a famous Romanian tennis player, is another internationally

---

1 https://en.wikipedia.org/wiki/Sport_in_Romania

known Romanian sports star. He won several Grand Slam[1] titles and dozens of other tournaments and was the first player to be ranked as number 1 by ATP[2] from 1973 to 1974; he also was a successful doubles player. Romania has also reached the Davis Cup finals three times. Virginia Ruzici was a successful tennis player in the 1970s.

PICTURE: Naida Comaneci
SOURCE: http://www.imperialtransilvania.com/2017/07/28/read-more/argomenti/ events-1/articolo/nadia-comaneci-the-first-gymnast-to-score-a-perfect-10. html)

---

  1 The Grand Slam tournaments, also called majors, are the four most important annual tennis events. They offer the most ranking points, prize money, public and media attention, the greatest strength and size of field, and greater number of "best of" sets for men [Source: Wikipedia].
  2 The Association of Tennis Professionals was formed in September 1972 by Donald Dell, Bob Briner, Jack Kramer and Cliff Drysdale to protect the interests of male professional tennis players. Drysdale became the first President [Source: Wikipedia].

Romania reached the Davis Cup finals three times (in 1969, 1971 and 1972). The most famous Romanian tennis player of all time is Ilie Nastase, presented by the Tennis Hall of Fame[1] as "the most talented player ever to hold the racquet". He was the only Romanian player to ever achieve the number 1 ranking. Other famous men's tennis players include Ion Tiriac and Andrei Pavel. In ladies tennis, Virginia Ruzici, Irina Spirlea and Ruxandra Dragomir are among the top Romanian players of all time. As for active players, the top Romanians on the men's side are doubles players Horia Tecau and Florin Mergea, who also brought Romania's first Olympic medal in tennis, a silver in 2016. On the women's side, the top Romanians include Simona Halep, Sorana Cirstea, Raluca Olaru, Alexandra Dulgheru and Monica Niculescu. There are also many junior stars like Ana Bogdan and Elena Bogdan.

Rowing and Canoeing

Romanian oars people have brought numerous successes including 35 Olympic medals (18 gold) for rowing and 34 medals (10 gold) for canoeing. Romania is a leading rowing nation, often boasting many wins each year in the Junior World Rowing Championships. In the under-23's age level, Romania often fields a strong team and medals in the women's events.

The Romanian Senior Women's rowing team is particularly strong. They have been the poster child team as regards women's rowing. They consistently perform in the coxed women's eight. In the Olympics, they won the women's coxless pair. This was one of the 6th Olympic gold medals for Elisabeta Lipa. Now she is the most decorated female rower in history.

Fencing

Fencing as a sport was introduced in Romania in the 19th century by

---

1 The International Tennis Hall of Fame is located in Newport, Rhode Island, United States. It honors players and contributors to the sport of tennis and includes a museum, grass tennis courts, an indoor tennis facility and a court tennis facility [Source: Wikipedia].

French masters. The first national fencing competition was held in 1921 and the Romanian Fencing Federation was created in 1931. The first Romanian fencer to reach the podium in a major international competition was Maria Vicol, who earned a silver medal at the 1956 Junior World Championships in Luxembourg.

Since then, fencing has brought Romania 8 Olympic team medals and 7 Olympic individual medals including 3 golds: Ion Drimba (foil) at the 1968 Summer Olympics in Mexico, Laura Badea (foil) at the 1996 Summer Olympics in Atlanta, and Mihai Covaliu (sabre) at the 2000 Summer Olympics in Sydney. Romanian fencers also earned 13 gold medals in World Fencing Championships and 13 gold medals in European Fencing Championships. 6 Romanians feature in the Hall of Fame of the International Fencing Federation: Laura Badea, Mihai Covaliu, Ana Pascu, Petru Kuki, Ioan Pop and Reka Szabo. 3 Romanian athletes are currently amongst the 10 top-ranked fencers: Ana Maria Branza and Simona Gherman in women's epee and Tiberiu Dolniceanu in men's sabre.

Olympics[1]

Romania first participated at the Olympic Games in 1900, with a single participant. The National Olympic Committee for Romania is the Romanian Olympic and Sports Committee, and was created and recognized in 1914. The nation first sent a team to compete at the Games in 1924 and has only missed two editions each of the Summer Olympic Games and Winter Olympic Games since then. Notably, Romania was the lone Eastern Bloc nation to participate at the 1984 Summer Olympics, which the other nations boycotted. That was also Romania's most successful Olympic Games: they won 20 gold medals and 53 medals total.

Maybe slightly surprising for a country of its size, Romania has been one of the most successful countries in the history of the Summer Olympic Games (15th

---

1 https://en.wikipedia.org/wiki/Romania_at_the_Olympics

overall) with a total of 307 medals won throughout the years, 89 of which are gold medals. Romania has appeared in 21 of the 28 Summer Olympic Games. The nation debuted at the 1900 Summer Olympics, appeared again 3 times between the World Wars, and has competed at every event since the 1952 Summer Olympics.

From the 1972 Summer Games to the 2012 Summer Games, Romania had qualified a women's team for the gymnastics team all-around. They had won medals at every Olympics from the 1976 Summer Games to the 2012 Summer Games. However, the women's team failed to qualify for the 2016 Summer Games, ending the 40-year run in medals and the 44-year run of having a team at the Olympics.

Physical Education[1]

In Romania, school physical education is a study discipline with an old tradition. Nowadays, Romanian education is passing through an important reforming process meant to render it compatible with the European educational system. But the Romanian education reforming has many consequences, inclusively on physical education, and is reflected in some legislative documents (the Law of National Education no. 1/2011, the Law of Physical Education and Sports no. 69/2000, as well as in other official documents (the curriculum framework, the physical education syllabi for all grades, the National School System of Evaluation for Physical Education and Sports).

The national curriculum or core-curriculum provides all the pupils with the conditions necessary to a unitary training, but, at the same time, it gives the decision factors at the school level the opportunity to particularize the education paths. The curricula provisions referring to the number of classes, correlated with the speciality syllabi content and the evaluation system requirements, also impose new methodological approaches to this discipline teaching.

---

1 https://www.academia.edu/11468562/Particularities_of_school_physical_education_in_Romania

Forms of Organizing School Physical Education

The Physical Education Lesson

It is thought to be the main practising form of school physical exercises. With structures and organizational-methodical particularities different from one grade to another, it keeps, however, a series of characteristic traits, namely: A. It is directed by a specialist. B. It is included into the pupils' compulsory schedule. C. It has a precise duration and content, both of them regulated through official documents. The curriculum presentation notes in different study cycles have shown that the lesson can't contribute any more to the fulfilment of the discipline goals, because of the pupils' low degree of involvement into the physical exercise practice. Consequently, the lesson effects can be enhanced only by means of some other physical activity forms. Although not compulsory, these activities bring a particular contribution to the achievement of the objectives specific to physical education.

The Daily Gymnastics

This non-compulsory activity can be performed simultaneously with all the pupils in grades one to four, either in the beginning of the school day or during the long break. Daily gymnastics is recommended to be performed in the open. It is directed by a physical education teacher, by instructors-pupils in the secondary education cycle or by the teacher "on duty" in the school. It consists of five to six free individual simple exercises, known by the pupils and addressed to their physical development. These exercises are only performed in the standing position and some of its derivatives. When selecting the exercises, we should consider that pupils perform them by wearing a piece of equipment non-specific to physical education.

The Physical Education Moment

It occurs during the teaching activities that are very stressing for the small children's body, because of the intense nervous concentration and of a prevailingly static effort (calligraphy, drawing and other general disciplines), which favours the fatigue onset. In such moments, the teacher must interrupt the respective activity and recommend the pupils to perform two to three simple physical exercises in their desks or in the open spaces between them. In the lessons for the writing learning, teachers may use exercises for the arms, hands and fingers: fist closing and opening by forcingly stretching one's fingers, the writing hand pressure on the desk, the writing hand shaking, etc.

Extracurricular Motor Activities

They are represented by sports groups and by tourist leisure motor activities such as excursions or trips. During the latest years, more and more importance has been given to the organization of pupils' leisure time by the school specialized factors. In this context, it becomes obvious the physical exercise potential to contribute to a better organization of pupils' leisure time, to the consolidation of premises created during the physical education lessons and to the orientation of the gifted pupils toward the performance sports pracstising. Sports groups are competition or non-competition activities performed during the pupils' leisure time, according to their preferences and desire to practise certain sports branches. In order to encourage pupils' participation in sports competitions, the school inspectorates organize contests at the municipality or county levels for different sports branches. The number of children involved in such activities has lately registered a descending trend. Less and fewer pupils practice leisure physical exercises, the physical education lessons remaining the only ones that require a sustained effort from their part (Stanescu et al., 2010). An important factor able to determine the increase of pupils' interest in extracurricular sports activities remains the teacher, whose training should permanently be kept at the level of the requirements imposed by the children's physicsal exercise practising. The new sports branches, the new types of competitive and non-competitive sports activities are elements to be taken into account by the specialists teaching in the Romanian schools.

Sports Tourism[1]

In Romania, there were discovered archaeological fonts which tie up the practising since oldest times of some forms of physical exercise culture, among them horse riding competitions, darts, hunting, individual battles and group sporting games. Once with the development of school institutions, the physical exercise culture was introduced in schools. The names of Doctor Carol Davilla and Professor Gheorghe Moceanu are connected with the efforts to promote physical exercise education as a mandatory discipline at the end of 19th century.

First references attesting the practising of sporting tourism date from 1578, when was published in Krakow, the work of Alexander Guagnini, *Sarmatiae Europeae Description* (Sarmatic European Chronicles), a short biography of the countries in Southern East Europe. He mentions in his work about sport practising in the Wooded Carpathians[2]. An important moment in the history of sport tourism (mostly leisure sport tourism) was the establishment of the Romanian royal family's summer residence in Sinaia and the beginning of building the Peles Castle in 1875. The influence of the royal family and also the natural touristic potential, made Sinaia monopolize at that time the touristic incoming of the Prahova Valley area, which determined the diversification of the touristic offer and the development of new touristic poles in the vicinity of Sinaia town in order to unblock the touristic traffic here. At present, Prahova Valley becomes a true touristic axis, monopolizing today the incoming flow of tourists from the capital of Bucharest and surrounding towns.

Most of the mountains in Romania are fitted with facilities for practising the winter sport, hiking and even extreme sports. The touristic infrastructure serving the sport tourism in mountain resorts does not reach modern standards

---

1 C. Chivu, (2013). "Sport Tourism in Romania and the Romanian Experience in Organizing and Hosting an International Sport Event: Case study" [in Bucharest International Marathon, *Cinq Continents*, 3(7), PP.88-113].

2 It refers to the eastern Carpathians Mountains.

as in the West-European countries. In terms of facilities, Romania is behind not only the West-European nations but also toward the neighbouring, Bulgaria and Hungary, that with the help of foreign investments made a big step ahead in improving the quality and representation of touristic facilities and also of the infrastructure in general. This is the reason why Romania does not represent an attraction for foreign tourists practising winter sports, their number being very small in the mountain resorts.

Making a step back in time, we can say the inception of extreme sports worldwide around 1980, and their spreading in Romania after 1990, represented another important moment in the history of sport tourism in Romania. Bungee jumping, paraglide, parachuting, tiroliana, zorbing, body flying, aerotrim are just a few examples of the extreme sport practised today in Romania. By far the most well-known is bungee jumping, which in Romania is represented by two platforms: Vidraru dam of 166 meters and Râșnoavei Gorge of 137 meters.

Regarding the most important component of the sport tourism, the one represented by the sporting events, it is noted that Romania is not a major destination for big sporting events, the so-called sport mega events.

The most sold sport in Romania is football, which often fills the stadiums, but until recently Romania did not have a stadium able to meet the international standards. Only in September 2011, Romania made a step forward in order to align with international standards, and opened the National Arena Stadium in Bucharest, the biggest in the country. The stadium extends on a surface of 108.000 m^2, it is six floors high and it has a capacity of 55,000 spectators. Another step in the history of Romanian sport and tourism was certainly the challenging of hosting and organizing in May 2012, the European League UEFA football final, hosted by the National Arena in Bucharest. One problem raised in this case was the violence that accompanied so far the image of Romanian football, in the country as also in international matches with the participation of Romanian fans. The violence in sport is a feature of modern sport and its increase is intensely debated today and it derives from its competitive feature.

Romania does not have yet a material facility specific for big international

Chapter 11 Sports and Outdoor Activities

events, and this issue represents a challenge even for the capital of Bucharest, because hosting such an event is not only about organizing the event itself. If you are thinking to a touristic flow of thousands of tourists, the accommodation options and the transportation system in Bucharest are a constant challenge (for example, Bucharest has only one international airport). The alternative possibilities for leisure are not sufficient. Until 2011, Bucharest was not in possession of touristic buses for the city tour. Until 2008, Bucharest was the only capital in the European Union not having its international marathon.

A number of such events (marathons and half-marathons, cross and street races) are organized annually in many other cities in the country: Tuşnad, Cluj, Arad, Fagaras, Brasov, Timisoara and so on, some of them are international (Cluj International Marathon, from 2010) but in reality, the international participation is poor and the impact of the event is local. There are also theme competitions, often associated to a humanitarian cause or for supporting some social, ecologic, cultural ideas: The Wood Cross, The Unification Cross, The Marathon of Reunification of Romanian Nation, etc. A newer trend in Romania, enjoying increasing popularity is represented by mountain marathons and half-marathons (Piatra Craiului, Muntele Mare, Cernei, Bucegi Mountains), mountain ultra-marathons (7,500 Marathon-Bucegi Mountains), trail running races (Azuga, Moieciu, Ciucas Mountains).

A real opportunity to make known the name of Romania in the international sports industry was the year of 2012 when among the six European sports cities, Iaşi city was also present. "The Municipality of Iaşi was chosen as a European sports city in 2012. Iasi was chosen to receive this symbol along with the cities of Florence, Pescara and Viterbo from Italy, Preston from UK and Charleroi from Belgium. According to selection criteria, the European sport capital must be a city with a population of over 500,000 inhabitants. Iasi is the only city in Romania which applied for this competition".

The top sports were always well represented by Romanians sportsmen even outside the country (from Iosif Barbu, the first Romanian Olympic champion, to the international legends like Nadia Comaneci, Gheorghe Hagi, Ilie Nastase).

The only Romanian sports museum able to support nostalgic sports tourism is the Arges Sports Museum, opened in September 2008. It presents a permanent exhibition dedicated to famous athletes in Arges department. Since 2011, works are underway to a museum of Romanian sports in Bucharest, at the Olympic House, but because of the lack of funding, the finalization is not complete and most of the exhibits are stored in repository.

The rebirth of the physical culture is a current trend in Romania and mostly promoted and represented in the capital of Bucharest and in the big cities. As a proof of the Romanians increased interest for sporting activities, one noted an increment of amateur athletes, of those passionate of certain sports and those practising a sport to be in a good physical condition.

Chapter 12
Entertainment

Television, magazines and newspapers are all operated by both state-owned and for-profit corporations which depend on advertising, subscription, and other sales-related revenues. The Constitution of Romania guarantees freedom of speech. As a country in transition, the Romanian media system is under transformation.

Cinema is one of the popular forms of entertainment in Romania, new multiplex cinemas have been opening in shopping malls, including Hollywood Multiplex, Movieplex Cinema, and Cinema City Romania. However, over 85% of tickets are for US blockbusters, with only 3.6% in 2008 for domestic Romanian film productions.

Television is one of the most popular entertainment media in Romania, and it gathers two-thirds of all advertising funds (337 million euro in 2008). The National Study of TV Audience has registered almost 50 TV stations distributed nationwide including general audience and specialised channels. Romanian television is dominated by a small number of corporations, owning multiple TV channels as well as radio stations, newspapers and media agencies. Their television business is structured around a flagship channel and a number of smaller specialized, niche channels[1].

Cinema of Romania[2]

The cinema of Romania is the art of motion-picture making within the nation of Romania or by Romanian filmmakers abroad. It has been home to many internationally acclaimed films and directors.

Romanian cinema achieved prominence in the 2000s with the appearance of such films as *The Death of Mr. Lazarescu*, directed by Cristi Puiu, and *4 Months, 3 Weeks and 2 Days*, directed by Cristian Mungiu (Cannes 2007 Palme d'Or winner). The latter, according to Variety, is "further proof of Romania's new prominence in the film world."

Beginnings

The history of cinema in Romania started before 1900, pushed by film screenings which helped arouse public curiosity towards the new invention and enthusiastic cameramen began making films out of passion for the newly discovered art. Due to the rudimentary technical conditions, the early films were actualities, very short (many less than one minute) one-shot scenes capturing moments of everyday life.

The first cinematographic projection in Romania took place on 27 May 1896, less than five months after the first public film exhibition by the Lumière

---

1 https://en.wikipedia.org/wiki/Media_of_Romania
2 https://en.wikipedia.org/wiki/Cinema_of_Romania

brothers[1] on 28 December 1895 in Paris. In the Romanian exhibition, a team of Lumiere brothers' employees screened several films including the famous *L'Arrivée d'un train en gare de La Ciotat* (Workers Leaving the Lumiere Factory). The event was hosted by the French-language newspaper *L'Indépendance Roumanie*. Initially, an elite attraction, permanent screenings both in the building of *L'Indépendance Roumanie* and in other locations (such as the biggest room of the newspaper building on Eforiei Spitalelor Civile Boulevard, then the Hugues room across from the old National Theatre) helped bring the ticket price down and cinema became a popular spectacle in Bucharest.

The next year, in 1897, the French cameraman Paul Menu (an employee of the Lumiere brothers) shot the first film set in Romania, The Royal paraded on 10 May 1897, showing King Carol I mounted, taking his place on the boulevard to head the parade. He continued by filming other 16 news items over the following two months, but only two survive today as nr. 551 and 552 in the Lumiere catalogue. Menu's first Romanian films were presented on 8 June/23 June 1897, including images of the floods at Galati, Romanian Navy vessels on the Danube.

However, by 1898, public interest in cinema started fading, so Paul Menu offered his camera for sale. The camera was bought by doctor Gheorghe Marinescu who became the first Romanian filmmaker, realizing a series of short medically themed films between 1898 and 1899. Gheorghe Marinescu, together with cameraman Constantin M. Popescu, made in 1898 the first scientific film in the world. In a letter to doctor Marinescu from 29 July 1924, speaking about these films, Auguste Lumière acknowledges that "unfortunately, few scientists followed the path you opened". His films were considered lost until 1975 when a TV reporter named Cornel Rusu discovered them in a metal cabinet in a hospital

---

1 Lumiere brothers, French inventors and pioneer manufacturers of photographic equipment who devised an early motion-picture camera and projector called the Cinematographe ("cinema" is derived from this name). Auguste Lumière and his brother Louis Lumière created the film *La Sortie des ouvriers de l'usine Lumière* (1895; *Workers Leaving the Lumiere Factory*), which is considered the first motion picture [Source: Wikipedia].

bearing the famous doctor's name.

Film screenings resumed in Bucharest in 1905 at various locations, such as the Edison, the Eforie, the Lyric Theatre, and Circul Sidoli. In May 1909, the first theatre in Romania built especially for exhibiting films, Volta, was opened on Doamnei Street in Bucharest. Transylvania, then part of Austria-Hungary, had already had its first movie theatre in Brașov since 1901. Volta was followed starting with the next year by others, such as Bleriot on Sarindar Street, Bristol, Apollo and Venus. The programs consisted of actualities and short "little films with actors" (for example, a five-minute shot of two actors talking during a stately walk on the seashore). The films gradually increased in running time, eventually developing into newsreels and fiction films.

Fictional Romanian Silent Films (1911 – 1930)

The first Romanian fiction film was *Amor Fatal* (*Fatal Love Affair*), starring Lucia Sturdza, Tony Bulandra and Aurel Barbelian, actors from the National Theatre Bucharest. The film was directed by Grigore Brezeanu, a director from the same theatre and the son of the great actor Ion Brezeanu. The film played between 26 and 30 September 1911 at the Apollo Cinema.

During the First World War, film production was mainly directed toward documentaries and newsreels. The few Romanian cameramen were mobilized, and during the retreat to Moldova, all film cameras in the country were saved. His Majesty Ferdinand I was filmed on the front, together with the generals Constantin Prezanand Alexandru Averescu, while Queen Marie was filmed in hospitals, easing the suffering of patients. Few sequences remain of the thousands of metres filmed. Some of these were later used in the film Ecaterina Teodoroiu, produced in 1930.

After World War I, internationally, film production developed in accordance with the interest of businessmen in the new industry. New studios endowed with good equipment and specialists well trained in the new technology appeared, directors and actors known to the public at large were attracted to work in the new industry, as were renowned screenwriters. Markets were opened for finished film products, which through a market-tested formula managed to bring profits and finance new productions. Film industries with lavish financial resources came to dominate the market, decimating weak national cinemas.

In this context, an active Romanian film industry was but a dream. The approximately 250 movie theatres then in existence in Romania could not even generate the amount of money needed for one film, with profits out of the question. Specialist training for film crew members was non-existent, and Romanian actors were unknown abroad so their work could not be sold outside Romania. Neither did the state accord any attention to film production. Its only preoccupation in this regard was to collect the tax on screenings, which provided a fairly consistent revenue stream, its proceeds at one time amounting to two-thirds of total revenue derived from this type of tax.

The lack of a steady supply of financial resources was the constant obsession permanently plaguing Romanian film directors. The absence of a "Leon Popescu", a wealthy man ready to invest his earnings in film production, caused directors and the few actors passionate about the new art to seek financiers who were equally passionate and disinterested. This is how the young actor-director Jean Georgescu found a retiree in the year 1925 who, for more or less artistic reasons, invested his savings in the production of a film called *Năbădăile Cleopatrei* (*Cleopatra's Caprices*). Jean Mihail directed *Lia* (1927), on a screenplay by Mircea Filotti financed by a German businessman who wanted to fulfil the wish of his wife, well-known actress Lilly Flohr. Likewise, he made *Povara* (*The Burden*) at Vienna in 1928 with the money of a lady who wished to see her name listed in the credits as production director.

Other films from this period include *Gogulică C.F.R.* (1929) (unfinished), and Haplea (*The Dullard*) (animated by Marin Iorda in 1928)—the first Romanian animated film preserved archivally.

At the end of the 1920s and beginning of the 1930s, cinema entered the consciousness of certain Romanian writers and cultural figures, such as Tudor Vianu, Liviu Rebreanu, Victor Eftimiu, Camil Petrescu and Dimitrie Gusti, who all became aware of this new mode of expression and culture. In this period, the film critic D. I. Suchianu made his debut, first in newspapers, then in 1929 in radio. Later on the critic, Ion Filotti Cantacuzino also started broadcasting.

Romanian Talking Films (1930–1947)

The appearance of sound films opened a new stage in the development of world cinema, by implication in the weak cinema of Romania as well. The appearance of sound further complicated the tricky problem of the technical-material base, both in terms of production and of projection in theatres. Competition from abroad shattered the dreams of Romanian producers, such that the number of films produced after 1930 within the cinema of Romania fell noticeably. Hence, until 1939, just 16 films were produced. The majority were "Romanian versions" of foreign films produced in Paris, Prague or Budapest studios with a few Romanian technicians and some Romanian actors. Practically, they were involved in dubbing. Among these were the Franco-American film *Parada Paramount* (*Paramount on Parade*), *Televiziune* (*Television*) (both 1931 *and dubbed in Paris*) (with George Vraca's voice *in the second film*), *Fum* (*Smoke*) 1931, *Trenul fantomă* (*The Phantom Train*) 1933, *Prima dragoste* (*First Love*) and *Suflete în furtună* (*Tempest-tossed Souls*) 1934, Hungarian films dubbed in Budapest.

Enthusiastic Romanian directors, due to lack of funds and disinterest on the part of the ruling authorities, all began to take other paths in their lives. Jean Georgescu left for Paris, where he added sound to his 1934 film, *State la București* (*States in Bucharest*) in the Gaumont Studio; the film had originally been made as a silent comedy. Ion Sahighian left cinema for the theatre. Eftimie Vasilescu worked as a newsreel photographer. Only Jean Mihail remained a director based in Romania, though he too had to do work abroad, participating in the dubbing of films.

During this nadir of Romanian cinema, a ray of hope appeared. Politicians, and not only in Romania, realized the great influential power that cinema had as part of the mass media. Cinema could be used for purposes of propaganda, for influencing the masses at large with different levels of culture. Furthermore, it had been proven that the tenacious work of Romanian film directors, despite all its imperfections, had been well received by the public, and had begun to prove right those who kept calling for subsidies toward the production of Romanian films.

Thus, at the beginning of 1934, a law was passed establishing a National Cinema Fund. This was funded through a tax of 1 leu per ticket and 10 lei per meter of imported film. Its stated purpose was to create a material base for Romanian film production (studios, laboratories, equipment and so on) and, as subsequent revenue came in, to finance productions as well. The fund's administration was placed in the hands of a committee formed by Professor Tudor Vianu, Professor Alexandru Rosetti and the writer Ion Marin Sadoveanu. These taxes provoked strong protests from film importers and movie theatre owners, yet with the authorities not yielding, tempers soon relaxed.

Following the passage of this law, Romanian film makers began a flurry of activity, planning all sorts of projects. An entrepreneur brought in a Bell-Howel sound recorder and founded a company called The Romanian Sound Film Industry, commencing with the production of newsreels. Together with Jean Mihail, he began the production of a documentary film, *România* (*Romania*).

In 1944, a Romanian-Italian company, Cineromit, assigned the production of the film *Visul unei nopți de iarnă* (*A Winter Night's Dream*) to director Jean Georgescu. The script was from the play by Tudor Mușatescu. The film was finished only near the end of the year 1945 due to the events of the war.

Romanian Cinema (1990 – Present)

The new millennium saw a reemergence of Romanian cinema. In 2001 and

2002, Romanian directors competed in the Directors' Fortnight section parallel to the Cannes Film Festival with Cristi Puiu's first feature film aka *Marfa și banii* (*Stuff and Dough*) and *Cristian Mungiu's Occident*, respectively.

Romania has also been chosen by foreign filmmakers as a location for filming scenes, such as *Cold Mountain*, the "Kazakh" village in Sacha Baron Cohen's *Borat*, the French film *Transylvania* or the 2004 American horror film *Gargoyle: Wings of Darkness*, to name just a few.

According to data by the European Audiovisual Observatory for 2012–2016, domestic productions account for only about 3% of all admissions to cinema in Romania, with US productions dominating the market (72%). As an example, *4 Months, 3 Weeks and 2 Days* was viewed by 350,000 people in France, 142,000 in Italy, but less than 90,000 in Romania itself.

TV Industry[1]

Romanian public television runs several channels: TVR 1, TVR 2, TVR 3, TVR HD, TVR News, TVR and TVR Moldova, and five territorial studios.

The most popular private channels in Romania are: Pro TV (member of Media Pro trust, run by CME, Central European Media Enterprises), Antena 1 and Antena 3 (both members of Antena Group), B1 TV(owned by businessman, film producer and director Bobby Paunescu), Realitatea TV and Kanal D (run by the Turkish trust Dogan).

Doina Gradea was elected by the Romanian Parliament as general manager of the Romanian public broadcaster (SRTV) on 28 March 2018. She was appointed acting general manager in September 2017 after the rejection of the activity report on 2016 and thus the dissolution of the Council of Administration led by the former general manager Irina Radu.

In 2018, HBO Europe and Germany's TNT Series shot in Timisoara, Bucharest and Frankfurt the six-episode series *Hackerville*, directed by Igor

---

1 https://en.wikipedia.org/wiki/Television_in_Romania

Cobileanski and Anca Miruna Lazarescu. The series was created by Ralph Martin and Joerg Winger, and it was produced by Cristian Mungiu and Tudor Reu through Mobra Films. The series premiered on HBO Romania in the autumn of 2018.

Music of Romania[1]

Romania is a country with a multicultural music environment which includes active ethnic music scenes. Romania also has thriving scenes in the fields of pop music, hip hop, heavy metal and rock and roll. During the first decade of the 21st century, some Europop groups/artists, such as Tom Boxer, Morandi, Akcent, Edward Maya, Alexandra Stan, Inna and Yarabi, achieved success abroad. Traditional Romanian folk music remains popular, and some folk musicians have come to national (and even international) fame.

History

Folk music is the oldest form of Romanian musical creation, characterized by great vitality. It is the defining source of the cultured musical creation, both religious and lay. Conservation of Romanian folk music has been aided by a large and enduring audience, and by numerous performers who helped propagate and further develop the folk sound. One of them, Gheorghe Zamfir, is famous throughout the world today and helped popularize a traditional Romanian folk instrument, the panpipes.

The religious musical creation, born under the influence of Byzantine music adjusted to the intonations of the local folk music, saw a period of glory between the 15th and 17th centuries when reputed schools of liturgical music developed within Romanian monasteries. Russian and Western influences brought about the introduction of polyphony in religious music in the 18th century, a genre developed by a series of Romanian composers in the 19th and 20th centuries.

---

1 https://en.wikipedia.org/wiki/Music_of_Romania

Traditional Music

Traditional Romanian music reflects a confluence of sounds similar to Central European (especially Hungarian) as well as Balkan traditional music. In Romanian folk music, emphasis is on melody rather than percussion, with frequent use of the violin for melody and often only the cimbalom for percussion. The melody itself and especially the melodic embellishments are reminiscent of music from further south in the Balkans and of a distant Turkish influence.

Classical Music

Notable Romanian composers of the 19th and 20th centuries include Ciprian Porumbescu, Anton Pann, Eduard Caudella, Mihail Jora, Dinu Lipatti and especially George Enescu. Also famous are the composer and conductor Sergiu Celibidache and Vladimir Cosma.

The Australian composer Julian Cochran wrote works extensively titled Romanian Dances with a collection of piano works and six orchestral works, exemplifying affinity amongst classical composers with the Romanian folk music tradition outside of Romania.

Popular Music

The term "Muzica de strada" (Easy Music) defines a branch of Pop music developed in Romania after World War II, which appears generally in the form of easy danceable songs, made on arrangements, which are performed by orchestras. This music shows many similarities with Western Popular music, as most songs could be defined as a form of Schlager. It supported influences from other similar melodic styles, like Musica leggera italiana (from Italy) and Canción Melódica (from Spain). This Romanian style of music was popularized abroad through the international Golden Stag Festival[1], held in Brasov, since

---

1 The most popular Romanian song contest and awards, held annually in the town of Brașov, Romania.

1968. The most representative singers of that era are those from the 1980s, 1970s and rarely 1960s.

Contemporary Romanian folk music is an acoustic Romanian style of music, inspired by American folk music, with sweet lyrics and played almost exclusively with guitar. Generally, it evokes a poetic and melancholic atmosphere. It emerged in the early 1960s, along with the first releases of Phoenix band. It was promoted later, through the medium of the Cenaclul Flacara[1], a cultural phenomenon from the 1970s and the first half of the 1980s, which was initiated by Adrian Paunescu, a Romanian poet. A lot of Romanian folk artists gain affirmation through the Cenaclul Flacara movement.

In the 1990s and the early 2000s, with the emergence of independent television and radio stations, the term easy music has been replaced by pop. Mainstream success is shared between early dance-pop bands such as A.S.I.A., Animal X, Blondy, Body & Soul, pop-rock singers and bands such as Stefan Banica Jr., Holograf, Bosquito, Voltaj or VH2, hip-hop outfits such as La Familia Paraziții or Ca$$a Loco, Latino singers (Pepe) and others (electronic band Suie Paparude; and some alternative rock bands such as Vama Veche, Bere Gratis, or Luna Amara that are still popular).

Forecast[2]

According to the PwC[3] Global Entertainment & Media Outlook 2018 – 2022' over the next five years, the digital segments will be the most dynamic

---

1 A cultural and artistic movement in the Socialist Republic of Romania led by poet Adrian Paunescu. Between 1973 and 1985, it organized shows and concerts which promoted Nicolae Ceausescu's cult of personality [Source: Wikipedia].

2 http://business-review.eu/business/report-media-and-entertainment-industry-will-grow-at-a-pace-of-7-4-%-until-2022-183998

3 PricewaterhouseCoopers (doing business as PwC) is a multinational professional services network with headquarters in London, United Kingdom. PwC ranks as the second largest professional services firm in the world and is one of the Big Four auditors, along with Deloitte, EY and KPMG.

components of the Romanian media and entertainment market and the whole media and entertainment market will register an annual growth rate of 7.4%.

The whole media and entertainment market in Romania will register a Compound Annual Growth Rate (CAGR) of 7.4% reaching total revenues of USD 3.7 billion by 2022. Out of this, approximately half is represented by spendings for internet access who will register a CAGR of 11.6% and will report revenues of over USD 1.8 billion by the same target year.

By comparison, Central and Eastern European (CEE) media and entertainment market will have a CAGR of about 7.1% and will reach total revenues of approximately USD 83 billion. The internet access segment will generate revenues of about USD 30.5 billion and will have a CAGR of 10.3%, compared to 6.6% global level. The internet access segment is generating, in Romania, CEE and at the global level, the biggest revenues of all segments that comprise the media and entertainment market. In Romania, the share of this segment in the total media and entertainment market will increase from 38%, in 2017, to 47%, in 2022. In CEE, the share of the internet access segment will rise from 31% to 36% (global level, from 26% to 29%).

A slight increase is estimated for the TV and home video segment, that will generate, in Romania, revenues of USD 623 million by 2022, an increase from the USD 606 million in 2017, with a compound annual growth rate of 0.5%. This is the second-largest segment in terms of generated revenues, after internet access, both in Romania, CEE and at global level. The development of the local TV market is in line with the regional one that will have an increase of 0.6% by 2022.

In Romania, the growth on the TV segment with the result also in substantial advertising revenues. In 2017, TV advertising reached USD 301 million, and has the potential of reaching USD 452 million by 2022, with a CAGR of 8.5%. This segment is the third in terms of revenue, following the internet access and TV and home video segments. As for the three segments, the 2017 classification on the podium remains unchanged in 2022 as well.

Chapter 12   Entertainment

At the local level, the video games segment will register a 16.3% compound annual growth rate by 2022 while Over-The-Top (OTT)[1] segment will register a 14.8 % annual growth rate. Over the course of time, these two segments have reported low revenues in Romania, but, by 2022, will reach a maximum of USD 144 million and USD 22 million respectively. Together with the internet access segment, which is closing the podium of the industries with the highest CAGR, the video games and OTT segments, in this order, are top of the class in the media and entertainment industry.

At the regional level, the virtual reality industry will have the highest growth potential with a CAGR of 51.3%, even though the revenues will reach, by 2022, only USD 178 million. In terms of CAGR, the second place is reserved for video games industry with a CAGR of 15.5% and revenues of over USD 7.5 billion. The third place is reserved for the OTT segment with a compound annual growth rate of 13% and revenues of about USD 1.2 billion, by 2022.

---

1   A term used to refer to content providers that distribute streaming media as a standalone product directly to viewers over the Internet, bypassing telecommunications, multichannel television and broadcast television platforms that traditionally act as a controller or distributor of such content [Source: Wikipedia].

Chapter 13
Current Issues and Challenges[1]

Romania's foreign policy is predominantly focused on relations with its neighbours and within the EU and NATO. Romania's EU Presidency in the first half of 2019 is one of Romania's biggest foreign policy priorities. Securing membership of the EU's visa-free Schengen arrangement is a priority. The country's NATO membership and relationship with the US are of strategic importance.

As Romania enters the 21st century under a new government, its immediate troubles seem to be behind it. The recession is over and growth is predicted for the next few years. One of the major work for the government is trying to stimulate the economy and the country's exports are rising as Romanian firms learn to compete in international markets, and more foreign investment is coming into the country.

---

1 http://www.ibe.unesco.org/International/ICE/natrap/Romania.pdf

However, there are plenty of risks along the way. For example, Romanian government has to tackle some of the reforms needed to thrive its economy, such as closing down uneconomic factories and encouraging much-needed investment in the country. It also has to maintain good relations with its neighbouring countries. [1]

Foreign Policy[2]

For centuries, during periods of both subjugation and independence, Romanians have had a reputation for handling their foreign relations with far greater skill than their domestic affairs. It is a story that has continued in the post-Ceausescu era when Romanian diplomats and military officers have gradually succeeded in forging strong links with Western Europe and the United States at a time when their country's economic backwardness would have otherwise left it isolated. Bucharest has played a particularly shrewd hand following the 11 September 2001, terrorist attacks on the United States, resulting in an invitation to join NATO and a visit by President George W. Bush a year later. The process of cultivating international relations did not begin smoothly, however. In the 1990–1992 period, the leading Western nations essentially put Romania on probation. They warned the new government in Bucharest that it would have to improve its domestic record on political and economic reforms and human rights if it wanted to join the international community as a member in good standing.

Initially, the United States took an even harder line against the "new" Romania than did its European allies. In the aftermath of Ceausescu's downfall in December 1989, Washington appeared to find fault with the new regime. Secretary of State James Baker III was the last senior Western official to visit Bucharest in the wake of the revolution, and he stayed for only a few hours. The

---

1 https://dfat.gov.au/geo/romania/Pages/romania-country-brief.aspx
2 http://www.countrywatch.com/Content/pdfs/reviews/B43L8M36.01c.pdf

| 罗马尼亚概况 | Survey of Romania |

United States extended $80 million in humanitarian assistance, but over the next few years resisted rewarding Romania with long-term economic aid and the coveted Most Favored Nation (MFN) trading status. In addition, U.S. leaders tended to distance themselves from senior Romanian officials at diplomatic gatherings.

By contrast, Western Europe took a more pragmatic, "business-as-usual" approach, feeling that the best way to change Romania's behaviour was with hands-on engagement. Former French president François Mitterrand became the first Western head of state to visit Bucharest in April 1991, and a year later Romania and Germany signed a treaty of friendship and cooperation. The leading European powers were motivated in part by the perception that Romania, for all its internal imperfections, remained a bulwark between the growing chaos to the west—where Yugoslavia was descending into bloody civil war—and the east, where the Soviet Union had dissolved into a patchwork of quarrelsome mini-states.

The EC began as an organization for economic cooperation between Western European nations. But more recently it has evolved into a force for political integration as well, a process that reached a milestone in November 1993 when the Maastricht Treaty took effect and the EC became the European Union (EU). Romania's association agreement aimed to eliminate trade barriers between it and the EU over a ten-year period, though the process continues to lag far behind that schedule. But the accord also had an important symbolic value, as it began the process of ushering Romania into the political structures of modern Europe.

Another key step in that process came in October 1993, when Romania finally won admission to the Council of Europe as its 32nd full member. The Council of Europe, based in Strasbourg, France, is primarily a symbolic body, but membership in it is widely seen as a "passport" to other European political and economic institutions. Doubts about Romania's human rights record, particularly its treatment of its Hungarian (Magyar) minority, were the main reason that Romania was the last former Eastern bloc country to gain admission to the council. During months of hard negotiations, Romania was compelled to promise to improve its record, and its membership won final approval in a meeting of the council's Committee of Ministers in which the Hungarian ambassador abstained in the voting.

Romania's growing acceptance in Europe helped improve its relations with the United States as well. Earlier, Romania had garnered considerable goodwill from Washington during the Persian Gulf conflict[1] of 1990 – 91. Romania had fortuitously taken over the rotating presidency of the United Nations Security Council a day before the Iraqi invasion of Kuwait and skillfully used its position to support the U.S.-led alliance against Iraq. The diplomatic respect it gained as a result was widely seen as having offset the large economic losses Romania suffered as a result of the UN's trade sanctions against Iraq.

The gradual thaw in U.S.-Romanian relations grew warmer still in October 1993, when the U.S. Congress voted in favour of ratifying a bilateral trade agreement that would include restoration of most favored nation trading status, long a key goal of Romanian foreign policy. That was followed in 1994 by a visit to Washington by President Iliescu, where he met with President Bill Clinton.

Three years later, in July 1997, President Clinton made a brief stopover in Bucharest during a European tour. "Stay the course and Romania will cross the milestone" of membership in NATO, Clinton told a cheering crowd of 100,000 that had been treated to free Coca-Cola and popcorn.

And in yet another diplomatic advance, Pope John Paul visited Romania on 7-9 May 1999, becoming the first pope to travel to a predominantly Orthodox Christian country since the Eastern and Western branches of Christianity split in the Great Schism of 1054. During his tour, the pontiff met with Patriarch Teoctist, leader of Romania's Orthodox Church, and President Emil Constantinescu.

1　war that began in 1990 when Iraq invaded Kuwait and ended in 1991 when a coalition of countries led by the United States expelled the Iraqi army from Kuwait and destroyed much of Iraq's military capability. Also called Persian Gulf War [https://www.thefreedictionary.com/Persian+Gulf+Conflict].

Romania understandably views itself as living in a rough neighbourhood. Thus its efforts to improve its relations with Western Europe and the United States (aside from achieving economic benefits) are aimed at gaining protection against its historic enemies, such as Russia, Hungary, and Bulgaria.

Romania was the first former Soviet bloc nation to sign a treaty of friendship with Russia, which committed both countries to respect their mutual territorial integrity and the inviolability of their current borders. But bilateral tensions persisted over the issue of the former Soviet republic of Moldova, which gained its independence in 1991. Moldova controls most of the territory of the former Romanian province of Bessarabia (Ukraine controls the rest), which was part of Great Romania[1] between the world wars. The majority of its population consists of ethnic Romanians, although there is a significant minority of ethnic Slavs, both Russians and Ukrainians.

The major stumbling block to regional cooperation was the long-festering dispute between Romania and Hungary over Transylvania. Romania believed that Hungary still hoped to regain the territory and was using Transylvania's Magyar minority as a subversive "fifth column" to further that ultimate goal. Hungary, in turn, complained continually about what it saw as the Romanian government's political and cultural oppression of its ethnic brethren in Transylvania.

Nevertheless, both countries were determined to reach some sort of compromise in order to avoid hindering their efforts to gain greater integration into Europe. In September 1993, Geza Jeszenszky became the first Hungarian foreign minister to pay an official visit to Bucharest since 1989, and Romania's Foreign Minister Teodor Melescanu followed with a visit to Budapest in September 1994.

---

1 The term Greater Romania (Romanian: România Mare) usually refers to the borders of the Kingdom of Romania in the interwar period. It also refers to a pan-nationalist idea. As a concept, its main goal is the re-creation of a nation-state which would incorporate all Romanian speakers. The phrase is strongly associated with the Kingdom of Romania between 1918 and 1940, often considered the realization of the pan-Romanian goal. In 1918, after the incorporation of Transylvania, Bukovina and Bessarabia, the Romanian state reached its largest peacetime geographical extent ever (295,049 km²) [Source: Wikipedia].

Finally, the two sides signed a treaty in September 1996 under which Hungary dropped its demand for autonomy for Romania's 1.6 million Magyar minority in exchange for Bucharest's commitment to guarantee them equal rights, despite bitter opposition from Romanian rulers. Then in May 1997, Hungarian President Arpad Goncz paid an unprecedented visit to his country's historic enemy in which he pledged his government's support for Romania's bid to join NATO. In fact, the agreement figured to help both sides with their efforts to gain further entry into the European establishment.

Romania was motivated to improve its relations with its neighbors in part to compensate for the growing instability in the Balkans, the main reason for which was the civil wars that ripped apart Yugoslavia beginning in the early 1990s. Bucharest tried to present itself as a mediator in the conflicts between the rump Yugoslav federation[1] (consisting of Serbia and Montenegro) and the newly independent republics of Croatia and Bosnia-Herzegovina.

The Romania's accession into EU has started in 1993 by signing the European Agreement having as main objective Romania's preparation for accession. These criteria have been confirmed by European Council held in Madrid in 1995, which has accentuated the importance of adapting the administrative structure of candidate countries, having in view the creation of conditions for a gradual and harmonized accession process.

In 1995, Romania officially applies for EU membership, but only in 1999, the European Council in Helsinki decides to start negotiations with Romania. By the end of 2004, all the 31 chapters of the acquis communautaire have been closed. Romania signs the Treaty of Accession to the European Union on 25 April 2005 at the same time with Bulgaria.

The areas referring to the accession negotiations to the EU are structured in 31 chapters and enclose all EU's legislation. When the applicant state accepts

---

1 The Yugoslav federation was constructed against a double background: an inter-war Yugoslavia which had been dominated by the Serbian ruling class; and a war-time division of the country, as Fascist Italy and Nazi Germany split the country apart and endorsed an extreme Croatian nationalist faction called the Ustase [Source: Wikipedia].

the common EU position, the respective chapter is considered provisionally closed. The negotiations are closed only when all chapters have been negotiated, no chapter been considered definitely closed until all 31 chapters are finished.

The negotiations results are incorporated in a draft accession treaty. The treaty is submitted to the Council for approval and to the European Parliament for assent and then is submitted to the Member States and the applicant country for ratification. In certain cases, this may imply a referendum. The treaty enters into force and the applicant becomes a Member State at the accession date. Since 1 January 2007, Romania has become EU Member State with rights and obligations regularized by EU's treaties and laws which Romania has to consider as every Member State of EU.

Contemporary Challenges & Future Prospects[1]

Few countries have benefited from integration into the EU as much as Romania. Reforms spurred by accession brought in foreign investment, boosted productivity and raised living standards. GDP per capita rose from 30% of the EU average in 1995 to 60% in 2017. Today, over 70% of the country's exports go to the EU, and they are becoming more technologically more complex. With 6.9% GDP growth in 2017, Romania is one of the best performing economies in Europe.

At the same time, Romania's population has shrunk from 22.8 to 19.6 million since 2000, and is expected to keep falling. Between 3 and 5 million Romanians — most of them of prime working age — live and work in other parts of the European Union. Meanwhile, owing to just 66% (a lowly 56% for women) of labor force participation, it is too low to offset aging and emigration.

To keep growing and converging to EU levels of living, Romania will

---

1 https://blogs.worldbank.org/europeandcentralasia/towards-more-prosperous-and-inclusive-romania

have to make some changes. Just as Romania availed of the EU's markets and institutions to accelerate economic growth during the last two decades, it will now have to use them to bridge the divide between citizens who are moving forward and those who are being left behind. As such, the country needs more qualified workers, more effective investments, and a much more efficient allocation of resources.

The skills of the workforce have not kept up with the increasing sophistication of the economy. Romanian exports have been switching from labor intensive low-technology sectors to more advanced automotive, machinery, electronic equipment and information and communications technology.

But at 25.6%, tertiary education attainment is the lowest in the EU. Romanian employers find that both hard and soft skills of employees are lacking. Romania lags in the number of graduates in STEM disciplines (sciences, technologies, engineering and mathematics), while non-technical vocational training is often deficient.

The state of infrastructure is abysmal: Romania ranks 102 out of 137 countries in the quality of transport infrastructure. Hamstrung by poor planning and weak public administration, Romania is the only EU country that was not able to use the flood of structural funds it has received since accession.

Romania received EUR 15.4 billion during the period 2007–2013, and another EUR 17.6 billion during 2014–2020, for investment in infrastructure. For a country with a GDP that averaged EUR 140 billion between 2007 and 2017, EUR 33 billion is certainly not insignificant.

Small businesses have struggled to be competitive and enter global value chains because of unpredictable regulations: The fiscal code has changed 20 times in the last two years! At the same time, there are 1,200 State-owned Enterprises (SOEs), many of which are large and inefficient and drag down overall productivity.

Over a quarter of Romania's population lives on less than US$ 5.50 a day, the highest poverty rate in the EU. The poor remain disconnected from the drivers of economic growth: Half of the poorest 40% of Romanians do not work while another 28% live off subsistence agriculture.

One in five people lack access to potable water, and one-third live without access to a flush toilet. The Roma face especially difficult circumstances, with an employment rate of just 28% and a poverty rate that reaches 70%.

Romania remains one of the least urbanized countries in the EU: A large number of poor people—75% of the population—live in rural areas. Less than 2% of the population has moved in the past five years, likely the result of poor skills and misguided policies.

Romania's education system is failing: 40% of Romanian students are functionally illiterate—meaning they can technically read and write, but cannot apply those skills meaningfully in their lives. And almost 1 in 5 children drop out of school—This is among the highest rates in the European Union.

A combination of relatively generous maternity benefits and lack of part-time jobs has had the unintended effect of keeping women out of the labor force. Whether they are in or outside the labor force, entrenched gender norms continue to place the entire burden of caring for children and the elderly on women.

Many workers are trapped in low-productivity farming and other informal activities, leading to both underutilization and misallocation of labor. As such, the transition to more productive jobs has been sluggish.

Social spending is low, at 14.4% of GDP. But it is also inefficient, becoming increasingly skewed towards pensions for the elderly. And it is becoming less targeted: With low and falling pension coverage in rural areas, public resources will be diverted away from the rural poor. The provision of social services for social protection, employment, education and healthcare is fragmented and sparse, especially in rural areas where the needs (and the economic benefits) are greatest.

So, with all of these contradictions, can Romania still be proud of its past achievements? Looking back, the answer is certainly yes. In less than a generation, Romania has built an open society, consolidated democracy, and become better off than ever before.

Looking ahead, however, Romanians ought to be concerned. Unless the country remedies its governance failures, economic growth will become more volatile, and prosperity will be shared even less. A truly prosperous and inclusive Romania should mean that nobody is left behind.

图书在版编目（CIP）数据

罗马尼亚概况 / 赵菁主编. — 北京：世界知识出版社，2020.4
ISBN 978-7-5012-6200-7

Ⅰ.①罗… Ⅱ.①赵… Ⅲ.①罗马尼亚—概况 Ⅳ.① K954.2

中国版本图书馆 CIP 数据核字 (2020) 第 041573 号

责任编辑	曾伏华
责任出版	赵　玥
责任校对	张　琨
封面设计	张远航

书　　名	罗马尼亚概况 Luoma Niya Gaikuang
主　　编	赵　菁
出版发行	世界知识出版社有限公司
地址邮编	北京市东城区干面胡同 51 号（100010）
电　　话	010-85114541（编辑部）　010-65265923（发行部） 010-85119023（邮购部）
网　　址	www.ishizhi.cn
印　　刷	北京虎彩文化传播有限公司
经　　销	新华书店
开本印张	710×1000 毫米　1/16　17½ 印张　2 插页
字　　数	187 千字
版次印次	2020 年 4 月第一版　2020 年 4 月第一次印刷
标准书号	ISBN 978-7-5012-6200-7
定　　价	88.00 元

版权所有　侵权必究